W9-AWS-503

The Press,
the Rosenbergs,
and
the Cold War

The Press,
the Rosenbergs,
and
the Cold War

John F. Neville

Westport, Connecticut
London

Library of Congress Cataloging-in-Publication Data

Neville, John F.
   The press, the Rosenbergs, and the Cold War / John F. Neville.
      p.   cm.
   Includes bibliographical references and index.
   ISBN 0-275-94995-8 (alk. paper)
      1. Anti-Communist movements—United States—History—20th century.
   2. Cold War.   3. Press and politics—United States—History—20th
   century.   [1. Rosenberg, Julius, 1918–1953.   2. Rosenberg, Ethel,
   1915–1953.]   I. Title.
   E743.5.N45   1995
   973.9—dc20   94–22655

British Library Cataloguing in Publication Data is available.

Library of Congress Catalog Card Number: 94–22655
ISBN: 0–275–94995–8

First published in 1995

Praeger Publishers, 88 Post Road West, Westport, CT 06881
An imprint of Greenwood Publishing Group, Inc.

Printed in the United States of America

The paper used in this book complies with the
Permanent Paper Standard issued by the National
Information Standards Organization (Z39.48–1984).

10 9 8 7 6 5 4 3 2

To My uncle Ned, my sister Sheila,

and my nieces Meghan and Katherine

Duggan Neville fondly remembered.

Contents

Preface

In January 1953, Hearst syndicated political columnist George Sokolsky said that the U.S. constitution did not protect stealing and treason.[1] Reduced to its essence this is what the furor surrounding the Rosenbergs was about: theft of a mythically secure future. Since then the case has become encrusted with ethical, political, and legal complexities that went unspoken during the Korean War. Sokolsky's bald statement, published in Hearst's *New York Journal-American*, is now considered a museum piece of cold-war paranoia. The Rosenbergs and Morton Sobell may or may not have provided the Soviets with classified data on the atomic bomb. Nevertheless, the notion that they advanced the Soviet Union's atomic program even marginally is now considered unlikely. Why then did the Rosenberg case excite such unrestrained passion? The political hysteria of the time can be at least partly explained by the triumph of communism in Eastern Europe and China. But most of the fury concerned what was thought to be the pilfering of U.S. atomic secrets.

Although it was many things, the cold war was certainly not an age of political reason. It was a time of hot war, of potential atomic war, possibly the final global war. Historian Perry Miller notes that the United States struggled from the early seventeenth century until zero-eight-hundred-fifteen hours, August 6, 1945, to realize ancient and modern religious history's often-foretold apocalyptic vision.[2] August 6 was a transcendentally horrifying experience: people were relieved at the result, yet terrified of the prospect of a third (and last) world war. But most Americans thought the weapon that destroyed Hiroshima and Nagasaki lent long-range security to the United States and Western Europe.

When President Harry Truman announced in September 1949 that the Soviet Union had exploded an atomic device, the security Americans had felt since 1945 evaporated overnight. Espionage was widely and immediately suspected as the culprit. Everyone knew the Soviets lacked the technological and industrial capacity to develop and produce a bomb. There could be no other answer, no logical explanation. After all, in October 1945, Truman said that sharing atomic information with the Soviets would be a waste of time: "I don't think they can do it anyhow."[3]

It was in New Mexico in mid-July 1945, that the world's first atomic bomb was exploded in the desert dawn.[4] The explosion produced a light so brilliant that it made a reporter recall the biblical description of the first day ever.

Acknowledgments

Special thanks and gratitude to Hazel Dicken Garcia. Sincere appreciation to Donald Gillmor, Edward Griffin, Jean Ward, Paul Murphy, and Nancy Roberts of the University of Minnesota. Posthumous appreciation to the late Edwin Emery, professor emeritus, University of Minnesota, for helpful answers and especially for the generous donation of an airline discount. I would also like to thank James Baughman of the University of Wisconsin-Madison for helpful suggestions and Pat Dooley of the University of Maine for constructive comments. Thanks also to my graduate school research partner Chuck Lewis of Mankato State University. I would like to also acknowledge helpful assistance from Michael Meeropol of Western Massachusetts University. I also would like to express gratitude to Harry Cherkinian and Carol Gissing of Milwaukee, Patricia Engelking of St. Paul, Mariana Schunk of Minneapolis, John Holland of New York City, and Erich Schwartz of Washington D.C. Thanks also to Ben Bradlee and Russell Baker for their patience in answering questions and taking time for interviews. Appreciation also to author Joyce Milton for her answers to letters and questions. Last, but not least, grateful recognition for assistance extended to Cele Russell, David Neville , and Robert Neville.

The Press,
the Rosenbergs,
and
the Cold War

1

A Flash in the Desert

The atomic bomb, dropped on Japan for the first time today, was previewed by scientists and military authorities in the New Mexico desert July 16 when a test sent a ball of fire many times brighter than the mid-day sun, billowing skyward, and set off a blast which rattled windows more than 250 airline miles away.

The steel tower, from which the test was detonated, was vaporized. A huge, sloping crater was left where the tower stood. Men outside the control center more than five miles away were knocked down by a heavy pressure wave. Witnesses said a huge multi-colored cloud was sent 40,000 feet into the stratosphere in five minutes.

The blast, at 5:30 A.M. at a remote location on the Alamogordo, New Mexico, Army Air Base, caused consternation throughout Southwestern New Mexico and Southern Arizona.

Windows rattled at Gallup, New Mexico, 250 miles Northwest. Forest rangers 150 to 175 miles away thought there had been an earthquake and checked with the Smithstonian Observatory on Burro Mountain in Southwestern New Mexico.

At Albuquerque, 120 miles away, a blind girl, when the flash of the test lighted the sky before the blast was heard, asked "what was that?"[1]

Associated Press wire story from the day after Hiroshima, August 7, 1945.

Eight years after a blind girl saw light in the New Mexico desert an odd thing happened at the Martin Beck Theater in New York City. It was the evening of June 19, 1953. The Broadway cast of Arthur Miller's play *The Crucible* was in the final act when the play came to an abrupt halt. *The Crucible*, a political allegory set in seventeenth-century New England, had opened in January to mixed reviews and a chilly audience reception. Even some of Miller's friends had snubbed him, so convinced were they that he had stirred trouble with a play that too plainly implied American cold-war persecution.[2] Weeks after its opening, *The Crucible* was playing to dwindling audiences. Some cast members had stayed on without salary. The play limped into spring and crawled into the hot, steamy summer of 1953.

During the performance on June 19, just after farmer John Proctor's execution, the audience fell silent and rose with bowed heads.[3]

Not far from the Martin Beck Theater a large, milling crowd had gathered on East Seventeenth Street near Union Square. It was the last New York Save-the-Rosenbergs rally. In Washington, thousands of Rosenberg defenders and sympathizers had also gathered in front of the White House. Similarly large vigils and rallies had been held in London, Paris, Rome, Stockholm, Sydney, Dublin, Prague, and Berlin. It was hopeless, though: the day before, the United States Supreme Court had turned down eleventh-hour appeals by two camps of Rosenberg attorneys. President Dwight Eisenhower had declined executive-clemency pleas for the Rosenbergs made by many groups and individuals, including heads of state, diplomats, and religious figures. In a dramatic but quixotic gesture, Poland offered the Rosenbergs asylum.

The executions took place just after 8 P.M. Friday, June 19. The Rosenbergs walked separately to their deaths in the electric chair. In doing so they triggered a controversy so lasting and sensitive that some U.S. history texts on the postwar period still dismiss the case in a sentence or two.[4]

The Rosenbergs' deaths sparked a brief explosion of international outrage: weeping, rock throwing, and scattered rioting rippled through distant foreign capitals. If the Rosenberg case had a definite (if grotesque) physical ending, its origins are not as clear.[5] Quite simply, Julius and Ethel Rosenberg were charged with having recruited Ethel's brother, David Greenglass, into a "far-flung" Soviet spy ring. The ring allegedly operated in the United States, mostly during World War II.

In spring 1948, American cryptologists deciphered part of a KGB code book found in Finland during the war. One of the messages intercepted mentioned two American spy recruits, Max Elitcher and Joel Barr.[6] More than a year later a painstakingly decoded document revealed a scientific report from a Klaus Fuchs. The report concerned the Manhattan Project, the wartime atomic research facility in the New Mexico desert. That revelation could hardly have been more shocking: Fuchs had worked as a high-level theoretical physicist at Los Alamos. The "Fuchs report" suggested that the Soviet spy ring had reached inside the most sensitive ever wartime project.[7] By late January 1950, Fuchs had unburdened his conscience to British intelligence agent and spy catcher William Skardon.[8] Fuchs was then arrested on February 2, 1950. His was the first "atom spy arrest"; it would culminate six months later in the arrests of Julius and Ethel Rosenberg.

What is remembered about the Rosenbergs' early lives mostly is culled from Virginia Gardner's 1954 book about them.[9] Gardner, however, worked for the communist *Daily Worker* and wrote a biography that sometimes verges on hagiography. Perhaps the chief irony in a case abounding with ironies is that one cannot reasonably reconstruct the Rosenbergs' lives without relying on the book of a radical journalist. Nonetheless, who were Julius and Ethel Rosenberg? How did this nondescript couple become symbols of a cold-war tragedy that played out in newspapers so noisily? Both were Jewish, the children of immigrants, and had spent all but fractions of their lives on New York City 's Lower-East Side. The youngest of five children, born to parents who had emigrated from Poland around the turn of the century, Julius had been a sickly boy; he barely survived a burst appendix when he was ten. The Rosenberg family lived in a cold-water flat on Broome Street in conditions very near poverty. Julius's father, Harry, worked as a clothes sample-maker years after briefly owning a dry cleaning shop in Harlem.[10] His mother, Sophie, worked in a garment industry sweatshop until she married. If the Rosenbergs had to struggle to survive, Ethel's family, the Greenglasses, lived little better than a hand-to-mouth existence. Born in 1915 to Barnet and Tessie Greenglass, also immigrants from Eastern Europe, Ethel was one of three children, who grew up in a cold-water tenement at 64 Sheriff Street, not far from the Rosenberg home. Ethel also had health problems as a child. A small, slightly plump girl, she suffered from ricketic curvature of the spine.[11]

As a teenager, Ethel was a fairly talented amateur singer and actress. After graduation from Seward Park High School in 1931, she began work as a clerk at a shipping and packing company, but at night she sang in amateur competitions and acted in plays with the Clark House Players, an East Side amateur drama group sponsored by the Clark House Settlement.[12] Later, she had small roles in productions with the Group Theater's Lavanberg Players, a company that stressed social themes in its plays. Still, Ethel frequently won prize money at amateur nights in New Jersey and apparently used some of her winnings to pay for voice and music lessons.[13] Eventually she won a spot on Hugh Ross's Schola Cantorum, a chorus of talented amateur singers sometimes used in some productions at the Metropolitan Opera House.

Ethel's life took an unexpected and dramatic turn in August 1935. That month she worked as an organizer in a large trike of shipping clerks in the women's garment industry. The strike was successful, but Ethel was promptly fired for her part in the action, which included lying down in the street in front of delivery trucks.[14] She appealed her dismissal to the infant National Labor Relations Board and won, though she soon took another job.

Like Ethel, Julius also was considered talented as a child and adolescent, but his talent lay in religion, not the dramatic arts. As a student at

Manhattan's Downtown Torah Talmud, he excelled in the study of the scriptures and was soon considered an excellent rabbinical candidate. When he entered Seward Park High School, Harry and Sophie Rosenberg's son was elected vice president of the Young Men's Synagogue Organization.[15] While still in high school, Julius became interested in the Tom Mooney case, which involved a left-wing-led crusade to free a jailed labor organizer. Julius soon converted to left-radicalism (or "progressivism" as he preferred) and joined several far-left student groups. In high school, he sold subscriptions door-to-door for the *Daily Worker*.[16]   At sixteen, he graduated from Seward Park High and entered the City College of New York. Political opinions were taken seriously at CCNY in the 1930s. It was a left-wing haven; many of its students (and some faculty) held rallies for the Scottsboro Boys, distributed leaflets for Loyalist forces in Spain, and campaigned against Fascism in Europe.[17]   The musty alcoves of CCNY's student union echoed with Marxist dialectics and endless political arguments. In this physically drab but intellectually pungent atmosphere, Julius committed himself to "progressive" politics and became a member of the Steinmetz Club, a collegiate wing of the Young Communist League.

Julius's remaining years at CCNY were devoted more to politics and activism than to education. Besides memberships in the American Student Union and Youth Socialist League, he also participated in the campus branch of the Federation of Architects, Engineers, Chemists, and Technicians (FAECT) a union with a pronounced far left-wing reputation. [18] In late 1936, Julius met Ethel Greenglass at a New Year's Eve dance sponsored by the International Seamen's Union. The two began to date regularly. They also marched together in rallies, distributed leaflets, sold subscriptions of the *Daily Worker*, ran mimeograph machines, and collected funds.

Julius's commitment to student politics, however, took a toll on his grades. He considered dropping out of college, but Ethel convinced him to finish his degree in electrical engineering. Julius graduated in February 1939, ranking seventy-nine in a class of eighty-five. About this time he became a full-fledged member of the Communist Party.

In June, Julius and Ethel were married in an Orthodox ceremony at the old synagogue on Sheriff Street.[19] The newlyweds lived in a rented room in the Williamsburg section of Brooklyn. Julius spent the first year and a half after graduation working as a tool designer and a free-lance tool inventor. Ethel helped out later by taking a job in Washington, D.C., as a clerk for the Census Bureau. In September 1942, Julius got a job as a civilian junior engineer in the Brooklyn Supply Office of the U.S. Army Signal Corps. Ethel returned to New York from her brief stay in Washington. Julius became active in FAECT again, this time as civil service chairman of a local chapter.[20]   Besides his Signal Corps job and union responsibilities, he remained active in political causes and also found time to sell International

Workers' Order insurance policies door to door.   He also visited defense plants in the New York City area, including Fort Monmouth in New Jersey. In 1942, Ethel and Julius moved into Knickerbocker Village, a modern high-rise apartment complex on the Lower East Side of Manhattan.   They furnished it with used furniture and an attractive drop-leaf table that would later become disputed evidence in their case.[21]

During the war, Julius's government job and sometimes frail health kept him out of military service. A son, Michael, was born to Ethel in 1943. As Julius's career seemed pointed toward mid-level bureaucratic comfort, he was accused by U.S. Army investigators of having communist connections. He denied the allegations but was fired from the Signal Corps in March 1945. He protested the decision and lost the appeal. The Rosenbergs later bitterly complained that Julius was a victim of his union activities with FAECT.[22]

While Julius filed a series of unsuccessful appeals, he found temporary work with Emerson Radio. After the war, he opened United Purchasers and Distributors, a war-surplus hardware store, with his brother-in-law Bernard Greenglass and another partner, Isidor Goldstein.[23] After David Greenglass, Julius's youngest brother-in-law, was discharged from the army in 1946, he too joined the firm. When the enterprise foundered, the partners reorganized and formed a machine shop, G & R Engineering Company. Goldstein pulled out of the business and a New York City matzoh manufacturer, David Schein, took his place. Schein invested $15,000 in G & R in exchange for a major interest in the machine shop. The shop was renamed Pitt Machine Products Co., Inc. and was moved to a larger building on Houston Street.[24] David and Ruth Greenglass had invested almost all of their savings in Pitt Machine. But by 1948, orders had fallen off sharply. Julius and his brother-in-law David often quarreled. Further, Ruth Greenglass resented what she said was an indifference on Julius's part to the economic fate of the shop. David withdrew from Pitt Machine in 1948; Julius owed him $1,000 for his share of the company.[25] While David got a job as a machinist in a Brooklyn foundry, Julius nursed the Houston Street along on a small crew.

The FBI watched him constantly, sometimes openly. After Julius was arrested on July 17, 1950, the shop was closed and eventually sold to pay off debts.[26] Ethel was arrested three weeks later; neither Rosenberg could raise bail. The Rosenbergs' sons, Michael and Robert, respectively seven and three in 1950, were placed with Ethel's mother. Later they were moved to the Hebrew Children's Home, a Bronx shelter for Jewish children.[27] Two years later, on June 19, 1953, Michael Rosenberg learned from a television bulletin that his parents had been electrocuted at Sing-Sing prison.[28]

Like many famous political trials, the Rosenberg-Sobell case received tremendous news media and press attention. The type and amount of coverage varied over time. But the Rosenberg-Sobell case is only one of many political cases of the twentieth century. In the late nineteenth century, the growth of the international news media and the ease of transatlantic travel encouraged causes cèlebrés. For example, the Dreyfus affair, the Sacco and Vanzetti case, the Scottsboro Boys case, the Hiss-Chambers case, and the Tom Mooney crusade all received intensive press coverage. The Nuremberg trial of 1946 and the 1949 Foley Square trial of eleven leaders of the U.S. Communist Party drew reems of sensational publicity. But the first five cases are closely related to the Rosenberg-Sobell case in that they involved obscure people catapulted into public view at a time when their religious or political views were unpopular. Indeed, Rosenberg defenders drew on the organizational and publicity strategies of earlier American causes, including the Trenton Six and Willie McGee cases, which will be discussed later. The Rosenberg case might have developed quite differently had it not been for the modern phenomenon of the political crusade and a competitive, sensation-conscious metropolitan press. Without the exemplars of the Dreyfus,[29] Sacco and Vanzetti,[30] Scottsboro,[31] Mooney,[32] and Hiss-Chambers[33] cases, the Rosenberg case might have died an oxygen-deprived death long before its major characters met their end. It takes an extraordinary issue, event, or person to attract a nation's attention even for a day. Getting the press's attention and sustaining it takes enormous hard work, skill, timing, and luck. The strongest link between these cases and the Rosenberg case is clearly politics. But the link of press coverage is not far behind.

2

Beyond Guilt and Innocence

> I try to ask myself: what's not getting reported? What's not on the agenda? What's the big story we're all missing?[1]

New York Times' columnist James Reston

The guilt or innocence of the Rosenbergs has been argued since the early 1950s.[2] The purpose of this book is not to continue that debate but, rather, to provide a view of the case in its most political terms: news coverage filtered through the dynamics of cold war patriotism. The point of this is its different perspectives. The primary focus will be an in-depth analysis of the case in terms of the press's role in reporting, framing, and interpreting it for the reading public. The Rosenberg case presents a rare convergence of cold-war politics, ideology, and fear magnified by the powerful prism of agenda setting, the news media gatekeeping process that strongly influences what people think about.

This book is a documentary analysis of a *wartime* government's attempt to place, shape, filter, and control the press's reporting of a single case through the exploitation of fear and patriotism. This book shows that the Rosenberg case was reported (and not reported) in a way that was intricately shaped by the political passions of the American cold war. As a cause cèlébre, the Rosenberg case might never have ignited had it happened five years earlier or later. But the death sentences made it something more. Patriotic values and beliefs in wartime often determine how political news is "framed," that is, presented, positioned, and explained to the public. News, as sociologist and media theorist Gaye Tuchman notes, "is a window on the world." She suggests that those who look through the frame of the window can acquire an understanding of American political institutions and values. In agenda setting what is omitted in the gatekeeping process is often just as important as what is reported. "News quarantines," as Ben Bagdikian describes them, are voluntarily imposed by the news media on certain topics in time of war and domestic crisis to prevent the possible adverse effects of news coverage that government officials sometimes fear. Although Bagdikian refers mostly to 1960s anti-Semitic and racial incidents, this gatekeeping concept also applies to the Rosenberg case. Initially, the case received a great deal of news media coverage before and during the trial but far less after a left-wing paper, the *National Guardian*, claimed the Rosenbergs were victims of a government conspiracy.

This book, an analysis of Rosenberg coverage by the American mainstream, communist, and left-wing press, examines a sample of fourteen U.S. daily newspapers, a communist daily, a left-wing news magazine, three other U.S. weekly news magazines, a Canadian and a British daily newspaper. The sample was selected for national location, regional variation, circulation size (dailies with a circulation above 150,000), and editorial diversity on political issues. Scrutiny of the press begins in February 1950, with Manhattan Project spy Klaus Fuchs's arrest, and continues after the Rosenbergs' executions in June 1953.

One method used in this book includes a systematic documentary analysis of the content of the following newspapers and periodicals.[3] The mainstream newspapers are: the *Atlanta Constitution, Chicago Tribune, Christian Science Monitor, Detroit News, Louisville Courier-Journal, New York Herald Tribune, New York Times, St. Louis Post-Dispatch, San Francisco Chronicle, Washington Post, Times* (London), and *Winnipeg Free Press*.

The newsweekly news magazines are: *Time, Newsweek*, and *U.S. News and World Report*. The following newspapers and periodicals were consulted: the *New York World-Telegram and Sun, New York Journal-American, New York Post, New York Mirror, New York Post, Baltimore Sun*, and *Le Monde* (France). At times, the *Herald Tribune, Times, World-Telegram and Sun*, and *Post* were used in a "local" New York City sample.

The differences in content and approach among the mainstream, communist, and left-wing newspapers and periodicals will also be considered. Sample dates will be determined in an agenda-sensitive fashion: each time a major Rosenberg case event-e.g., a court ruling, clemency decision, or exposé is announced, the sample will be checked for "day-after" coverage.[4]

There have been many famous trials in American history, but agenda setting, gatekeeping, news media "black out," and patriotism make the Rosenberg case unique because these phenomena occurred in an epoch of political ferocity that time has not diminished.

The agenda-setting model of the press describes ways that media editors and reporters select political stories for the news.[5] The notion of an agenda-setting function of the press first was proposed by Bernard Cohen in 1963.[6] Cohen said that while the press was not very good at telling readers what to think, it was stunningly successful at determining what they think about.[7] In his hypothesis, editors act as "gatekeepers" in selecting, placing, and emphasizing certain political issues and topics for reporting.[8] Not only do readers learn about political and social issues, but editorial selection and placement tell them which issues are most significant. In this system, the selection of topics, national or local, is seldom arbitrary, nor are the ways they are developed, edited, and presented as news. This process implies that information is "shaped" and "packaged" before it is printed in newspapers. Sometimes, the agenda-setting hypothesis also triggers a government reflex action, forcing public officials and politicians to act because of strong public reaction to some event, topic or issue in the news agenda. The U.S. cold-war experience presented an issue, communist subversion in government, that evoked a public response verging on white-hot hatred. This response helped spur action involving loyalty oaths, congressional committee investigations of alleged subversion, and restrictive legislation on political association and immigration. The nation's news media, particularly the press, served as a springboard for public and government reaction to the cold war at home.

The Rosenberg case fits nicely into the political matrix of the agenda-setting hypothesis. Initially, the FBI and the Justice Department provided the news services and newspapers with the raw information on the case. It was the official view of the case. But that changed in August 1951, when the *National Guardian* said the Rosenbergs were innocent victims of a government conspiracy.

In an interesting left-wing twist on agenda-setting, the *Guardian* stressed its theory of the Rosenberg case to mainstream press editors from 1951 to 1953. The *Guardian* claimed the nation's press had conspired with the government by reporting only the Justice Department's and FBI's view of the case. The dominant political values of each generation influence the ways that news (especially news with political or ideological overtones) is reported. This situation sets up a jarring paradox: journalists cannot ignore the political values of either their readers or their culture. Still, they struggle to assemble news into formulaic, nonpartisan constructs. This sometimes fragile process requires "framing," a process that requires subtle value decisions about what to report, but prohibits acknowledgement or discussion of its presence or use. Of related interest is Todd Gitlin's political development of Erving Goffman's "frame analysis," the notion that the news media are organized to regulate the production of news frames.[9] The Rosenbergs claimed they had been "framed" by the government with the complicity of the "lords of the press." Gaye Tuchman speaks of a news frame as a construct not a "mirror of events."[10] The Rosenberg case has a tortuously complex history, involving dozens of major characters, many minor ones, and a grid of interlocking issues and events. Reporters who covered the case had to disentangle myriad characters and events and arrange them into a reasonably understandable construct. Critics later said this version was really designed by the government for ready consumption in the press in order to prejudice the reading public against the Rosenbergs.

Ben Bagdikian's *The Media Monopoly* discusses the 1920s American press's initial reluctance to report news suggesting Sacco and Vanzetti's innocence.[11] He describes this reluctance as a failure to provide a "balance wheel" of political news. As noted, Bagdikian also describes news quarantines on sensitive issues in *The Effete Conspiracy and Other Crimes of the Press*.[12] Similarly, press coverage of some cold-war events tended to lack political balance, as in reporting on the House Un-American Activities Committee and, especially, on Senator Joseph McCarthy's early career.

In 1955 congressional testimony, James Reston said that the government was increasingly "managing the news."[13] Reston feared the news sometimes reflected a picture of the government that was not very accurate.[14] He referred mostly to international and diplomatic reporting, but his words can at least indirectly apply to the FBI's and Justice Department's handling of press relations in the Rosenberg case. Before interpretive and investigative reporting was standard journalistic custom, "news management" meant reporting by government press release. During the early cold war, a reporter or columnist who questioned the accuracy or credibility of the FBI director or the attorney general on a matter of national interest risked being considered unprofessional, unpatriotic, and un-American by colleagues, the public, and political and public officials.

Herbert Gans writes that traditionally mainstream American journalists have remained aloof from ideological debate. Unlike in Europe, reporters in the United States have tended to equate most all ideological thought with political extremism.[15] During the early cold war this tendency meant news and information from left-wing sources and publications was considered biased, unreliable propaganda. Michael Schudson explains that the history of government "news management" is a systematic attempt to influence, withhold, and sometimes distort national and international news.[16] The emergence of this system coincided with the start of the Korean War and the Rosenberg case, which eventually were fused in the news media like Siamese twins, inseparably linked by a single spinal column. This state of affairs made problematic the chance of publishing or broadcasting the views of communists and other political radicals. It often made such people all but invisible citizens when questions of fair play and justice arose about their treatment by the state or the criminal justice system. Historian Lauren Kessler notes that radical and dissident political groups in the United States often have had great difficulty getting access to the press.[17] Rosenberg defenders claimed the mainstream press was intimidated by cold war politics into not reporting the alternative, left-wing view of the case advanced by the *National Guardian*. These media concepts, of agenda setting, gatekeeping, patriotism in war time, news framing, political reporting, and government news management will be applied to press coverage of the Rosenberg case in hope of providing evidence that government institutions, e.g., national, regional, or local prosecuting agencies; law-enforcement agencies; and legislative committees unduly influence the way news is reported and interpreted during periods of war or civil crisis.

Because the Rosenberg case coincided with the Korean War, this book asks the question whether the major government institutions responsible for prosecuting the case took advantage of a patriotic, less probing press. This question is not to argue that there was a government conspiracy against the Rosenbergs. It is to raise questions regarding the complex relationships that government has with press during times of war and political crisis.

3

The Atom Spies and the Press

Haven't heard much lately from the Pinks and sincere Liberals who once
went in for heavy breast-beating in behalf of the so-called "sanctity of the
scientist." Where are they now that the arrests and confessions are coming
in? They once liked to say from their platforms and printing presses that
FBI and Army's sleuthing force working for Gen. Leslie R. Groves were a
lot of fascist dastards who wanted to see the poor atomic scientist muzzled
and chained in his lab.

Syndicated columnist Bob Considine, June 21, 1950

Syndicated writer Bob Considine's angry June 1950 column about atom spies
(see quoted at the start of the chapter) appeared three days before North
Korean troops launched early morning artillery and mortar attacks on the west
coast of Korea.   Hours later, in his Maryland farmhouse "Harewood,"
Secretary of State Dean Acheson's white phone rang. Assistant Secretary of
State Dean Rusk told Acheson that North Korean troops had attacked South
Korean territory.[2]

  The day the Korean War began, the *New York Times* carried a brief
story about David Greenglass. A photo showed a heavyset ex-army sergeant
being escorted by marshals into the federal building in Foley Square. The
story said Greenglass's removal hearing (to New Mexico) had been adjourned
until July 13.[3]   Commissioner Edward McDonald had granted the
adjournment at the request of U.S. Attorney Irving H. Saypol, a squat, middle-
aged prosecutor with gray, combed-back hair, bushy eyebrows, wire-rimmed
glasses, and a bulldog mien. Greenglass's arrest followed those of suspected
atom-spy ring members Harry Gold in Philadelphia and Alfred Dean Slack in
suburban Syracuse, New York. News reports linked directly Gold's and
Greenglass's arrests to the still unfolding [2] "Russian spy ring" investigation.

  Sociologist W. A. Gamson says "facts" presented to the press by
public officials are initially devoid of "intrinsic meaning." He explains that

facts only assume coherence by being embedded in a "frame," or storyline. Certain facts are ignored by the press while others are emphasized in stories.[4] In this paradigm, news stories bring to mind stories about the world as much as they present facts to the reader. In time of war or crisis, news stories involving themes of patriotism, loyalty, and treason can and do appear with great frequency. These "frames" are easily recognized through popular culture, e.g., films, television, and literature, and are understood readily. Todd Gitlin observes that the news media "frames" an event by organizing it for the reader. But he explains that "unspoken and unacknowledged" news media frames also assist the journalist in organizing the often confusing woof and warp of reality.[5] The atom spy arrests of 1950 evolved amidst great chaos, excitement, and confusion. The press was particularly dependent on the government to help it make sense of an extraordinarily complex, multi-dimensional plot involving the future of the nation. With the Korean War raging, and more atomic conspiracy arrests imminent, the government could depend on the patriotic editorial support of the press and other news media in its battle against internal subversion. The cold war was now a shooting war, a "hot war" gone ballistic. It transformed the republic's political sensibilities into what presidential historian Richard Hofstadter later called a "paranoid style."[6] This does not mean that reporters and editors began churning out pell-mell state-sponsored propaganda. Nor does it mean that news reports of the unfolding "spy drama" were suddenly transfused with editorial opinion.[7] It means that the news media faced great pressure to assert their patriotism. This was true in 1950, when the spark of war abroad fueled a firestorm of anticommunism at home.

Like earlier newspaper reports, *Newsweek* said David Greenglass had belonged to the New York Young Communist League in 1938. But the news magazine said Greenglass's "friends, family and associates" could not recall his ever having spoken about radical political issues.[8]   Whether Greenglass had his ideological bona fides in order was of little use to Westbrook Pegler. Five days after war began, the Hearst columnist called for the execution of all American communists.[9] Pegler defended his draconian stance as "the only sensible and courageous way to deal with communists in our midst." The former World War I correspondent also urged execution of persons belonging to "covert subsidies" of the Communist Party.

> These people are guilty of conspiring with a foreign country to make war on our country. In this war, the enemy will kill as many Americans as he may have to in order to destroy our government and make slaves of all those Americans who, after the defeat, refuse to join the triumphant regime.[10]

Pegler said "fastidious quibbling" about who was a communist only served the enemy. In his view, patriotic citizens would only be taunted by American traitors and conspirators. He strongly urged the amendment of federal and state laws to provide the death penalty for Communist Party members and their compatriots.[11]

Pegler did not mention Klaus Fuchs, Harry Gold, or David Greenglass in his column. Nonetheless, he had pinched the same nerve cluster that Joseph McCarthy had the previous winter. Americans dreaded being made slaves of communism. But if that seemed far-fetched so did the notion of the Soviets having their own atomic program, mainland China falling to Mao Tse-tung and Eastern Europe capitulating to the Soviet Union. David Greenglass's intransigence with FBI agents was only temporary. The July 13, 1950, *New York Mirror* predicted that Greenglass was ready to "tell what he knows" about his confessed role in the plot to provide the Soviet Union with atomic secrets.[12] The article reported that U.S. Attorney Saypol and Greenglass's attorney, O. John Rogge, had a "series of conferences" and, in Rogge's words, "several more talks" might occur. Greenglass had been indicted by a New Mexico grand jury July 6, 1950. He was accused of meeting Harry Gold in Albuquerque in June 1945 to turn over a sketch of a high-explosive lens mold and a statement about the Manhattan Project for $500. A news story in the *Journal-American* said Rogge and Saypol left the courtroom "practically arm in arm."[13] In any event, the Greenglasses' statements (plus help from Harry Gold) speeded Julius Rosenberg's arrest July 17, 1950.

Greenglass and his wife, Ruth, told agents that Julius Rosenberg had had a hand in the doings of the two espionage rings. The first, operating in Los Alamos, had already been discussed in his June confession. But Greenglass also claimed a *second* ring operated in New York City after World War II.[14]

There were no reporters at Knickerbocker Village before the arrest that evening.[15] A *Time* rewrite later described the Rosenberg apartment as "battered and drab." The report said agents took away a "puffy bespectacled native New Yorker with a small moustache and thinning black hair." At Foley Square photographers waited to snap his picture. Rosenberg was of medium height, dressed in a wrinkled suit and floral-pattern tie.

Until then, the press had dealt with accused spies as remote, exotic symbols, usually professional diplomats, soldiers, or government employees seduced by a combination of flattery, sex and money. Now that a suspect stood before them, ready to be processed into the routine formulas of news framing, it was obvious that no story, photograph, series, exposé or editorial was big enough to describe the harsh reality Julius Rosenberg faced. In a sense, he represented the banality of the familiar and commonplace: a quintessentially ordinary looking man of early middle age. He was too plain, too recognizable to translate with any meaningful impact into the relevant criminal symbolism of newspaper conventions. This circumstance was a dilemma no one in the press had foreseen. How to present, to convey adequately the specific human terms of atomic espionage to the uninitiated who read newspapers? After all, this suspect was not Axis Sally or Tokyo Rose making broadcasts from distant foreign cities. It was not Ezra Pound defending Mussolini to Italians or Robert Henry Best extolling the Third Reich from Vienna.[16] It was a neighborhood boy from City College.

As Rosenberg was hustled up the stairs of the building in Foley Square, J. Edgar Hoover and Attorney General J. Howard McGrath held a press conference in Washington, D.C. They said that the fourth American member of the spy ring had just been arrested in New York City.[17] As after the Gold and Greenglass arrests, Hoover distributed a simple press release. It summarized the data of the arrest and also contained a brief biography of the suspect.

Julius Rosenberg, thirty-two, was arrested on a charge of conspiracy to commit espionage. Hoover described Rosenberg as "another important link" in the Soviet espionage apparatus."[18] Like Gold and Greenglass, he was accused of violating Section 32(A) of the Espionage Act. Rosenberg was charged with recruiting David Greenglass into a spy ring and providing Greenglass and Harry Gold with classified data on the atomic bomb.[19] The FBI-Justice Department press release said the FBI's detective work revealed that Rosenberg had engaged in espionage "so he might do something to help Russia."[20] Rosenberg was charged with giving David Greenglass part of a torn Jello box top when Greenglass was on furlough in New York City in 1945. The other half of the "irregularly cut" cardboard was passed by Rosenberg to an intermediary who gave it to Gold. Hoover said Gold used the Jello box top to identify himself to David Greenglass when he contacted the latter in Albuquerque in June 1945.[21] Hoover told reporters Gold gave Greenglass the torn box-top half, and the soldier matched it with the half Julius Rosenberg had given him five months earlier in New York City. Although Hoover did not say who gave Gold his half of the box top, the New York Post's Loy Warwick likened him to "a character (in) a spy thriller."[22]

Julius Rosenberg arrived at Foley Square handcuffed to agents, forelock tousled, glasses glinting in the light from popping Speed Graphic flashbulbs.[23] A lawyer named Emanuel "Manny" Bloch arrived minutes later to represent Rosenberg. Bloch told reporters on the courthouse stairs that his client would plead not guilty.[24] Bloch briefly conferred with Rosenberg, who otherwise expressed little emotion.[25] Irving Saypol and Assistant U.S. Attorney Myles Lane represented the federal Southern District of New York. Bail was set at $100,000, a figure Manny Bloch vainly protested as excessive.

At Knickerbocker Village, Ethel talked to reporters from the New York Mirror, New York Journal-American, and New York Daily News through a crack in her apartment door.[26] She denied that either she or her husband had belonged to the Communist Party.[27] Ethel insisted Julius was not involved with any spy ring. "My husband has done nothing. There is nothing to clear up." She also said she and Julius had only discussed Klaus Fuchs's arrest the previous February "in the way people discuss any big news story."[28] Neighbors in the complex told a *New York Post* reporter Julius was "very pleasant" and a "fond parent."[29] At the apartment of Sophie Rosenberg (Julius's mother) an unidentified male said there was nothing to say. "We are all shocked."[30]

Reporters had struggled to glean a few quotes from Ethel Rosenberg, the Rosenberg family, and Julius Rosenbergs' employees. Most interviewed complied to some extent, but it was hardly the stuff of Graham Greene or Ian Fleming. A good story with national impact often features highly publicized conflicts between people and institutions. So far neither Julius nor Ethel Rosenberg went beyond pro forma denials of charges. Obviously, neither saw the mainstream news media as a forum for expressing a fuller account of events. For its part, the press was content to let the familiar routines of court coverage handle the story.

4

The Government, the Press, and the Rosenbergs

You can shut yourself off to a certain extent, but I'd be riding the subway, and I'm a guy that likes to read sports. You're bound to see a newspaper. But I thought I'm not going to let some writer impress me. Every writer has a different slant and I was there. But anyone who tells you he can shut himself off completely during a trial has never served on a jury.[1]

Rosenberg-Sobell juror Harold Axley reflecting on the trial in 1975.

Lawyers for the Rosenbergs and Morton Sobell complained in appeals that their clients had been victims of "inflammatory" trial-by-newspaper coverage. They maintained that J. Edgar Hoover and officials in Washington and New York created widespread hostility against their clients in the press before the trial.[2] Defense lawyers said "repeated harangues by public officials" made chances of receiving a fair trial impossible. Specifically, they cited Hoover's comment to the news media that espionage activity in 1950 was far worse than during World War II. The appeal said this publicity was aimed at members of new "atom spy" grand juries in New York City.[3] It described "official" press releases that "pander[ed] to the basest bigotry." Defense attorneys assembled an extensive exhibit they termed "Quantitative News Coverage." The brief stated that some 30,000 column inches of "cold war news" appeared between February 1950 and March 1951, when the trial began. This mountain of "publicity" was said to "bear upon the case" of the defendants. The Rosenberg-Sobell defense turned in thirteen separate exhibits consisting of more than 1,000 news articles. The exhibits were limited to metropolitan New York City and included the *New York Herald Tribune, New York Post, New York World-Telegram and Sun, New York Daily News, New York Mirror, New York Journal-American,* and *New York Times.*

Allegedly a "publicity campaign" was organized against the defendants by the "prosecuting arm of the government."[4] A review of a

nationwide sample of newspapers and newsmagazines the day after Julius
Rosenberg's arrest has interesting results. Of the eight newspapers in the
sample, all featured headlines that were at least technically inaccurate. For
example, the *Chicago Tribune* said, "FBI Seizes Fourth American as A-Bomb
Spy." The *Atlanta Constitution*: "New Yorker Arrested on Spy Charge." The
Washington Post: "FBI Seizes 4th Man on A-Spy Charges." The *New York
Herald Tribune*: "New Yorker Seized as Atom Spy, Linked to Fuchs."[5] Harry
Gold, David Greenglass, and Julius Rosenberg were arrested for conspiracy to
commit espionage, not for atomic espionage.   The legal definition of
conspiracy requires two or more people to confederate in an unlawful or
criminal act.[6] To be convicted of conspiracy one need only plan a crime; an
attempt to accomplish the plot is not required. In this sense, the headlines in
the above mentioned pages, plus those in the *San Francisco Chronicle*, *St.
Louis Post-Dispatch*, *New York Times*, and *Louisville Courier-Journal*, were
inaccurate and inflammatory. Still, it can be argued the effect of the charges
was that of accomplished espionage. After all, J. Edgar's Hoover press release
spoke not of plots but of actions by a number of people.[7] Nonetheless, a
fundamental advantage of trial in a republic is of the right to be tried on
charges limited to an indictment.

Another question: Did newspapers report Julius or Ethel Rosenberg's
reaction to his arrest? As noted, the late-afternoon July 18 edition of the
Journal-American reported Ethel's reaction to her husband's arrest. But of the
eight newspapers in the sample only the *St. Louis Post-Dispatch*, using a
United Press report, mentioned Ethel's postarrest remarks.[8]   The *Herald
Tribune* quoted Ethel: "I really have nothing to say," but did not include her
or Manny Bloch's comments about Julius Rosenberg. (*Time* said in a July 31
issue that Julius Rosenberg "stoutly" denied charges.)[9]

Julius Rosenberg's arraignment took place late at night. Possibly, the
morning papers and morning editions of afternoon papers missed or
overlooked his plea. A check of the sample for July 19 (two days after the
arrest) revealed the *San Francisco Chronicle* reported Rosenberg's denial.
Too, the *Herald Tribune* quoted Manny Bloch as "vigorously" denying
charges against his client. However, the *New York Times*, America's paper-of-
record, did not inform readers of Rosenberg's response to his arrest. Is that
really important? Yes, not only in the sense of the formulaic, nonpartisan
reporting of the profession practiced by midcentury but because Klaus Fuchs,
Harry Gold, and David Greenglass had confessed.[10] Rosenberg was described
as the fourth member of the ring. Not to report his reaction to charges, or his
plea, would imply that he too had confessed.

In the context of mainstream, "objective" journalism, something else
is odd about the Rosenberg arrest coverage. When one reads the official press
release, it is unclear exactly who the source(s) of the FBI and Justice
Department were. It became obvious in the following months that they were

David and Ruth Greenglass, but the FBI did not then disclose this fact. What of that? The subtle implication that the Department of Justice created was that the FBI information on Rosenberg was the result of 1) investigation and observation; 2) full or partial confession; or, 3) disclosures provided by informants not involved in the spy ring. Evidently no one in the press or other news media questioned who had provided FBI agents with their information. All the newspaper stories on Rosenberg's arrest in this study's sample are rewrites of the Hoover/McGrath press release: "The FBI investigation revealed that Rosenberg made himself available";[11] not "Hoover said Greenglass told agents Rosenberg made himself available." *Time's* article on the arrest sometimes even omitted source references to Hoover, McGrath, or Saypol. Example: "Rosenberg tore the top of a Jello box in half, gave a piece to Greenglass";[12] not "Hoover said Rosenberg tore . . ."

Reporters who covered government institutions in 1950 seldom sought the why or wherefore of a political story. Edwin Bayley found in his study of Joseph McCarthy and the U.S. press that what is not reported in politics often is as important as what is reported.[13] The Rosenberg-Sobell case was reported like many other big stories: in a multitude of bite-size, highly sensational and sometimes indigestible pieces. That does not mean it was fully or even adequately reported. Plainly, the Justice Department and the FBI did not want to identify the Greenglasses as their major witnesses in the case against Julius Rosenberg. Why? Both now were confessed accomplices; the word of accomplices traditionally has not carried the same weight as the testimony of other witnesses. Also, the fact that Ruth Greenglass had not been arrested left the government open to the charge that a deal had been made with the Greenglasses.

This is not to say that newspapers outside the national sample did not attempt more balanced reporting of Julius Rosenberg's arrest. The *New York Daily News* interviewed Ethel at home the morning after the arrest. It said Ethel denied being "wife and sister to suspected traitors."[14] The report described the Rosenbergs small but mostly "barren" apartment-only a few pieces of furniture and no rug. Reporters did notice, however, a large library collection, including the books *Stalin Must Have Peace*, and *Battle Hymn of China.*[15]

The press busily struggled to reconstruct the Rosenbergs into a coherent, media acceptable framework. Mostly it did not work. Their utter, undifferentiated mediocrity, their ethnic, socioeconomic, and urban indistinguishability, was immutable and unconfined. Sifting through the flotsam and jetsam of their disrupted lives only turned up a nonobservant Jewish petit bourgeois family with far left-wing sympathies. Now that the atomic apocalypse had been brought to the neighborhood level, journalists had to assemble a new framework for their readers. Of course, the only major peg to hang the story on was the spy ring. This created a major dilemma: a spy ring, like evidence in an arson case, often leaves no corporeal substance. There were no fingerprints, no ransom notes, no blueprints, no memoranda, no telltale phone records. Further, the alleged crimes had occurred years earlier. To journalists who deal in here-and-now murder-suicides, bank robberies, child molestations, this lack was as palpable as Ariel's voice in a windstorm. It was almost impossible to be fair (in the conventional, nonpartisan journalistic sense) to either the Rosenbergs or Morton Sobell. The press did the next best thing. It accurately reported the limited view it was allowed of the case by the government.

The *Daily News* was unique among the papers studied here in that it strongly suggested the FBI's information on the Rosenberg case came from David Greenglass.[16] A story in the July 20 *Herald Tribune* said the Manhattan U.S. Attorney's office "did not plan" to use David Greenglass as a government witness.[17] Someone, either in the local FBI or U.S. District Attorney's Office, leaked another allegation to the news media. Julius Rosenberg was said to have provided David Greenglass with a little less than $5,000 to pay for the Greenglass family's alleged flight to Eastern Europe.[18] An "informed source" also said Rosenberg's part in the conspiracy was confined to the New York City metropolitan area. The unnamed source also said Rosenberg had contacted others in his role as a "leg man" in the spy ring.[19]

Four "atom spy" arrests in less than two months had left a nation angry, shaken and suspicious. President Truman made a speech over network radio warning of the dangers of internal subversion. Truman now was a political lame duck. It only stretches credulity slightly to say that the "A-Spy" arrests of summer 1950 were the president's political coup de grace.[20]

Five days after Truman's speech, Attorney General McGrath in Washington and Irving Saypol in New York City held simultaneous press conferences. Both announced the arrests of Abe Brothman and his business partner, Miriam Moskowitz.[21] Brothman, thirty-six, was described as a New York City chemical engineer and a small-business owner. News reports said Moskowitz, thirty-four, was his business assistant.[22] Both were charged with conspiracy to obstruct justice. In addition, Brothman was indicted on a charge of attempting to influence testimony. The *New York Times* said the indictments were issued after Harry Gold had testified before a grand jury.[23] Mindful of publicity, Saypol promised the news media that more arrests would stem from the present ones.[24]

Shockingly, the FBI case against Ethel proceeded on the most cynical terms. Declassified FBI documents released in the 1970s indicate that J. Edgar Hoover wanted to arrest and interrogate Ethel as a "lever" for getting Julius Rosenberg to confess his role in the spy ring.[25] Indeed, Hoover sent a brief letter on the case to Attorney General McGrath two days after Julius Rosenberg's arrest. The director suggested Ethel's arrest might lead to

Rosenberg's naming other suspected ring members.[26] (Of course, news media members were not informed of this correspondence). Then Ethel was called to testify before the same grand jury on August 7, 1950. The case changed subtly day by day, but reporters' perceptions of it were confined to FBI and prosecution press releases and news leaks. Ethel Rosenberg again appeared before the grand jury shortly before her arrest. Assistant U.S. Attorney Myles Lane questioned her about her husband's alleged dealings with what newspapers referred to as "the atom bomb espionage ring." Ethel refused to answer any questions pertaining to Julius's arrest.[27] She was again summoned to appear August 11 before the same grand jury. She again invoked the Fifth Amendment to the questions. After being excused, she left the courthouse to catch a subway. FBI agents caught up with her as she strolled across Foley Square's crowded plaza. She was arrested for conspiracy to commit espionage.[28] Altough she was accused of helping to recruit her brother into a Soviet spy ring, Myles Lane told reporters he had "ample evidence that Mrs. Rosenberg and her husband have been affiliated with communist activities for a long time." He also said both Rosenbergs told other unnamed conspirators to flee the United States for the Soviet Union.[29]

Bail was set for Ethel Greenglass Rosenberg at $100,000. Alexander Bloch, Emanuel Bloch's seventy-year-old father, represented Ethel at a hearing. A slight, neatly attired man, the elder Bloch protested the bail, saying the "flimsy charges" against his client did not justify $100,000. Alexander Bloch's point about "flimsy charges" was not without merit. The arrest warrant (and newspaper reports) listed only one overt act—a discussion with Ethel Rosenberg's brother and husband. There was no date for it, either; even the general theme of the discussion was undetailed.[30] Nonetheless, how was Ethel's arrest reported in the press? Ethel's arrest did not command as much attention as those of her brother and husband.

A review of newspapers in the national sample for August 12, and 13, 1950, reveals only a United Press report in the *Louisville Courier-Journal* and a staff report in the *New York Herald Tribune*, which reported Ethel's denial of charges after her husband's arrest. Since Ethel's earlier remarks denying her husband and brother's spy ring involvement were not widely published in newspapers, their residual effect three weeks later was minimal. Still, the charge of conspiracy was reported accurately in all the newspapers. Headline writers, however, took some liberties with the conspiracy charge. For example, the *Atlanta Constitution*: "FBI Holds Mother of Two On Spy Count." The *Chicago Tribune*: FBI Nabs Wife, 7th Accused in Red Spy Ring." The *San Francisco Chronicle*: "FBI Arrests Woman as Atomic Spy."[31] Further, the issue of FBI source identification in these articles is moot because there simply is none. After Julius Rosenberg's arrest, a discerning newspaper reader might have inferred that David Greenglass was the FBI's source of information. But the stories following Ethel's arrest are so sparse in detail that one cannot assume he was the major source leading to her arrest. Although Alexander Bloch's "flimsy" comment appeared in some stories, no one questioned why Ethel's arrest happened three weeks after her husband's arrest.

Further, the warrant against Ethel mentioned one overt act, an alleged "discussion" among David, Julius, and Ethel. There is no detail of this conversation in the news of the national sample, even though it is a fascinating extension of the charges. What should have been a scintillating story merely segued into routine police blotter rewrite. Surprisingly, the case against Ethel, at least as it appeared in the news media, was almost nonexistent.

Summer 1950 was winding down, but questions hung unanswered in the stifling heat. The unasked questions surrounding Ethel Rosenberg's arrest suggest a term first broached in 1955 by *New York Times* diplomatic correspondent James Reston: news management. In congressional testimony, Reston said that he feared Eisenhower administration officials increasingly "managed" the news.[32] When Reston used the term "manage" he referred to international reporting. He meant officials shaped the news without letting reporters know (or without revealing) the full story behind the event.[33] Sometimes deceit or lying was the problem, but more often it involved subtle manipulation of the news media to achieve the best possible coverage. In a sense, the news management concept is made to fit the near formless contours of this case. Beginning with Harry Gold's arrest, U.S. reporters mostly seemed content to report by government press release. The New York City papers, of course, "localized" the story, especially David Greenglass's and Julius Rosenberg's arrests. But for an "atom spy ring" series of stories, there was mostly an official perfunctory quality to the coverage. Later, though, the unasked questions, the neglected quotes, the unsought interviews certainly had an impact on the history of the Rosenberg-Sobell case.

Sociologist Gaye Tuchman speaks of news as a "frame," a means for reconstructing reality for media consumption.[34] At first, the government's "frame" of the "atom spy" arrests went unquestioned despite some loose ends. This observation is not to argue for the Rosenbergs' innocence, only to suggest that the tension of war and crisis at home encouraged a more malleable, less probing, less aggressive press. What about the Rosenbergs? Why didn't they, or their lawyers, protest? Why didn't Manny Bloch use his access to the news media to refute the FBI-Justice Department version of events? For several reasons, answers to these questions are extremely difficult to find. For one, both Bloch and his legal assistant, Gloria Agrin, are dead. Nonetheless, part of the reason for the Rosenbergs' silence might be attributed to the shock of arrest and jail. Then there was anguish over their sons' placement and care, as well as other problems. Though Manny Bloch had only two clients, he was a very busy man. He attended to the legal, business, and private affairs of the Rosenbergs full-time for three years. Then, arguably a large degree of fatalism had settled on all three defendants. The domestic cold war was at its nadir: both Rosenbergs had been labeled as atom spies in newspaper headlines.[35]

Morton Sobell's arrest is quite possibly the oddest in FBI history. It is odd because the circumstances under which it took place were unprecedented as well as bizarre. Sobell was arrested in Laredo, Texas, but he first had been arrested, then "deported," by Mexican federal police in Mexico City.[36] Sobell had worked at Reeves Instrument Company in New York City as a research engineer. He, his wife, his wife's daughter by a previous marriage, and their infant son then left their Flushing, Queens, home in late June 1950. They traveled by plane to Mexico City, where the Sobells rented an apartment.

While he was in Mexico, Sobell tried to book passage out of the country. About this time he learned of Ethel Rosenberg's arrest from the international edition of the *New York Times*.[37] Then on August 16, 1950, Mexican security police arrested Sobell for bank robbery.[38] The Sobells were returned to the United States the next day. Morton Sobell was led into an office on the U.S. side of the Rio Grande River in Laredo, Texas. There he was arrested, put in handcuffs, and taken to a local jail, where he was processed and sprayed with DDT.[39]

There were no Mexican or U.S. press reports of the Sobells' experience prior to Sobell's arrest in Laredo. Whoever retells the Rosenberg-Sobell case can turn nowhere else for documentation. The only reconstructions of the Sobells' experiences in Mexico are their own accounts.[40]

By the time Sobell reached Texas, U.S. newspapers carried reports that a New York City grand jury had indicted the Rosenbergs and a Soviet national, Anatoli A. Yakovlev, for conspiracy to commit espionage.[41] Yakovlev was said to be living in the Soviet Union. Morton Sobell's departure from New York was discussed more in the press than his "deportation" from Mexico. Sobell was reported to have left New York on June 22.[42] In New York, Irving Saypol refused to confirm or deny to the *Herald Tribune* whether Julius Rosenberg had told Sobell to go to Mexico. The *Times*, however, said "it is believed that [the Sobells] were awaiting Russian visas for a Scandinavian country from which they would proceed to the Soviet Union or a satellite."[43] In any event, the *Times* did not cite its source of information.

Once again, most headlines in the national sample did not accurately reflect the charges. For example, the *Herald Tribune*: "New York Radar Expert Held; Is 8th in Red Atom Spy Ring"; the *Times*: "Engineer Is Seized at Laredo as Spy for Russian Ring"; the *Washington Post*: "FBI Seizes Ex-D.C. Man as Red Spy"; the *Louisville Courier-Journal:* "Runaway Jailed as Spy in Laredo." Further, five of the eight newspapers in the sample said Sobell had been charged with "passing" or "giving" defense secrets to the Soviet Union, instead of conspiring to do so.

The *Herald Tribune* said the FBI had traced the Sobells to Mexico after finding their two-story Flushing, Queens, home "shuttered."[44] A new, unused Buick sedan sat in a locked garage. Reporters found bottles of milk and a stack of newspapers outside the Sobells' front door.[45] Neighbors said they did not know where the family had gone.

5

The Greenglasses Revise Their Story

David Greenglass was interviewed today by SAs W. F. Norton and John A. Harrington. He furnished in substance the same information as related by Ruth Greenglass . . . He stated that when he and his wife, Ruth, came home in September 1945, Julius came to the house early in the morning very excited and asked him if he had any information. David stated that he told Julius that he believed he had worked out all the plans of the atomic bomb. Julius was elated at the news and gave him an envelope which contained $200.[1]

FBI file, February 25, 1951

The Rosenbergs and Morton Sobell sweltered in the stale summer air of three different jail cells. Ethel was in the Woman's House of Detention, Julius in the Federal House of Detention. Morton Sobell resided in the Manhattan County Jail, known as "the Tombs."[2] The "atom spy case" was far from forgotten, though. By now, there was modest community support for the Greenglasses in the old East Side neighborhood. In late August, the *Jewish Daily Forward* ran a series of articles sympathetic with the Greenglasses' plight.[3] The FBI also was interested in the series; the articles were translated from Yiddish and included in the agency's vast files on the Rosenberg case.[4]

What about the Rosenberg children? After being rejected by their maternal grandmother, they were placed in a Bronx shelter for Jewish children. Neither the left-wing, the communist, or the mainstream press reported this development.[5] Meanwhile, Helen Sobell had retained the services of Edward Kuntz. Like Manny Bloch, Kuntz was a lawyer with a leftist reputation and civil liberties experience.[6]

Although Morton Sobell had been in jail for several weeks, he had not been able to assert his innocence publicly. Silence on the matter made it seem as if he tacitly conceded the government's charge. Sobell had passed up several opportunities to declare his innocence to the press, thinking it would "sound phony." While the Rosenbergs at least had had a limited opportunity to rebut the case against them, Sobell's guilt seemed a fait accompli in the press from the start. While his case dissolved into a legal twilight zone, the spy ring arrests ended abruptly. After Sobell's arrest, FBI predictions of further arrests disappeared from newspapers.

Then on September 15, Manny Bloch appeared in court to request "a true copy" of the sketches of experiments made and allegedly turned over to Julius Rosenberg by David Greenglass.[7]

Several days later confessed spy contact Alfred Dean Slack pleaded guilty to conspiracy to provide Soviet Russia with classified information on explosives. By now Slack was something of a forgotten man. News of his plea was buried in the inside pages of most newspapers. At his trial, however, he related some interesting incidents. He said he and Gold first met in Rochester in 1940 when Slack worked for the Eastman Kodak corporation.[8] Slack also said he had refused three times to give Gold information on RDX, a high explosive. He relented, he said, only after Gold threatened to reveal his prior espionage activities. Although never charged with being a spy, Slack was implicitly tied by the press to the Fuchs-Gold-Greenglass ring. Judge Robert L. Taylor sentenced Slack to a fifteen-year prison sentence.[9]

U.S. federal Judge Edward Weinfield said the sketches and information Manny Bloch wanted were "far more" than he was constitutionally entitled to see.[10] News of Weinfield's decision was buried in the back pages of section one, but it was a telling blow against the Rosenbergs. It meant defense lawyers would be at a huge disadvantage instead of a formidable one. Moreover, Bloch, his father, Alexander, Kuntz, and Kuntz assistant Harold Phillips were inexperienced as trial lawyers and had little knowledge of federal law and procedure. They were also at a psychological disadvantage because they could not categorically refute any of the government's charges in the press *before* the trial began.

On October 18, David Greenglass pleaded guilty to conspiracy to commit espionage.[11] The *New York Herald Tribune* predicted Greenglass would escape the death penalty by testifying for the government. O. John Rogge announced that his client was "prepared to give what is his best recollection" in testimony.[12]

Of the sample of newspapers cited in chapter 4, the *Herald Tribune* noted on page twenty-three of a story jump that the Rosenbergs had pleaded not guilty at their arraignment. The *Times* also reported the Rosenbergs' plea. It was the only newspaper or newsmagazine in the sample to record Morton Sobell's belated plea. Sobell says he and his lawyers first read of the indictment in the *New York Daily News*. While the indictment was released to the press on October 11, Sobell's lawyers did not receive a copy until later. Perhaps this incident best represents the increasingly close relationship between government and the press after World War II. Reporters, editors, and newspaper readers knew of the prosecution's decision *before* the defense knew of it. It was almost as if the arm of federal justice now had a semiofficial presence in the press. That was not wholly the news media's fault, but it suggests that war and politics had taken a subtle toll on the nation's constitutional presumption of innocence.

Historian Daniel Hallin describes the cold-war era as a "low point" for muckraking style journalism. He attributed this situation to reporters' "depending on the state to make objectivity work as a practical form of journalism." Not until the Vietnam War would this sometimes incestuous relationship finally be challenged by journalists.[13] Todd Gitlin's point about "media frames" being arranged to help journalists make sense of the world applies here. The spy ring described in newspapers in 1950 easily could have existed, but if it did, it was as a web of tangled trails, confusing switchbacks, and dead-end roads. J. Edgar Hoover and Irving Saypol provided the press with a vastly simplified, neatly packaged media frame, replete with a recognition cue and pass phrase. It was as if a high-noon bank robbery had fused with the apocalyptic evil of nuclear fission. Thrown into the bargain was cold-war Americanism and the vibrant secular religion of anti-communism.

On November 7, 1950, Harry Gold spent four hours being questioned by an unidentified member of U.S. Attorney Irving Saypol's staff.[14] Newspaper reports said the session was a rehearsal for Gold's upcoming testimony at the Brothman-Moskowitz trial.[15] Gold had testified before grand juries, but he had never told his story in open court. Confessed spy Elizabeth Bentley would also appear as a prosecution witness at the Brothman-Moskokwitz and Rosenberg-Sobell trials. This strategy was not without its risks for Saypol, who would represent the government at both trials. Poor or disastrous performances by Gold, or Bentley or both, might result in negative newspaper publicity, i.e., pointed questions about the credibility of the witnesses. That might carry over to the Rosenberg-Sobell trial, where the "frame" of media coverage might change, inviting closer inspection of the case.

If this trial was a news media dress rehearsal for the Rosenberg-Sobell trial, it was a success for Saypol. Several days into the trial, Bentley testified that Abe Brothman had given her "blueprints" in 1940 and 1941. She said she passed these along to Jacob Golos, her dead lover and a longtime Soviet espionage operative.[16] Bentley, like Gold, made her first-ever appearance before a court. The next day Gold followed his colleague-in-confession to the stand. Gold testified that in 1941 his Soviet control, Semen Semenov, instructed him to get military information from a chemical engineer in New York City.[17] The "sullen, morose" looking Philadelphian said his espionage contact was Abe Brothman. Both defendants were convicted of the conspiracy to commit perjury charge. Brothman was also found guilty of the influencing-a-witness count.[18] Judge Irving Kaufman congratulated the jury, the U.S. Attorney's Office, and the FBI.[19] Six days later he gave Brothman a seven-year sentence and $15,000 fine; Moskowitz received two years and a $10,000 fine.[20]   The Brothman-Moskowitz trial was connected to the Rosenberg-Sobell trial by the political umbilical cord of news media coverage. The same judge, the same prosecutor, and two of the same prosecution witnesses would appear in the later, more famous trial. These trials featured different defendants (and different charges), but Irving Saypol made sure the *media frame* would stay the same: treason and communism. In the first winter of the Korean War, the dark side of Americanism would clash with anything defined as communist or communist inspired. In some ways Irving Saypol sat on a power keg with a short fuse. After all, his major witnesses, the Greenglasses, had reached an obvious "understanding" with the U.S. Attorney's Office and the Justice Department. Further, Ruth Greenglass, a confessed accomplice, was an unindicted coconspirator. Then there was the matter of Elizabeth Bentley and Harry Gold. As noted, Bentley had a reputation for weaving complex spy plots, while Gold publicly admitted to lying to friends and contacts. All of the government witnesses had one problem or another, but Gold and David Greenglass presented a special difficulty. They had confessed to participating in an exchange of classified data but had no physical evidence to back their stories. They also would recount in court an incident that happened five and a half years earlier. Under these circumstances, even fairly minor discrepancies in testimony might cause a juror to hold out for acquittal. Discrepancies might encourage a reporter to question the credibility of the Greenglasses or Gold. So far, the news media had overlooked the fact that these four major witnesses had told something less than seamless stories. What to do? The answer that Saypol came up with was simple but canny. He brought Gold and David Greenglass together in the same jail to reconcile their somewhat diverging accounts.

Before Harry Gold was brought to New York City to prepare for the Rosenberg-Sobell trial, he was sentenced on December 9 in Philadelphia. Judge James P. McGranery gave the spy-messenger thirty years in prison,[21] the maximum term allowed under federal law.

Gold later announced through his attorney that he would not appeal his conviction. A week later, the *Times* reported Gold had been transferred from Philadelphia to the Tombs jail in Manhattan.

Harry Gold arrived at the Tombs about a week before Christmas 1950. He was sent to the eleventh floor, known to court reporters as "canary row" or "singer's heaven." David Greenglass was already a resident of the floor reserved for cooperative prisoners. Greenglass and Gold were questioned together by Irving Saypol's U.S. assistant attorneys. Rehearsed mostly by Assistant U.S. Attorney Roy Cohn, both men practiced their forthcoming testimony. What made Greenglass's and Gold's rehearsal unique was the extent to which the FBI and the Justice Department went to reconcile their differing accounts of a critical incident. Three days after Christmas, the two were brought together for an FBI interview. Each had a different recollection of the password Gold used when he met Greenglass in Albuquerque in June 1945. Gold told agents he always brought greetings from someone to his contact. When he met Greenglass in the narrow hallway of an apartment house, Gold said he brought "greetings from Ben in Brooklyn."[22]

A problem arose when David Greenglass did not recall the password "Ben." Further, he said that name would not make sense to him.[23] Greenglass suggested Gold had really conveyed "greetings from Julius." In turn, Gold said he might have said "Julius" rather than "Ben." Nonetheless, the FBI report of this meeting concluded that Gold was "not at all clear on this point."[24] After several more interviews in January and February 1951, Gold decided he really had used the "Julius" password. An FBI summary of this session commented that Gold had made up his mind "after considerable reflection."[25] In late February, Ruth and David Greenglass remembered something about Ethel Rosenberg that placed her in the eye of the spy ring. At an FBI "reinterview," Ruth said she remembered Ethel had typed David's handwritten notes about the atomic bomb.[26] According to this updated scenario, David gave Julius notes and sketches of the atomic bomb in the Rosenbergs' apartment. David said that because of his hard-to-decipher handwriting, Ethel had typed up his notes. The Greenglasses said this typing took place in Knickerbocker Village in September 1945.[27] In a 1979 interview with authors Ronald Radosh and Sol Stern, former U.S. Assistant Attorney James B. Kilsheimer III said David Greenglass had only gradually brought his sister's name into the spy ring.[28] Nonetheless, both Greenglasses had given accounts that contradicted their original statements to the FBI.[29]

In fact, until then the prosecution's case against Ethel Greenglass Rosenberg was almost nonexistent. But as Radosh and Stern have noted, there was a striking contradiction in David Greenglass's change of story. Ethel's younger brother told the FBI in a July 17, 1950, interview that he gave an "unsealed envelope" containing notes on the atomic bomb and sketches of a lens mold to Julius Rosenberg.[30] He said the exchange took place on a "street somewhere in Manhattan." During questioning on August 4, 1950, Assistant U.S. Attorney Myles Lane asked Greenglass if Ethel was present at any of Julius and David's espionage meetings. Greenglass replied: "Never."[31] Why is all this relevant to a study of press coverage of the case? Simply this: Gold's change of mind about the password and the Greenglasses' eleventh-hour revisions were not reported in the news media. Why not? Releasing or leaking this latest news would have earned headlines, but Irving Saypol might have risked charges of "coaching" or even fabricating evidence. Also, it might have set off bells and whistles in some journalistic minds (to say nothing of defense lawyers' minds). Why had not the Greenglasses (or Harry Gold) reported these incidents earlier? By any standard, they were not trivial recollections. Saypol truly enjoyed good press, but he was not always the showboating publicity hound his critics later made him out to be. He enjoyed meeting with reporters, relished posing for newsreel and television cameras. But doubtless he knew from long experience that even the most patriotic reporters had their limits. Patriotism and anticommunism could take a case only so far. That does not mean Saypol (or the FBI) privately disbelieved Harry Gold or the Greenglasses. It means they were being selective in the information they released and leaked to the news media. In practical terms, it meant that a somewhat lopsided version of the case appeared in the press. In this sense, the deck was stacked against the Rosenbergs and Morton Sobell. Too, with limited legal discovery, their defense team could not find out about the crucial, damaging, last-minute additions of the Greenglasses and Harry Gold. Further, reporters had no access to federal prisoners (or their records) in the 1950s. Consequently David Greenglass had no chance of inadvertently revealing this latest development to journalists.

This situation suggests another question. Could the press, or news media in general, have somehow uncovered Saypol's devastating secret? Under the reporting restrictions and conventions of the time, almost certainly not. Press-government relations of this era were based on predictable routines; "objective journalism" mostly precluded reporters finding out important, late-breaking details unless officials *wanted* them to know. What about Ruth Greenglass? Well, she certainly was not going to divulge her delayed recollection of events unilaterally. To do so would only weaken her credibility as a prosecution witness. As an unindicted coconspirator she was already vulnerable. Further, between her husband's arrest and the trial, she sat for only one press interview. That was with the *Jewish Daily Forward*, a paper that expressed compassion for her plight.

Nonetheless, the mainstream press displayed little curiosity in the progress of the case in the months before the trial. There were few background stories, profiles, or analyses of the issues or events surrounding the case. Part of the answer for this lies with the event-oriented nature of agenda setting in the cold-war period. Everyone was waiting for the next watershed event, the trial, to begin. Also, in 1951, there was far less analytical reportage on controversial topics with political overtones. U.S. press historians Edwin Emery and Michael Emery say part of the reason for the ascendancy of interpretive reporting before World War II was the "political-social-economic revolution of the New Deal Years." Although interpretive reporting flourished on a small scale in the 1930s and 1940s, this somewhat risky form of reporting faded after World War II.[32]

In any event, what happened in the months before the trial was not discoverable—to the *Times* or anyone else in the news media. The disturbing chapter from the pretrial period of the case later convinced some that Ethel Rosenberg was framed. Too, other files from beyond the scope of this study give pause about David Greenglass's credibility as a witness.[33] Nonetheless, it is undeniable that the government's tight control over compromising (and classified) information minimized "negative coverage" in the news media. It also means historians and scholars cannot assemble a coherent story solely from the multitude of news stories that survive the case. They must delve into other primary sources to make sense of what happened.

The *New York Times* said the trial was "expected to develop to a great extent what atomic secrets were passed to Russia."[34] It noted that the trial had been "tentatively" set for February 13. The press reported the trial would begin March 6, 1951. News on the eve of the trial were the big names that appeared on the prosecution witness list. Newspapers said retired Lieutenant General Leslie R. Groves would testify for the government. Further, Robert Oppenheimer, wartime scientific director of Los Alamos, Harold C. Urey, Nobel laureate and professor of nuclear science at the University of Chicago, and George Kistiakowsky, former Manhattan Project physicist and Harvard University chemistry professor, would also testify for the prosecution.[35] Actually none of these men appeared at the trial. Why they did not is a matter of opinion, depending on whom you ask. Still, Saypol's release of the scientific names on the eve of the trial was pure agenda-setting genius. To cite the impressive persons in news accounts was to imply that they were in agreement with the government's scientific interpretation of the case. Although it would not be known for years, that was not necessarily true. (Indeed, one, Urey, did not even realize for many months that his name was on the list.)

Unquestionably, Manny Bloch and his colleagues now knew theirs was an impossible task. Bloch told reporters he thought the case would "be tried in an atmosphere of tension." He then made a point that would be lost until long after the trial had ended. "I don't mean in the courtroom but outside."[36] Bloch was most likely right. As the following chapters show, in a sense, the Rosenbergs and Morton Sobell never made it inside the Foley Square courthouse. Why they did not related to a prosecutor's news-making ability and the fierce hurricane backlash of American anticommunism.

6

Treason, the Trial, and Agenda Setting

Atom spy traitors Julius and Ethel Rosenberg, their chalk white faces frozen into grimaces of incredulity, yesterday heard themselves condemned to death for passing wartime A-bomb secrets to the Soviets—the first time in the nation's history a civil court has doomed U.S. citizens for espionage . . . But an hour or so later, in their cells, they were loudly singing various melodies.[1]

New York Mirror, April 1951

The city had nine daily mainstream newspapers: the *Times, Herald Tribune, Post, Daily Mirror, Journal-American, World-Telegram and Sun, News Daily, Jewish Daily Forward,* and *Daily Worker.* In 1951, as it is today, New York City was headquarters of America's print and broadcast empire.[2] But then the newspaper was still king. Even in jaded cold-war Manhattan, there was nothing like a sensational trial to heighten the circulation and advertising competition of the big seven dailies (not counting the *Jewish Daily Forward* and the *Worker*). The Rosenberg-Sobell trial, held in Foley Square courtroom room 110, was expected to be the "trial of the century."[3] The staccato language of daily journalism would struggle to capture the atavistic clash of virtue with evil, patriotism with treason, brother with sister. Irving Saypol delivered a blistering denunciation of the defendants in his opening statement. He told jurors that the story of the conspiracy would come from the lips of "associates and colleagues" in the spy ring. The U.S. attorney said he and his staff would show how the defendants had "reached into wartime projects and installations" to provide secret data to a Soviet spy ring. Later in his speech, he linked the "treason" of the defendants with an affinity for communism.[4] No matter how unethical, Saypol's coupling of communism and treason was a masterful courtroom tactic that also ensured a high level of news media coverage. Of course, the trial was not technically about treason. In only a limited sense was it supposed to be about communism. Yet once these two explosive issues were joined, the terms of the Rosenberg-Sobell case were irrevocably established. In only minutes, Saypol framed and fused the underlying, politically unstated themes of the trial. The press, and news media in general, would find this framing an irresistible agenda setter.

But what about Irving Saypol's use of the word "treason?" Judge Kaufman did repeat the exact charges, conspiracy to commit espionage, after the defense team asked for a mistrial.[5] He did not directly address the issue of treason, but then, surprisingly, neither did Manny Bloch or the other defense lawyers. What about the press? How did it report Saypol's "communism" and "treason" remarks? In this book's national sample of newspapers and newsmagazines, the *New York Times*, *Atlanta Constitution*, *Chicago Tribune*, *Washington Post*, and *Time* noted the defendants were on trial for conspiracy. (The *Chicago Tribune* and *Washington Post* did not report the charges).[6] All the newspapers (and *Time*) reported on the topic of communism, but only the *Constitution*, *Chronicle* and *Post* noted any of the defense lawyers' opening statements.[7]

As conscientious, evenhanded reporting, at best, this sampling shows a mixed record. Nonetheless, the headlines for the day accurately reflected Irving Saypol's opening statement. For example: the *New York Times*: "Theft of Atom Bomb Secrets in War Stressed at Spy Trial,"; *New York Herald Tribune*: "Spy Jury Hears Suspects Stole Atom Secrets,"; *Atlanta Constitution*: "Three Accused as 'Traitors' in Spy Trial,"; *Chicago Tribune*: "Trio on Trial for Spying to Serve Russia."[8] As they were after the three defendants' arrests in summer 1950, the headlines were technically inaccurate. But treason and conspiracy to commit espionage are not synonymous. It was a distinction that headline writers mostly did not notice. Once again, a public official had taken advantage of the weakest link in print journalism's gatekeeping structure. There were no means for distinguishing between accusatory statements and accuracy of charges. As long as a public official said it, and the statement was accurately reported, the press's responsibility went no further. In this practice, the press and other news media were little more than public stenographers. (Gaye Tuchman later described this phenomenon as "objectivity as a strategic ritual)."[9] They were no more than that because they chose not to risk being anything else in the tricky undertow of public and political outrage. While there were news columnists to provide opposition, their voices often were ignored or did not carry far in an age of near total anticommunism. Irving Saypol's first-day comment raises Bernard Cohen's original pre-empirical hypothesis of agenda setting. Cohen said that the press

> may not be successful much of the time in telling people what to think, but it is stunningly successful in telling its readers what to think about . . . The world will look different to different people, depending . . . on the map that is drawn for them by writers, editors, and publishers of papers they read.[10]

One might assume the Rosenberg-Sobell case would dominate for months the front-page agenda of newspapers. In fact, even in New York City that was seldom true. Further, it was Irving Saypol's bad fortune to have to compete with the nationally televised Kefauver Commission hearing on organized crime, which was also held in the Foley Square courthouse. In mid-March the hearings focused on New York City gambler and racketeer Frank Costello, whose trembling hands became a close-focus television phenomenon.[11] The Kefauver hearings nudged the Rosenberg-Sobell trial into the inside pages of newspapers, the Devil's Island of big-trial publicity.[12] But for the first week, the goings-on in Foley 110 entranced newspaper readers. Saypol's every word had the potential to find its way into the nation's front-page headlines. As noted earlier, Saypol enjoyed news media attention. He held informal press conferences in his office every day after court.[13] He knew his words would determine not only what jurors and spectators thought about the defendants, but what newspaper readers and public officials thought about their government's "national defense."

But Saypol had a local prosecutor's instincts, meaning that he thought of the "hometown" news media first. To keep the trial "page-one, far-right" he had to recast conceptually a case that had already received ample publicity. Reporters had to feel that they were getting daily fresh angles on a sensational but nonetheless old story.[14] This was a tall order, even for someone of Irving Saypol's experience. But Saypol knew generally how an astute prosecutor should "frame" a case for the news media. "Frame" in this sense means providing boundaries to an imbroglio with dozens of characters and subplots. To borrow Gaye Tuchman's phrase, "frame" also means "window," providing a defining if limited perspective otherwise unavailable to news media consumers.[15] Tuchman speaks of a news frame as a construct of reality. Irving Saypol knew he would be lost in the courtroom (and perhaps the press) if he tried to recapitulate events as they unfolded from Klaus Fuchs's arrest until Morton Sobell's "deportation." The construct he offered went beyond conspiracy to treason, a crime universally regarded as heinous. But no one commits treason without a compelling motive. Here Saypol provided an irresistible interpretive frame to the news media, especially to newspapers, which had already given extensive coverage to the atom spy investigations of the House Un-American Activities Committee (HUAC). It was overpowering because few outside the courtroom understood federal conspiracy law or scientific terms such as "implosion" or "spherical lens mold." But even grade-school children understood the words "communism" and "treason." Todd Gitlin writes that the news media are organized to regulate news frames. This concept applies retroactively to the Rosenberg-Sobell case, as well. The world of March 1951 anxiously watched a land war in Asia. The press was accustomed to packaging political and military news in a Manichean framework: Reds versus the U.N., the U.N. versus North Korea, the U.S. versus the Red Chinese, the U.S. versus the Soviets, Marxism versus the Free World, Stalin versus Truman.

For a first witness, a big or familiar name would have been logical. Max Elitcher hardly fit the bill. Tall and gangly with thick, horn-rimmed glasses, he was unknown to the news media. Elitcher's lead-off appearance was a surprise. He testified in barely audible tones that in June 1944, Julius Rosenberg met him in Washington, D.C., and asked him to provide data from his job at the Navy Bureau of Ordnance.[16] Elitcher also said that in 1948 his friend Morton Sobell went with him near Julius Rosenberg's Manhattan apartment, where Sobell delivered to Rosenberg a 35 mm film can.[17]

On cross-examination, the witness admitted that he didn't reveal his status as a member of the Communist Party member on a 1947 U.S. government loyalty form.[18] Elitcher insisted he had not made a deal with the prosecution, though technically he could have been charged with perjury for having lied on the loyalty form. He also conceded he had never turned over any information to Rosenberg or Sobell. He further admitted that he had told his entire story to the FBI over a period of time.

How did the press cover Elitcher's testimony? Specifically, was the loyalty-oath incident reported? What about his delayed telling of his full story to the FBI? What about his concession that he had never given the Rosenbergs or Morton Sobell data? According to this study's national sample, the *New York Times, St. Louis Post-Dispatch, Louisville Courier-Journal,* and *Washington Post* reported the loyalty-oath incident.[19] The *New York Herald Tribune, Atlanta Constitution, San Francisco Chronicle, Chicago Tribune,* and *Time* did not.[20] The *Times, Herald Tribune, Post-Dispatch,* and *Constitution* noted some part of Elitcher's FBI answer, while only the *Times, Post Dispatch,* and *Constitution* reported his admission that he had never provided the defendants with data.[21]

Nonetheless, using Max Elitcher as a lead-off witness was a stroke of framing genius. His account had never before been reported in the news media. It was a fresh, unexpected perspective on an old topic, a time-honored agenda-setter. Then, too, Elitcher's testimony also served as a perfect lead-in for the trial's major prosecution witness.

David Greenglass is usually remembered because his testimony condemned his sister and brother-in-law to death. It is specifically recalled because of Manny Bloch's request to impound Greenglass's "scientific testimony." This extraordinary incident came in the midst of Greenglass's testimony about information and sketches on the atomic bomb he allegedly provided to Julius Rosenberg. Assistant U.S. Attorney Roy Cohn introduced an exhibit of a "replica" of a cross-section sketch of the atomic bomb dropped on Nagasaki. It was described in newspaper accounts as a "copy" of a freehand sketch of the bomb that David Greenglass had given to Julius Rosenberg in September 1945. Bloch requested that Judge Kaufman "impound" Greenglass's testimony and sketch.[22] He also asked that the government be saved the expense and trouble of proving that the data Greenglass assertedly gave the Soviets had "national defense" value.[23] Was there anything unethical about Bloch's extraordinary request? No, but it did violate the defense lawyer's canon never to concede anything the prosecution has not proved. Still, although the Rosenbergs and Morton Sobell did not dispute David Greenglass's involvement in the spy ring, the impounding motion added that much more credibility to his testimony. By all accounts, it was a devastating procedural miscue. True, it was not the last Bloch made, but it was his most infamous. Shortly after the Rosenberg executions, Bloch said he made his request in order to impress the jury with a "grandstand play." In the years after the trial, Bloch's critics attached more cynical interpretations. Some suggested he wanted to see the Rosenbergs doomed as martyrs; others thought he secretly was working for the FBI. A few speculated he wanted to avoid embarrassing the U.S. Communist Party by keeping trial coverage in the news media to a minimum.

Initially, Judge Kaufman barred spectators and the news media from the courtroom. Only after an angry clique of reporters complained by note to Kaufman were they readmitted to the courtroom. Oddly, the judge asked the reporters to use "good taste" and "judgment" in reporting on the impounded evidence and testimony.[24] Perhaps the strangest aspect of this incident was Bloch's asking that the news media be barred from the proceedings. Whatever his reasons, he wanted major news kept off the agenda of newspapers. Authors Ronald Radosh and Joyce Milton say that by asking that spectators and news media be barred from the courtroom, Bloch, in effect, told the jury that David Greenglass had given the Soviets "the secret of the atom bomb."[25] After readmitting reporters, Judge Kaufman told them they had the prosecution and Atomic Energy Commission (AEC) to thank. He said both groups had decided not to bar the news media from hearing David Greenglass's "technical" testimony.[26] Spectators were not allowed back into the chamber. It was a weird, topsy-turvy, Alice-in-the-Looking Glass experience. Much of Greenglass's testimony would be reported in newspapers. But it would not be included in the trial's official transcript until the late 1960s.

For nearly a day and a half, Manny Bloch grilled David Greenglass. Most reporters agreed that he succeeded only in putting a few small dents in Greenglass's account. Again, what of newspaper coverage of Greenglass's crucial evidence? How many newspapers (or newsmagazines) in the sample reported that Greenglass's impounded sketch was a draft of the one he drew in 1945? The *New York Times, Atlanta Constitution, Chicago Tribune, St. Louis-Post Dispatch, Louisville-Courier Journal*, and *Time* reported on the atom bomb cross-section sketch. However, only an Associated Press report used by the *Chicago Tribune* and *Washington Post* said Greenglass had made his draft "copy" of the sketch just before his testimony.[27] Completely misleading was the *Herald Tribune*, which said the sketch was an "exact" copy. But then, amazingly, there was no mention in any of the newspapers or newsmagazines of Bloch's impoundment request. If Bloch was trying to impress the news media with his "Americanism," he was a conspicuous failure. Or perhaps reporters covering the trial did not realize the implication of Bloch's behavior. Still, even if they did, perhaps they did not want to risk giving a "radical" lawyer positive coverage in the next day's news columns.

What about David Greenglass's admission that he feuded with his brother-in-law? Was that reported? What about the business debt Julius Rosenberg owed David Greenglass? Of the sample for March 13, 1951, the *New York Times*, *New York Herald Tribune*, and *Chicago Tribune* had mentioned either the debt or quarrels. Reports in the *San Francisco Chronicle*, *St. Louis-Post Dispatch*, *Atlanta Constitution*, *Louisville Courier-Journal*, *Washington Post*, and *Time* did not note this testimony.[28] Perhaps the most subtle thing to emerge from Greenglass's testimony was the fact that he obviously was the unnamed source J. Edgar Hoover referred to after Julius Rosenberg's arrest. Since that had been almost eight months earlier, probably no one in the press remembered (or cared). But still, the question lingers: why did not anyone in the news media question Hoover's reluctance to identify David Greenglass as his source? Moreover, why was there not any curiosity about David's Greenglass's trial account of his sister Ethel's typing up his hard-to-read notes? That incident did not appear in FBI or Justice Department reports to the press after Ethel Rosenberg's arrest. Further, why did not Manny Bloch more closely examine David Greenglass on this obvious discrepancy?

The appearance on the stand of Ruth Greenglass, a tall, attractive woman, gave tabloid reporters a familiar, if minor, angle to report. But the government's third major witness was different in more than just gender. Irving Saypol's selection of Max Elitcher as a first witness mostly had paid off in good press coverage. Still, Elitcher's nervousness in the witness chair had been obvious. Then, David Greenglass's penchant for grinning at inopportune moments had not helped him or the prosecution. By contrast Ruth Greenglass was composed; she was assured but not arrogant. She made a strong impression as a witness. The *New York Times's* William R. Conklin said she gave jurors "an illuminating picture of Soviet espionage."[29] Ruth testified that Julius Rosenberg boasted he could "always" find $10,000 to $15,000 as a "front" for espionage.[30]

Later that same day, after court adjourned, Irving Saypol announced the arrest of William Perl on perjury charges. (Perl was a college classmate of

Julius Rosenberg and Morton Sobell). The arrest sent reporters scurrying to cover yet another new angle on an old story.

Saypol told reporters that William Perl had testified before a grand jury in summer 1950. Saypol said Perl had been asked by his office to corroborate "certain statements" at the trial by the Greenglasses. (He had declined to do so). However, Perl was charged with denying under oath that he knew the Rosenbergs and other spy ring suspects.[31] Saypol said a sealed indictment against Perl had been opened only the night before.[32] Perl was arraigned that night at Foley Square; he pleaded innocent. Bail was set at $20,000. Assistant U.S. Attorney John M. Foley said a Vivian Glassman had offered Perl "a substantial sum of money" in 1950 to leave the United States. Foley claimed Perl had only recently applied for a passport.[33] Saypol's decision to arrest Perl while the trial was in progress stunned the defense. While arresting Perl in the midst of the trial was not illegal, it was plainly unethical. Further, such behavior presented clear grounds for a mistrial. Why? Arresting Perl during the trial for denying under oath that he knew Julius Rosenberg could be interpreted as a tacit attempt to influence jurors. The jurors in this trial had been told not to read, discuss, or follow the case, but they were not sequestered. There was nothing to stop them from reading about the case in any of New York daily newspapers.

In any event, Manny and Alex Bloch, Harold Phillips, and Edward Kuntz awoke March 15, 1951, to see the legal equivalent of a publicity blitzkrieg. Morton Sobell says he first learned of Perl's arrest when he walked into court that morning. He recalls seeing Manny Bloch engaged in animated discussion with the Rosenbergs and waving a copy of the *New York Times*. Later, sitting at the defense table, Sobell overheard defense lawyers trying to arrive at a consensus. Apparently, they never reached one.[34]

It is difficult not to believe that Irving Saypol was not trying to grab front-page headlines. As it was, he certainly got them, coast to coast. It was what one might describe as an agenda-setting coup, par excellence. But eventually it was something of a Pyrrhic victory for Saypol. The publicity surrounding the arrest jeopardized the government's convictions on appeal and shortcircuited Saypol's future in the federal judiciary. Moreover, the FBI was irate with the timing of Perl's arrest.[35] Partly, Hoover's anger with Saypol can be traced to the director's desire to have news-media coverage on his terms. FBI officials did fear that Saypol was not equal to the task of prosecution of a very important case. But they also loathed him for beating them to the agenda-setting punch. The tough, soft spoken U.S. attorney knew how to "make news," and he proved it with Perl's arrest.

The story of William Perl's arrest was reported on the front pages of major dailies in New York City and nationwide. It was an audacious publicity stunt by an acutely image-conscious prosecutor. For a day, the Rosenberg case displaced the Kefauver hearings as the nation's number-one story. As noted, Irving Saypol's arrest of Perl later presented him with legal trouble. The *New York Times* ran side-by-side articles that linked Perl with the Rosenberg-Sobell trial. "Columbia Teacher Arrested Linked to 2 on Trial as Spies," and "Greenglass Wife Backs His Testimony as Theft of Atom Bomb Secrets"[36] appeared on page 1 in another unethical journalistic fusion. The *Times'* positioning of the articles assured an appeal charging Saypol with trying to influence the jury through newspaper publicity.

When the trial resumed, Edward Kuntz approached the judge's bench. He promptly lobbed a return volley into Irving Saypol's lap. "I have never tried a case in my life in the newspapers." Kuntz plainly referred to the morning coverage of Perl's arrest in the *New York Times*. Saypol said that was "nonsense" and invited Kuntz to thrash out the incident in open court. Judge Kaufman suggested the matter be taken up in the afternoon session at his bench. The matter then became off-the-record after Edward Kuntz made one tantalizing on-the-record statement to Judge Kaufman.

> I suppose you saw the newspapers. It is an unfortunate experience. We were wondering what effect it might have . . . I didn't know it until I got in the courtroom and Manny Bloch showed it to me. It had a front page.[37]

What else was said between Judge Kaufman and the prosecution and defense is lost to history. Inexplicably, there was no motion for mistrial. Why defense lawyers did not request one remains a lingering mystery.

Ruth Greenglass's testimony had been overshadowed by Perl's arrest. In fact, the press did a rather uneven job of reporting her testimony. For example, while most newspapers noted her status as an unindicted co-conspirator,[38] none in the sample reported an incident that strongly suggested she had memorized most of her testimony. Alexander Bloch used an old defense attorney's ploy when he asked Ruth Greenglass to recount her testimony about the Rosenbergs. When she finished, Bloch had the court stenographer read back the first and second accounts. They were very nearly indentical.[39] Moreover, none (including *Time*) reported Ruth's statement that she hoped for a lesser punishment for her husband. (Some said later that this statement suggested a deal had been arranged). As in the case of her husband, the press presented Ruth Greenglass's account as one of confessed-spy-baring-all. Yet there was no mention in the national sample that reflected Alexander Bloch's hostile questioning of Ruth Greenglass. The defense team's *few* successful questions of Ruth Greenglass were either forgotten or ignored by the press.

Harry Gold took the stand next. His testimony lasted the better part of two days. True or not (or something in between) his was a long, tangled fascinating account worthy of several episodes of "This is Your FBI," then a popular network radio program. Reporters scrambled to construct a coherent (and accurate) story from the spate of details Gold provided. Most important, though, Gold backed up David Greenglass's account of their 1945 meeting. Myles Lane asked Gold the final prosecution question. To the astonishment of the press, Manny Bloch rose and said the defense would not cross-examine Gold.[40]

A strong case can be made that the defendants suffered some degree of prejudicial, pretrial publicity. However, in newspaper coverage before the trial the author was unable to find any instance of a direct attack by the press on the Rosenbergs or Morton Sobell. It is true, the press accurately repeated inaccurate and sometimes inflammatory statements by public officials about the Rosenbergs. Still, during the trial the author found only one notable exception to editorial restraint. A *New York Daily News* editorial appeared just after Gold completed his testimony. It observed that Gold's testimony "in the current atom-spy trial" was "fantastic to the nth degree."[41]

> Gold is a confessed spy. It all reads like cloak-and- dagger stuff that goes on in international intrigue novels and movies. Most of us have taken those things with generous pinches of salt, as being good entertainment but a long way off base from real life. Now it turns out-as the FBI and Secret Service have known all along and have been trying to convince Americans-that these novels and movies are not far fetched; that spies from various countries have infested this vastly and widely envied nation for decades . . . We all need to get these facts firmly nailed into our minds as part of our mental equipment for the cold war.[42]

The March 17 editorial did not mention any of the defendants by name. The piece, however, did imply guilt. More, neither of the Rosenbergs had testified by then. Still, the press was caught off guard by Bloch's abrupt announcement that Gold would not be cross examined. The expectation was that Gold would be thoroughly interrogated by defense lawyers. But all four of the lawyers agreed that Gold was better left alone. This proved a questionable judgment: Gold's testimony featured several minor but glaring inconsistencies. First, he testified to having signed a hotel register in Albuquerque in his own name. Would an espionage agent undertaking a vital assignment use his real name? Whatever the answer, the press did not ask itself that question. Second, Gold said he had used the passphrase, "I come from Julius." He said he had been a professional spy for fifteen years. Why a professional spy would use an unknown colleague's real first name has long puzzled Rosenberg case devotees. Third, there was the already discussed 1947 grand jury perjury of Gold. Fourth, in addition, at the Brothman-Moskowitz trial, Gold had admitted having lied quite often in his espionage career. Still, none of these facts were reported in any of the newspapers or newsmagazines in the sample for the dates corresponding to Gold's trial testimony.[43] Is it realistic to expect that they would have been reported? The answer, at best, is indefinite. Most interpretive and investigative reporting had been chilled by cold war political tensions. Still, Harry Gold was an admitted perjurer. It seems unlikely that reporters covering the trial would not know of his 1947 perjury. Probably, it is more realistic to assume since the defense did not bring it up, that the press did not feel obligated to note Gold's perjury and other inconsistencies in his account. But if reporters did not note it because they found it insignificant, that would be very odd. Odd because Gold was a major witness providing crucial testimony involving the death penalty. If Harry Gold had testified against a defendant in a murder trial, his character defects probably would have been reported in detail. Nonetheless, all four defense lawyers decided that Gold was better left alone. Indeed, Manny Bloch later told the jury Gold "had told the truth."

Elizabeth Bentley testified that she had received several phone messages from a man named "Julius." She said in 1942 that her spy control, Jacob Golos, drove her to a neighborhood near Knickerbocker Village. She said Golos was supposed to "pick up" some material from a contact, who she said was an engineer. She said Golos got out of the car and returned carrying an envelope.[44] Bentley never said she had met Julius Rosenberg. Still, her testimony, at least as reported in newspapers, had the effect of an identification. Manny Bloch managed to elicit from the witness the fact that she was writing a book about her espionage experiences and was a sought after public speaker. Bentley was the defense's last major witness. Now it was time for Julius Rosenberg to testify for the defense; spectators inched forward, necks craning, eyes focused on the bespectacled witness.

Julius Rosenberg invoked the constitutional privilege against self-incrimination several times. (Technically, he did not enjoy a clear right to invoke the Fifth Amendment). Irving Saypol, though, astutely consented to let Rosenberg invoke the Fifth Amendment at his pleasure. It was a skillfully set booby trap that would explode first in the courtroom, then in the news media. Before the trial, Rosenberg told Manny Bloch he and his wife would "plead the Fifth" to any questions about his political beliefs.[45] Bloch told author John Wexley in 1953 that his aging father saw it differently.[46] Alexander Bloch argued that to invoke the Fifth Amendment in reply to a political question would suggest that the defendants had something to conceal. The elder Bloch, of course, was referring to the jury, but his advice could have been extended to the news media. Invoking the constitutional privilege before courts and government committees often was interpreted in the news media and elsewhere as an indirect admission of wrongdoing. When Julius Rosenberg refused to answer questions about his politics, he might as well have been waving a red flag. The Rosenbergs were not on trial for their political beliefs, but Judge Kaufman allowed the prosecution to probe that subject freely. It was a rich opportunity for Irving Saypol, who was at the pinnacle of his career as a U.S. Attorney. He could convince the jury of the defendants' guilt by association before he persuaded the nation by newspaper the next day. Indeed, in this study's national sample for March 22, *Time* and all but one newspaper reported Julius Rosenberg's selective use of the constitutional privilege.[47]

All the newspapers did, however, report his categorical denials of the Greenglasses' assertions.[48] But none of the newsmagazines mentioned a word of Julius Rosenberg's denials.[49] Referring to Judge Kaufman's decision to impound David Greenglass's sketch and testimony, *Time* lamented: "It scarcely seemed worthwhile-the horse had apparently been stolen years ago."[50] Further, none of the newspapers or newsmagazines made any reference to the defendant's version of his relationship with the Greenglasses. Moreover, in its March 26 issue, *Time* referred to the defendants as "spies." This reporting was premature to say the least. The Rosenberg-Sobell jury did not convict the defendants until March 30, 1951.[51]

Ethel Rosenberg made her appearance as a witness on March 26. As with her husband and Morton Sobell, months in jail had made her pale and aged her noticeably. Ethel testified that she and her husband got along well with her younger brother. She denied, however, that David Greenglass had "hero" worship for Julius.[52] During her testimony, Ethel admitted she had owned a secondhand typewriter and said that she had used it to type business reports for her husband. Ethel also said she had typed on this typewriter Julius's appeals to his 1945 Signal Corps firing. However, earlier, before her arrest, she had refused to answer questions on this topic. Like her husband, Ethel also refused to answer a number of questions at the trial. The questions had to do with her or her husband's links to communism.

Irving Saypol quickly had Ethel painted into a tight corner. He reminded her that at two August 1950 grand jury appearances she had claimed the constitutional privilege. That made her an extremely inviting target for the U.S. attorney's arrows at the trial. Saypol followed up, asking Ethel if she had ever helped her brother join the Communist Party. He also reminded her that she had answered questions about her brother and sister-in-law at the trial that she had refused to answer in August. To emphasize his point, he reviewed parts of Ethel's August 1950 grand jury testimony. This review proved damning in that each response he read featured a repetition of the well-known phrase "may tend to incriminate me."[53] In early August, Manny Bloch had advised his client to refuse to answer questions. The fact that Ethel had earlier claimed the constitutional privilege could easily be interpreted now as an implicit admission of guilt. This fact was damaging in the courtroom and just as destructive when it appeared in the press the next morning (especially if jurors were privately tracking the case in newspapers). To reporters, Ethel likely joined a long parade of liberals, left radicals, communists, and ex-communists who refused to answer questions about their political pasts.

Saypol took maximum advantage of his gatekeeping role and its agenda-setting opportunity. He pointedly asked Ethel why she was able to discuss certain activities now while earlier (at grand jury appearances) she had declined to talk about them. While Ethel pondered a response, Judge Kaufman advised her to "see if you can give us some reason." Ethel did not give a specific reason, but she said that during her grand jury appearances her brother and husband were under arrest. She claimed she feared her brother might falsely implicate her in the conspiracy.[54] She then refused to answer some of Irving Saypol's questions about communism, thus reinforcing his questions about Ethel's grand jury testimony. The *New York Times's* William Conklin said some of the questions seemed "harmless."[55] His statement subtly implied that Ethel Rosenberg *would* have answered all Saypol's questions if she were innocent.

Although press coverage was likely the last thing on his mind, Manny Bloch objected to Saypol's tactic. He said that Ethel's use of the constitutional privilege at a grand jury proceeding was a different matter. Judge Kaufman then reminded the jurors they should not draw an inference from Ethel's resort to the Fifth Amendment plea. The judge did, however, rule that Saypol could point to discrepancies between Ethel's grand jury testimony and trial testimony.[56] Finally, on redirect examination, Ethel said she could not recall "what reasons I might have or might not have had."

Ethel's testimony soon ended. It was a damning performance in the political and news-media framework of 1951. Irving Saypol and his staff had engineered what now looked like an easy legal triumph. The defense team announced it had completed its case. Edward Kuntz said Morton Sobell would not testify. That announcement also surprised the press. No doubt, reporters had looked forward to Sobell's explanation of his visit to Mexico and his "kidnapping" by Mexican security police. Sobell's decision not to testify (really more his lawyers' than his) reinforced the notion that he had something to conceal.[57] Really, Kuntz and his colleague Harold Phillips were also thinking of the news media when they kept their client out of the witness chair. They thought the publicity surrounding Sobell's arrest had already smeared him. Why? The Rosenbergs were arrested at home. Sobell was arrested in a country associated in American popular culture and the news media with flight from crime.

But what of Ethel Rosenberg's testimony? Were her claims of innocence reported? What about invoking the constitutional privilege against self-incrimination at the trial? Authors Radosh and Milton say her "behavior on the witness stand and the reaction to it by spectators and the press was to be the beginning of the persistent theory that she and not Julius was the moving force behind their espionage effort."[58] This statement refers to Ethel's persona, which one juror referred to in 1975 as "steely, stony" and "tight-lipped."

In this study's sample, all but one newspaper had stories on Ethel Rosenberg's testimony. The *Chicago Tribune, Louisville-Courier Journal,* and *St. Louis Post-Dispatch* did not report her denials of guilt. All the newspapers (save the one that did not file a story) reported her Fifth Amendment pleas at the trial. (Sometimes they were also noted in headlines). More, *Time's* account did not even say Ethel had testified. As for Ethel Rosenberg's "behavior," none of the newspapers surveyed described any such lack of emotion. While early in the trial various press accounts described a self-possession in Ethel that was lacking in her husband and Morton Sobell, Ethel Rosenberg was not depicted as the cold, unfeeling woman some authors later said she was.

The testimony of Evelyn Cox, a part-time maid, and Ben Schneider, a commercial photographer, ended the trial. Cox briefly testified about a console table in the Rosenbergs' apartment. With Schneider, however, Saypol ended the trial as he began it: with a surprise witness. Schneider told jurors that the Rosenbergs had posed in his shop for passport photos in mid-June 1950.[59] Since Schneider's name did not appear on the witness list, Manny Bloch was caught off guard. Still, he was forced by necessity to cross-examine him. The witness acknowledged he had neither receipts nor negatives to prove the Rosenbergs had been in his shop. Also, he admitted that he had not recognized newspaper photos of the Rosenbergs after their arrests.[60] Although it would not be known for some time, FBI agents had brought Schneider into court the day before his testimony. He then made surreptitious identifications of the Rosenbergs for FBI agents. For months, the FBI and the U.S. attorney had gone to great lengths to lead reporters and newspaper readers through an international labyrinth of winding corridors, hidden doors, concealed trapdoors, and distorting mirrors. Nonetheless, the efforts were not of much use to either David Greenglass or Ben Schneider. Both testified that initially they had not recognized front-page photos of the people they had testified against. It was another case of the press's ineffectual role as intermediary between reality and constructed reality, between the real and the sensationally apparent.

Manny Bloch began his summation by thanking the court for its "utmost courtesy"[61] and extending thanks to the prosecution for its "courtesies."[62] He had again dumbfounded his colleagues. Tactically, his obsequious gratitude would create immense problems on appeal. Moreover, his words were transparently untrue. He, his father, Kuntz, and Phillips had often bitterly complained of Judge Kaufman's many interruptions and rulings during the trial. Also, there had been a high number of mistrial requests. But Bloch was not all unctuous flattery. He quickly switched gears, calling David Greenglass "repulsive" and Ruth Greenglass "evil," saying that she had given testimony "like a phonograph record." Bloch said he did not cross-examine Gold because he thought Gold was telling the truth, but he described

Elizabeth Bentley as a publicity-seeking "professional communist." He noted that Gold and Bentley had used code names when spying. Why then, he asked, was Julius Rosenberg identified by his real first name? This same question would surface months later in the *National Guardian* when that newspaper ran a series of articles claiming the defendants' innocence.

Bloch stressed that Evelyn Cox did not remember a "microfilming" apparatus on the console table. (This fact would be forgotten until just weeks before the Rosenberg executions when a *Guardian* reporter said he had found the missing console table sans the apparatus). Bloch described Ben Schneider as a "Hollywood finisher," a witness sprung on the court for one last headline. He dismissed the "surprise" witness as a "vulgar" and "tawdry"[63] part of the trial. A newspaper report said Bloch "pleaded" with jurors to set aside political prejudice in judging his clients.[64] Still, he stopped short of accusing the government of conspiracy to convict the defendants. In fact, he made it plain he thought the FBI and prosecution had done nothing wrong. By inference, they were victims of the machinations of the Greenglasses, Max Elitcher, and Elizabeth Bentley. Only months later, Bloch's view on the government's role would change dramatically. The *National Guardian's* exposé would soon reveal a second interpretation of the case. This one offered a much different framework, an entirely different construction from which the American political left could mediate the reality of the situation.

Irving Saypol said the defendants were traitors. In his summary, he told jurors that they would decide "one of the most important" cases in the nation's history. He also stressed that members of the spy ring still remained at large. He warned that he knew "traitors" still were at large because of "[Julius] Rosenberg's boasting to Greenglass."[65] The jury took part of an afternoon, all evening, and part of a morning to reach a verdict. There was a lone holdout. Late that night, the judge directed the federal marshall to find hotel rooms for jurors. A newspaper account said they were then "locked up." Judge Kaufman said he thought the jury's verdict was "a correct one." Irving Saypol happily "congratulated" the panelists and predicted that the implications of the case would determine "the very question of whether or when the devastation of atomic war may fall upon this world."[66]

It had ended after fifteen trial days, twenty-two witnesses, and thirty-two exhibits. The verdict was not surprising; the brevity of the trial was. After one night of sequestration, jurors returned to their families. All that remained was the judgment. Holding hands, Ethel and Julius were loaded into a van to return to their respective detention centers. Morton Sobell walked with marshals through a light drizzle back to the nearby Tombs. As he was brought down the steps of Foley Square, a photographer jumped in front of him.

"Look this way Mr. Rosenberg."

"Sobell," the defendant deadpanned.[67]

The press had no editorial comment the next morning. That would come after the sentencing.

April 5, 1951, was sentencing day. The Rosenbergs and Morton Sobell arrived at Foley Square to find an assemblage of reporters and newsreel photographers. A photograph of the Rosenbergs emerging from a police van appeared the next day in the *New York Mirror*.[68] (Another one of them, locked in a passionate kiss, would become famous after their deaths). But photographers did not have it much easier than the reporters. The Rosenbergs (and Morton Sobell) did not conform to any visual stereotypes about crime. They simply appeared too average, too unremarkable for visual or news pegging. No bald heads, jutting jaws, monocles, scars, disfigurements, cosmopolitan soigne, or striking good looks. In this respect, they might have been chosen at random from the telephone directory.

The Rosenbergs declined an offer to address the court. Sitting in chairs before the judge's bench, they stared straight ahead. Judge Kaufman stated that the case appeared in a "unique framework of history."[69] He said it was hard to understand the "life and death struggle" with the Soviet Union. Sounding the theme of Americanism, he said the Rosenbergs had dedicated themselves to Soviet atheism, collectivism, and action against "the cause of liberty and freedom."[70] The judge's sentencing speech has been cited as an exemplar of "the paranoid style" of American cold-war politics. Another view of it is that it was a judicial exercise in prosecutorial and media reflexivity. Judge Kaufman clearly had cribbed several of Irving Saypol's pretrial and opening statements, which, of course, had appeared in the press. Too, his speech had the sharp slap of a Hearst chain editorial. Certainly, parts of Kaufman's speech were written with newspaper and news media commentary in mind. An Associated Press report in the *Washington Post* characterized it as a "stinging lecture."[71] In a secular benediction of cold-war patriotism, the judge scored the Rosenbergs for "putting into the hands of the Russians the A-bomb" sooner than scientific authorities predicted. He claimed that the couple was accountable for communist aggression in Korea.[72] He also accused them of being neglectful parents who "put love of Russia" before their children. Before he pronounced sentence, Kaufman noted he had visited a synagogue "several times" for guidance. After he passed sentence, the *New York Mirror* said the Rosenbergs' faces froze into "grimaces of incredulity."[73] A reporter said Ethel placed a hand on a rail in front of her. A "wan smile" creased Julius's face. The packed courtroom, listening in "concentrated silence," exhaled, as if suddenly deflated. Eventually, the Rosenbergs left their chairs; they left the courtroom by the side door, arm in arm. In the lobby, Julius asked Ethel how she felt. Reporters overheard his wife say, "Fine. I'm all right as long as you are."[74] They were stubbornly mundane, even after being condemned to death. Reporters jostled in the hallway to eavesdrop on their conversation. They heard only the cliches of lovers, typical of conversations outside thousands of halls of justice and misdemeanor courts.

Later, marshals told journalists the couple had sung to each other in adjoining cells in the basement of Foley Square. Reportedly, Ethel sang an aria, "Un Bel Di Vidremo," from *Madame Butterfly*. Another press report said she also sang "Good Night, Irene," while Julius responded with a tenor rendition of "Battle Hymn of the Republic."[75] Manny Bloch met with the press in the corridor outside the courtroom. Plainly dispirited, he reiterated his clients' pleas of innocence. "I repeat that these defendants assert their innocence and will continue to assert it as long as they breathe. They believe that they are victims of political hysteria, and their sentence was based upon political considerations."

Leonard Lyons had an unusual report in the *Post* about the Rosenbergs. He said the husband and wife could "save their necks" if they made "full disclosure about their spy ring."[76] He did not list his source, but J. Edgar Hoover's "lever-strategy" was apparently now in motion with a co-operative journalist serving as ex-officio press agent. Oddly, the government's highly publicized and disastrous two-year international tug-of-war with the Rosenbergs began in a New York City cafè society writer's column.

Nevertheless, there was some anxiety inside the government over the sentences. Concern about Ethel's death sentence cropped up swiftly. Judge Kaufman invoked patriotic values in justifying his decision to sentence the Rosenbergs to death. It was the darker, wrathful side of Americanism: the side that saw the world as a conflict between a treacherous empire and a just, embattled republic. It also mirrored more than one editorial voice in daily mainstream American journalism. The *Atlanta Constitution* lauded the sentences. It hoped they "marked the end of our soft treatment of those who are disloyal." The *Constitution* defended the severity of the death sentences as a necessary evil.

> The testimony during the trial showed clearly the nature of the enemy and the length to which communists in this country will go to obey the wishes of Moscow. We can no longer afford the foolish indulgence of being soft with traitors. Irving Kaufman is to be congratulated for making this plain. Let other traitors be warned. . .And let us not forget every communist is a potential espionage agent pledged to lie and steal to accomplish the direction of the Kremlin.[77]

The *St. Louis Post-Dispatch* said Judge Kaufman's sentence was completely "justified." The paper said the defendants had threatened the national security of the United States in order to assist the Soviet Union. Like the *Constitution*, the *Post-Dispatch* said the death penalty served "as a warning to any others who are not repelled from treason by love of country but must be restrained by fear."[78] The *Post-Dispatch* and *Constitution* both were unambiguous in their defense of Judge Kaufman's Americanism. What about the rest of the press? Was there a rush to defend the death sentences? Given the political milieu of the time, one might assume a torrent of editorial support for Judge Kaufman. Surprisingly, most major dailies in the United States took a hands-off attitude about the sentences. Of the newspapers in the sample, only the *Post-Dispatch* and the *Constitution* had editorials on the case. If patriotism is a value defended by the media in wartime, then the press mostly reserved comment. Whatever the reason, one could hardly assign this lack of discussion to an absence of news worthiness. Perhaps newspapers intentionally avoided editorial comment on the case. After all, as is so often true in trials, the outcome was already stale news. Some editorial writers may have refrained from comment out of a sense of private doubt or revulsion at Ethel Rosenberg's sentence. Whatever the exact reasons, the editorial support Irving Saypol and J. Edgar Hoover hoped for hardly overwhelmed the country.

Interestingly, the *Jewish Day,* a Yiddish-language New York City weekly, suggested that Judge Kaufman had sentenced the Rosenbergs to death because of a "Jewish complex."[79] The *Jewish Daily Forward,* not disputing the Rosenberg convictions, upbraided Kaufman for a disproportionately harsh punishment.[80] On the radical left, the *Daily Worker* most strongly assailed the death sentences. Though the *Worker* did not say the Rosenbergs were innocent, it did contend they were "scape goats for the Korean War."[81]

Next, there was the sensitive matter of David Greenglass's sentencing. The Greenglasses had been expecting no more than a five-year prison term for him. However, Ethel's sentence had put Judge Kaufman in a delicate position. If he gave Greenglass a light sentence, the *Daily Worker's* point about a deal might seem plausible. In that event, even the mainstream press might have to concede that something looked wrong about that. Further, Kaufman could most certainly expect editorial criticism if he handed out a light sentence to a man whose testimony doomed his own sister to the electric chair. In fact, O. John Rogge asked Kaufman to sentence his client to "no more" than five years. In court, Rogge said Greenglass had been the hapless victim of an ideological seduction.[82] He suggested a "pat on the back" and a "light sentence" would help confessed members of the spy ring to step forward. Judge Kaufman sentenced the defendant to fifteen years in prison.[83]

No editorials appeared the next day about the Greenglass sentence. The case had already faded as front-page news.

7

The *National Guardian*: A New Frame

Ever since I received the *Guardian* articles, I've been re-reading them.
The truth is being made known and finally good, decent people are
beginning to come forward in increasing numbers.[1]

Julius Rosenberg from correspondence to his wife, Ethel, September 1951

News of the Rosenbergs' sentences had barely settled when President Truman
fired General Douglas MacArthur.[2] Nevertheless, as MacArthur prepared to
return to the United States, at least one syndicated columnist wrote a
valedictory to the Rosenberg-Sobell case. Dorothy Thompson ostensibly
protested the severity of Judge Irving Kaufman's death sentences in an April
1951 column.[3] Her objection was based solely on opposition to capital
punishment. Thompson had not attended the trial but had obviously read
some file clips on the case. She spoke of the Rosenbergs' convictions for
"treason," a crime she thought despicable.[4] Like other journalists, she
unquestioningly accepted Irving Saypol's opening trial statements about
treason without realizing their inaccuracy.

Therefore, treason is, in essence, the worst of crimes for it strikes at the
most basic social assumption; it is the sin of Judas; it opens possible
consequences, which the perpetrator himself cannot gauge, and which may
bring death and disaster to millions. But treason, in our times, has
somehow escaped satisfactory legal definition. Treason hitherto has been
equated with betrayal to an enemy with whom the country is in open
conflict. Only because the Rosenbergs gave secret information to a
foreign country in 1944 in wartime could Judge Kaufman impose the
formidable sentence.[5]

Meanwhile, Manny Bloch and his legal assistant, Gloria Agrin,
worked fulltime on the appeals. The case wended its way through appeals

courts, but it was more or less a discontinued case in news columns and editorials. For his part, Morton Sobell was told by a *New York Mirror* columnist that once he began his sentence in a federal penitentiary, inmates would make him wish he had been sentenced to death.[6] Other than that there was little news of either the Rosenbergs or Sobell for many weeks.

In early May 1951, a young Mississippi black man, Willie McGee, was executed in the town of Laurel. McGee had been sentenced in 1945 to the electric chair for the rape of a white woman.[7] The evidence against him had been so weak that even the deepest deep-South state required three trials to convict him. Still, the McGee case received at best only sporadic press coverage in the United States. It soon, however, became a cause celèbré in this country and in other parts of the world. By 1950, the McGee case eventually galvanized the Communist Party in the United States and Europe.[8] Willie McGee committees, rallies, and demonstrations were formed and took place in some American cities and in Europe, reminding many of the Sacco and Vanzetti and Scottsboro cases. In the United States, though, few joined the McGee ranks except far-left partisans and opponents of capital punishment.

Ethel and Julius Rosenberg followed the McGee case in newspapers. (In Sing-Sing Julius had a subscription to the *New York Times*). After McGee was executed, Julius wrote Ethel that he was "terribly shocked."[9] Neither Rosenberg realized it, but they soon would become international political and media figures on a scale that would dwarf the McGee case. Their images would clipse Sacco and Vanzetti and the Scottsboro Boys. But for the moment they served their sentences, hoping their appeals would save them from electrocution.

New York Post columnist Max Lerner, like Julius Rosenberg, was also disturbed by McGee's execution. Lerner's distress, however, had only partly to do with the Mississippi man's wrongful conviction and execution.

> There was a time when a case with these ingredients might have stirred the national sense of injustice, cutting across section and party and color and creed. The Scottsboro case did-but the case of McGee, like that of the Martinsville Negroes, seemed to have become the exclusive property of the communists. That is one of the tragic things that has happened in our time. In all honesty, those who care about justice and injustice in America had better face the fact that the communists seem to communicate the curse of leprosy to whatever they touch, even to cases good in themselves.[10]

Lerner had long enjoyed a reputation as a liberal columnist. More, he wrote for a paper that had a liberal editorial reputation. His column on the McGee case was a caveat that cautioned liberals to be careful with whom they went to bed. Lerner's point was well made. Willie McGee died with more support in foreign capitals than in the United States. The "Martinsville Negroes" Lerner referred to was another case in point. In 1946, seven Virginia black men had confessed to the rape of a white woman in Martinsville, Virginia.[11] Unlike the McGee case, the major issue was not guilt or innocence but the sentences. In 1950, the Martinsville case had became another well known international case. As Lerner noted, liberals in the United States also were reluctant to join "Martinsville Seven" committees. The U.S. Communist Party (under the rubric of the Civil Rights Congress) was heavily involved in the Martinsville and McGee cases. Lerner's cautionary statements did not fall on deaf ears. Liberal organizations, such as the American Civil Liberties Union (ACLU), the National Association for the Advancement of Colored People, (NAACP), and Americans for Democratic Action (ADA), argued about whether to join such causes and risk being tarred by negative reaction in the press. It was a question that would return with special force in the Rosenberg case.

Ethel Greenglass Rosenberg released a statement to the press a month after being transferred to Sing-Sing. It was quoted in the *National Guardian*, a left-wing, New York City based, weekly newspaper. Rosenberg said government officials transferred her to Sing-Sing to "break her." She warned judicial and prison authorities that they were "in for a sad awakening." Ethel said she had "nothing to tell them" except to say she and her husband were innocent.[12] She also used the opportunity to repeat her charge of the previous month. "We are victims of the grossest type of political frame-up ever known in American history. In our own way we will try to establish our innocence. But we ask the people of America to realize the political significance of our case and come to our aid."[13] The day before Ethel's letter appeared in the *Guardian*, the *New York Times* reported that Julius Rosenberg would also become a Sing-Sing inmate. The story said he would join his wife in the prison, though, of course, they would be housed in different sections.[14] Then news of the case abruptly disappeared from newspapers.

The executions of the Martinsville Seven and Willie McGee had badly demoralized the left and far left in the United States. In June 1951, however, another case involving black men accused of murder ended in a rare cold-war victory for partisans of the left. In 1948, six young African-American men were convicted of murdering an elderly white security guard in Trenton, New Jersey.[15] After that trial, a relative of one of the defendants had gone to *National Guardian* offices and described the convictions as a "frame-up." *Guardian* editors James Aronson and Cedric Belfrage assigned a reporter, William Reuben, to check out the story. After a brief investigation, Reuben concluded the six men had been convicted falsely. He wrote a series on the case in 1949, which ran in the *National Guardian*. The *Guardian* sent galley proofs of its "Trenton Six" series to mainstream papers, the news wire services, and network radio. The exposé was at first shunned by the mainstream press, but then it was reported on network radio by CBS commentator Don Hollenbeck. Reuben's reports helped launch a movement on behalf of the defendants. In June 1951, four of the Trenton Six were acquitted after a second trial. In an obvious compromise verdict, the other two were convicted of murder.[16] On the left and far left, the Trenton Six news helped elevate the stature of the *National Guardian*. The Civil Rights Congress (CRC) helped defend the Trenton Six at their second trial, but the *Daily Worker* deferred to the *Guardian* coverage of the story. Nevertheless, it was an embarrassing loss of face for the Communist Party. Its public stewardship of the Martinsville Seven and Willie McGee cases had left a bad taste in many mouths. Still, the CRC worked on the Trenton Six case albeit with a lower profile. Manny Bloch was one CRC lawyer who helped on the Trenton Six appeals. During the second trial, Bloch befriended William Reuben. Both soon would work together again.

Sometime in late June 1951, Manny Bloch had lunch with *Guardian* editor James Aronson.[17] They met to discuss the Rosenberg case. In a 1978 memoir, Aronson said that just he and Bloch met for lunch at a Lower East Side cafeteria. However, William Reuben's recollection in 1990 was that another person, Sol Abramson, was also present.[18] Abramson had worked as a reporter for the *New York Mirror* since the late 1920s. He also moonlighted (and later worked full-time) for the *Daily Compass*. In any event, Bloch had told Abramson that "There was more to the case than anyone had expected."[19] As a mainstream Hearst reporter with leftist sensibilities, Abramson was a good choice as a go-between. That a Hearst reporter (the *Mirror* often held conservative to right-wing editorial positions) was helping locate a left-wing newspaper willing to print the Rosenbergs' conspiracy charges was a jarring irony. Apparently, though, Abramson had tried unsuccessfully to interest other mainstream newspapers in the new allegations. Bloch also had spent the summer looking for a newspaper, any newspaper, to publish the Bloch-Rosenberg side of the case. Aronson said Bloch's "odyssey" resulted in "the media shut[ting] their doors and their consciences" to him. Exactly which newspapers Bloch approached is not clear. It is certain, however, that he visited the *Daily Worker* several times in hopes it would cover the Rosenbergs' side of the case. In a 1991 interview, former *Daily Worker* editor John Gates said the paper had already decided not to cover any story pertaining to atomic espionage. "We didn't want to be associated in any way, shape, or form with espionage. . . . In the public mind the words 'spy' and 'communist' were synonymous. We were very leery."[20]

Manny Bloch's luncheon meeting with Jim Aronson was quite long. Aronson said he told Bloch that it "looks as if this has been a political case from the start."[21] When Aronson returned to the *Guardian* offices, he called a meeting with coeditors Cedric Belfrage and Jack McManus. All three quickly decided that Bloch's assertions merited investigation. The next day, Aronson asked Reuben to meet with them. The *Guardian* editors then gave Reuben the outlines of Bloch's story. "They asked me would I be willing to look at the transcript and make an analysis of it, and then give a report on whether it should be taken up."

In more than one way, Reuben was the right choice for the Rosenberg story. His reputation as an investigative reporter was well known in New York City, especially after the Trenton Six trial. Moreover, he had good contacts in leftist circles. He had served briefly as public relations counsel for the ACLU, had worked for the *Compass,* and wrote a civil-liberties column for *Pageant* magazine.[22] He was also a practical choice: the young military veteran had the time to investigate the "reopening" of the case. As a thrice-wounded U.S. Army lieutenant with the 40th Infantry Division in Europe, Reuben received a limited-disability pension.

Reuben next took a couple of weeks to research the case, including visits to Columbia University's journalism library to read clip files.[23] Also, he read the trial transcript and spoke with several people familiar with the case. In summer 1951, Reuben lived on Fire Island, a resort community near Long Island. Manny Bloch came out to see him several times, bringing along the trial transcript. The two men had several long talks. Reuben became convinced that Bloch's story had real merit. In his mind, the mainstream and left-wing press had treated the Rosenberg case as a "spy-criminal case." After a few weeks he told Aronson and Belfrage that it was time "we go ahead and do something."[24]

In most ways the *National Guardian* was an ideal vehicle for a major left-wing exposé on government conspiracy. The *Guardian* had been founded in 1948 by two former mainstream reporters, Cedric Belfrage and James Aronson. Belfrage, a British-born journalist, at one time was the U.S. correspondent of the *London Express.*[25] Aronson had worked for the *New York Times* and several other mainstream papers. He and Belfrage were joined by John (Jack) McManus, a former *Time* and *PM* film critic. All had pronounced left-wing views, though none was a card-carrying communist or socialist. They had left mainstream journalism in order to investigate wrongdoing and advocate social and political causes.

The *National Guardian* was from the start an exercise in self-described "maverick journalism." Unlike the *Daily Worker* it was less a forum for rigidly structured ideology than a radical voice appealing to a wider liberal and left-wing audience. Unlike *PM,* Marshall Field's 1940s left-of-center experiment, it had advertising. Like the *Nation*, it was well written and edited. Unlike the *Nation*, it ranged politically farther to the left. Like the *New York Times* it had foreign correspondents; unlike the *Times*, it had no editorial page per se.

The *Guardian's* birth coincided with the 1948 Progressive Party presidential bid of former Roosevelt administration Vice President Henry Wallace.[26] Although the two were closely allied, the *Guardian* was not the official organ of the Progressive Party.[27] The paper invited controversy in January 1949 when it came to the defense of the twelve leaders of the Communist Party indicted for conspiracy to advocate overthrow of the government. Typically, it did not shrink from unpopular causes. It even upset some of its supporters with articles favorable to life in the Soviet Union, praise of Mao's conquest of mainland China, and opposition to the Korean War. Despite the risks and the inhospitable political climate, the *Guardian's* circulation increased to a peak of 75,000 in 1950. (This was robust for a left-wing publication). By then the American left-wing press had shriveled to a handful of newspapers and periodicals. Besides the *Guardian* there was the *Daily Worker*, the *New York Daily Compass*, the socialist *Daily Call*, and the *Monthly Review*. (The *New York Star* and George Seldes's crusading *In Fact* would perish in 1951).

In one way the Rosenberg-Sobell case could not have reached the *Guardian* at a better time. The paper had little to lose. By 1951, despite reasonably good circulation, it tottered on the verge of financial collapse. The support of Anita McCormick Blaine, cousin of *Chicago Tribune* publisher Robert R. McCormick, helped keep the paper afloat. If not for a wealthy, left-wing Chicago dowager, there might not have been an international movement on behalf of the Rosenbergs two years later.

William Reuben returned to Fire Island to resume research on the case. He met several more times with Manny Bloch, studied the trial transcript, interviewed several of Julius Rosenberg's friends and relatives, and held conferences with *Guardian* editors. Roughly a month later, he had enough material for a lengthy two-month series. In the August 8, 1951, *Guardian*, the newspaper cryptically said it would soon "expose" the government's case against "these two beloved and respected American parents."[28] Because the comment came at the end of a story on a visit by the Rosenberg boys to Sing Sing, it seemed oddly misplaced.

Nevertheless, the next week *Guardian* readers found this headline staring at them: "Is This the Dreyfus Case of Cold War America?" The series began with a blunt claim that the Rosenbergs were victims of a government fraud.

> We are convinced of the overwhelming probability that the Rosenbergs are completely innocent. We believe you will be convinced when we have had the opportunity to lay out all the facts before you. We are confident that you will act, as you did in the Trenton Six case, to win vindication for these young American parents and to repudiate the forces which would take their lives as a propaganda measure in behalf of war and oppression.[29]

Reuben referred to several historical cases involving government conspiracy. He said France's Dreyfus case had the strongest link to the Rosenberg-Sobell case. (See chapter one). He used Emile Zola's muckraking series of newspaper articles on behalf of Dreyfus, "J-accuse," as a historical model for introducing the *Guardian* series on the Rosenbergs. Reuben said "the very best" that could be said of the government's case was that it left doubt enough about the convictions of the Rosenbergs and Morton Sobell to "entitle them, by all American legal standards, to acquittal."[30] Reuben also concluded that Ethel Rosenberg was correct-there were "strong grounds" to suggest an "out-and-out political frame-up." The *Guardian* claimed that if the Rosenberg convictions stood, the government could arrest any member of the 200 or more radical left organizations listed in the U.S. Attorney General's Office as subversive.[31]

> Is the Rosenberg case the Dreyfus case of cold-war America? Is it the Sacco-Vanzetti case of this era when the nightmare Truman war program demands the destruction of a militant labor opposition? Is it the Reichstag Fire Trial of a time when the voice of protest from the political left must at all costs be silenced? The facts we shall present about the Rosenberg case will at least pose the question for most of our readers as to whether their government has not now begun to operate on this shameless Nazi level.[32]

Reuben described the trial as "a four-ring circus" and decried "sensationalized press treatment" of "cloak-and-dagger melodrama." The article discussed several aspects of the trial he thought peculiar. He said only two exhibits "directly linked" the Rosenbergs to the case. One was a Spanish refugee appeal collection can from 1938 found in the Rosenberg apartment. The other was a nominating petition for an obscure New York City Communist Party mayoral candidate.[33] Reuben also reminded readers that the prosecution's two major witnesses were confessed spies. He said Ruth Greenglass went free, while her husband would be eligible for parole in eight years. Too, he characterized the Greenglasses' testimony as "flimsy, rehearsed, and entirely unsupported" by physical evidence.

Reuben said that as "outspoken radicals," the Rosenbergs were logical targets of a conspiracy. He claimed this connection was based on the "legal justification" that all communists were espionage agents serving the

Kremlin. The government case against the Rosenbergs, he maintained, was part of a program to remove "constitutional checks and balances" against Americans with left-wing backgrounds.[34] As a case in point, he noted the U.S. Supreme Court's recent upholding of the convictions of the Smith Act Eleven.

       Besides the opportunity to close leftist ranks, the Rosenberg-Sobell case gave the *Guardian* what historian Lauren Kessler terms a major function of a radical newspaper: "to strengthen the will of their comrades and convert those outside the movement."[35] Reuben sought to educate *Guardian* readers on a topic they could not read about in mainstream newspapers, while attacking a "government frame-up."[36] For example, his first article suggested a radically different position from which to interpret the case. His claim that the case fit a larger picture of government intolerance for political radicals had touched a raw nerve on the left. The Walter-McCarran Act (with its Subversive Activities Control Board), the attorney general's list of subversive organizations, the Smith Act Eleven convictions, and talk of making Communist Party membership illegal frightened many. Embattled and closeted, political activists on the left now had a case to rally around. Coverage of the Rosenberg-Sobell case by the American radical press had been next to nonexistent until August 15, 1951. That soon would drastically change. The case would eventually dominate the *National Guardian*'s and *Daily Worker*'s "conspiracy" coverage of U.S. politics in the next two years.

       In the second article on the case, Reuben retraced the lives of the Rosenbergs. He described the couple as unpretentious "average New Yorkers."[37] Julius, he said, had lost his job in the U.S. Army Signal Corps in 1945 because of Communist Party affiliations. Reuben's major revelation in this installment was that Klaus Fuchs was known to his American friends as "Julius." Because Elizabeth Bentley had reported receiving phone calls from a "Julius," Reuben concluded the jury assumed this "Julius" was Julius Rosenberg and not Fuchs.[38] The author claimed David Greenglass was motivated to implicate his brother-in-law by a soured business relationship and an unpaid Rosenberg debt. In a summary article in the same issue, the *Guardian* denounced the death sentences as "cruel and inhuman to the point of barbarity." The case, it said, "reek[ed] of frame-up."

> That the government should have connived in demanding death sentences for these particular individuals while consenting to freedom and clemency for confessed participants in the same alleged plot leads to the conclusion that there was a special political objective in making a supreme example of the Rosenbergs because of their left-wing politics.[39]

       On August 29, the third article of the series asked: "Did the FBI lie to launch a frame-up?" A photograph of Harry Gold appeared in this issue. A cutline posed the question: "He came from which Julius?" Reuben said the FBI agents began building a case against Julius Rosenberg after they searched David Greenglass's New York City apartment.[40] It was here, Reuben said, that the FBI found some of Rosenberg's old college math notes. He charged that the discovery of these notes led to their being "shaped up" to enrich a case that lacked political sensation.[41] The author of the 1955 book *The Atom Spy Hoax* said Rosenberg's 1945 discharge from the U.S. Signal Corps dovetailed nicely with the math-notes discovery. Again, Reuben described Ruth Greenglass as a confessed spy who made a deal with the FBI and federal prosecutors. He reminded readers of her statement at the trial that she thought the FBI "wanted bigger fish" than her husband.[42] The story also contained a statement from Ethel Rosenberg maintaining that she and her husband were victims of the "machinations of Ruth Greenglass."[43] Reuben was sure the FBI had operated at the center of the conspiracy. As proof of a deal between the prosecution and the Greenglass's lawyer, he cited a quote in the July 13, 1950, *New York Mirror*. In the story, Irving Saypol declined to reveal "the substance of discussions which have been going on."[44] As noted, the *Mirror* of the same date reported that a "series of conferences" had taken place between Saypol and O. John Rogge. Reuben said Rogge told reporters he wanted "several more talks with his client."

Reuben also claimed the Rosenbergs were not linked to the spy ring until Ruth Greenglass signed a statement implicating them three days after her husband's arrest.[45] The *Guardian* reporter noted that no FBI agents had testified on the stand during the trial. (The implication was that the prosecution considered the agents too vulnerable to cross-examination).

This picture certainly presented a "frame" of the case much different from that found in mainstream newspapers before and during the trial. The alternative, "dissident" view of the case continued in the next issue. In the September 5 *Guardian*, in the fourth article, Reuben referred to a story in the August 17, 1950, *New York Times* to strengthen his claim that Ruth Greenglass and Max Elitcher had gradually developed their stories after consultations with the FBI.[46] The *Times* story, like the July 13, 1950, *Mirror* article, also reported David and Ruth Greenglass's cooperation with the U.S. Attorney's Office.

Reuben asserted that Julius Rosenberg's arrest was based only on the "oral allegations" of the Greenglasses. He said the arrest of Morton Sobell was based on "nothing except his suspected political beliefs" and "being over the border."[47] Reuben suggested that if Sobell was trying to flee to Mexico he did a poor job. The *Guardian* cited evidence that Sobell reserved a flight to Mexico and rented an apartment in Mexico city using his own name.[48] (Nevertheless, Sobell had used aliases in traveling to other Mexican cities). The third article had said the "only support" for the Greenglasses' testimony

came from Max Elitcher. Less surprisingly, Reuben alleged that the major
prosecution witnesses gave "rehearsed" testimony at the trial.

The fifth article of the series questioned Judge Kaufman's conduct
during the trial. Reuben asked whether a fair trial was possible "considering
the ceaseless barrage of press and radio statements by the prosecution, the
FBI's J. Edgar Hoover, and Attorney General J. Howard McGrath for eight
months prior to the trial, hammering into the minds of the public the certainty
that the Rosenbergs were guilty. . . it is surprising that sixteen citizens (twelve
jurors and four alternates) could be found who could swear under oath they
had formed no opinions as to the guilt of the accused."[49]

Presaging sentiments that would appear in an appeal, Reuben
accused the government of practicing "phony pre-trial press agentry." He said
the result of this campaign was to remove from "press and public," the issue of
guilt or innocence and replace it with the death penalty.[50] Reuben wrote that
only 20 of the announced 118 prosecution witnesses testified at the trial. Still,
the charge that made the deepest, most lasting impression was that the judge
and the prosecution used the jury selection process to screen out Jewish
citizens. He said this selection happened in city where more than 30 percent
of the population was Jewish. He emphasized the power of government
control of the news media. It was a charge that would appear quite often in
the remaining months of the Rosenbergs' lives.

Both Rosenbergs avidly read the *National Guardian* series. The first
indication of it came in a letter from Julius to Ethel dated September 16,
1951. During a visit to Sing-Sing from their sons and their lawyer, the
Rosenbergs briefly discussed the articles with Emanuel Bloch. Julius later
said in a letter to his wife that he was "reading and re-reading" the Reuben
stories in the *Guardian*.[51] (See quotation at the head of the chapter.). Julius
Rosenberg said at last the truth was "being made known." He also drew
"heart-warming" encouragement from supportive letters-to-the editor and
small cash contributions.

The *Guardian* series continued through September, although its
remaining stories lacked the impact of the first three. In the next *Guardian*
issue, Reuben expanded his initial analysis of the trial. He said Julius
Rosenberg was the only member of the spy ring not to adopt an alias. He
reminded readers that Julius's name was a vital part of the government's case
against him. Elizabeth Bentley testified that a man named Julius had made
apparently spy-related phone calls to her during World War II. Further,
David Greenglass and Harry Gold testified that Gold had used the passphrase,
"I come from Julius."

The next article sharply questioned Judge Kaufman's motives at the
trial. Reuben alleged the judge "waved the red flag" before the jurors several

times. He denounced the trial judge's decision to allow testimony on the Rosenberg's communist affiliations.[52] "The purpose for which this testimony was taken . . . [was] not to establish . . . the guilt here of the crime charged because any of them might have been members of the Communist Party but it [was] to show a link exists between aiding Russia . . . and being members of the Communist Party." In Reuben's view, U.S. Attorney Saypol and Judge Kaufman painted the defendants with "a communist brush."[53]

The final article condemned Judge Kaufman's death sentences. Reprising editorial phrases in the *Jewish Daily Forward*, Reuben described the sentences as "too horrible" and "too cruel." Further, he decried Kaufman's comments about the Rosenbergs having indirectly triggered the Korean War. Reuben said the verdict was based purely on political hysteria. "But even assuming Rosenberg did participate in such a plot, the judge's statement justifying the death sentence falls apart when viewed against the historical facts, and the sentence itself becomes not only cruel and horrible but ridiculous and illegal to boot."[54]

The article argued that after World War II no one was executed for aiding the enemy. For example, Reuben said Axis Sally and Tokyo Rose (who made broadcasts on behalf of the Italian and Japanese governments) each received only ten-year sentences.   Too, Reuben argued that the death sentences were unjust when one considered that the scientific validity of David Greenglass's testimony was questioned by *Time*, *Life*, and *Scientific American*.[55] He claimed the *Guardian* had "presented an array of facts," indicating that the defendants deserved freedom on appeal of their convictions.   He also said a convincing circumstantial argument could be made that the defendants were "victims of a political frame-up designed to convince" Americans that Communist Party members and their political allies posed a threat to national security.[56]

The series ended with an unspecified plea for justice. Still, the *Guardian* mentioned no forthcoming demonstration, rally, or formation of any sort of organization. There was not even a box-office number set aside for contributions. Indeed, the story concluded without fanfare on the inside pages-page 5 to be exact.

What happened next is not precisely clear. Sometime during the early stages of the series, however, *Guardian* editors had sent out either press releases, summaries, or copies of the Reuben series to newspapers, wire services, and network radio. Exactly which newspapers, wire services, and networks received them is uncertain, but it is unlikely that Cedric Belfrage, Jim Aronson, or Jack McManus expected anyone to run a story based on them. Aronson said in 1978 that he told Manny Bloch that the chance of a mainstream editor reporting on the Reuben series was remote. Indeed, he said even if an editor saw merit in the series, he would be intimidated by "the Gospel according to Saint J. Edgar." (Presumably this is a reference to Hoover's statements to the press about Julius Rosenberg). Aronson's prediction proved accurate. In the United States, no major mainstream newspaper, news service, or broadcast network reported news of the exposé.

A week after Reuben's series ended, the *Guardian* developed an angle it said had been "overlooked." It described the missing perspective as "the human side of the young New York couple."[57] The *Guardian* then featured several excerpts from the Rosenbergs' prison correspondence. It was the first time these often intimate letters had been made public. They disclosed an uneven blend of the evocatively personal and unabashedly political. Both Rosenbergs had directed their voices unmistakably to a left-wing audience. Perhaps, more important, both had used a newspaper to dispute their images as atomic spies for the first time. In a 1951 letter to Ethel, Julius mourned the execution of Willie McGee.

> Mark my words, dearest, the harshest sentence passed on us is part of the atomic hysteria designed to brutalize the minds of the people in order to make it easier for them to accept as a commonplace thing long prison terms. It serves the loaded purpose of establishing fear paralysis among progressive Americans. The most important thing is that the camouflage has to be ripped away, the loud braying of jackals of hate has to be answered with reason and fact.[58]

Not long after "Is This the Dreyfus case of Cold War America?" appeared in the *National Guardian,* a steady flow of small cash contributions trickled into the paper's office in lower Manhattan. William Reuben says that the unsolicited donations caught everyone at the paper flat-footed. "The money came into the *Guardian,* and the readers said give this to the committee-and there was no committee." Reuben and others scrambled to put together an organization. In late October a provisional Rosenberg-Sobell committee was formed. Several hastily formed meetings took place in William Reuben's Manhattan home.[59] Then a coupon was placed in the *Guardian* requesting financial support to fund legal appeals.

8

1952: The Year of the Long Wait

Atom Spies Julius and Ethel Rosenberg moved a step closer to Sing Sing prison's electric chair yesterday when the Supreme Court refused to consider their case.[1]

Washington Post, October 14, 1952

The U.S. Supreme Court refused to consider the appeal of Julius and Ethel Rosenberg, sentenced to death, and of Morton Sobell...evidence with respect to the conduct of case by Justice Department, FBI, and lower courts indicates these three were victims of carefully cultivated anticommunist hysteria and anti-Semitism.[2]

Daily Worker, October 14, 1952

William Reuben continued writing about the Rosenberg-Sobell case in late 1951 but only sporadically. In October, the paper had told its readers of Ethel and Julius's private lives. Shortly before Christmas the paper published Reuben's article on the plight of the Rosenberg children-the news angle the mainstream editors mostly ignored.[3] He said the boys had moved from an orphanage into their paternal grandmother's apartment in Manhattan, where they now enjoyed life on the outside.[4] *Guardian* editors knew by now that the mainstream press would not cover this story. In that sense, the weekly newspaper met the traditional dissident-press role of providing news unavailable in the commercial news media. But focusing on the Rosenberg children was a volatile issue for the *Guardian* and the Rosenberg committee. Mainstream reporters and columnists had gone out of their way not to cover the fate of the Rosenberg children. Conversely, the *Guardian* was almost compelled to assign coverage; it might otherwise appear less than fully dedicated to the cause.[5]

In early 1952, Reuben tried to follow up his series with a personal interview with the Rosenbergs. He said the idea initially was broached to Manny Bloch by the Rosenbergs.[6]   Eventually, though, the project was scotched when Sing-Sing warden Wilfred Denno denied Reuben permission to visit the Rosenbergs. "I was eager to do it, but the warden at Sing-Sing said no."[7]

Despite his disappointment, Reuben continued forming a permanent Rosenberg Committee. By early 1952, the National Committee to Secure Justice in the Rosenberg case was headed by three New Yorkers. Novelist David Alman and his wife, Emily Arnow Alman, helped William Reuben form a permanent committee. The three were joined by Joseph Brainin, who became chairman of the committee, and Louis Harap, editor of the *Jewish Life*, a magazine with far-left ties.[8]

The committee formally announced its birth in the *National Guardian* in mid-January 1952.[9] The advertisement solicited members and donations for a new trial for the Rosenbergs and Morton Sobell.[10]   The committee was still unable to find a big-name liberal to act as spokesperson. A slow start resulted. Nevertheless, the Almans and Brainin convinced a small group of left-wing intellectuals and writers to join their ranks.[11] The first committee members knew they would have difficulty getting publicity and advertising space in the mainstream news media. Undoubtedly, they also knew the *National Guardian* was read by a shrinking base of followers. Worse, the *Daily Worker* and the *Daily Compass* had not exactly dashed to the ramparts to assist the *Guardian* in championing the Rosenberg-Sobell cause. This put pressure on the committee to quickly build a grass roots organization throughout the country.

During 1952, small but well organized regional committees sprang up in several large and medium-sized eastern and Midwestern cities. William Reuben and James Aronson made a cross-country tour on behalf of the committee. They stressed the need for a new trial, pointing to the defects of the government case against the Rosenbergs and Morton Sobell.[12]

In the early weeks, news-media recognition of the committee was nonexistent, though fund raising showed promise. At first, mostly $1 and $2 cash contributions and a few checks arrived. From the start, though, the Almans suspected that any success they achieved would be accomplished in the streets, in meeting halls and lodges, and in living rooms, coffee shops, and neighborhood bars. Emily Alman explains: "This was before television, really. It was simply a different world. [We] didn't get that kind of coverage for what was happening. It got some coverage, but it wasn't throughout the media. It was grass roots. It was door-to-door. It was city-to-city and basically the press would say, `Well, what are you doing?'"[13] As often as not reporters never wrote stories, or, they filed dispatches that appeared only in back pages.

Rosenberg Committee coffers gradually filled with small cash and a few big checks. David Alman and James Aronson traveled extensively, speaking to any group in the Midwest that would listen. At most stops a local newspaper reporter might attend, but, at best, only a back-page squib would appear in the next morning's newspaper noting the presence of local communists.

Back in New York City, press coverage was the last thing on Emily Alman's mind. In fact, she was looking for a hall for the first Rosenberg Committee rally, scheduled for early 1952. The rally was held partly to gauge how successful committee members had been as grass-roots organizers. While there was budding interest in the Rosenbergs in Brooklyn and Manhattan's working-class neighborhoods, Emily Alman could not find a hall to rent.[14] The problem of renting halls and hotel ballrooms was particularly difficult in the early days of the campaign. As the *National Guardian* noted in its February 13, 1952, issue a scheduled rally in Chicago had to be relocated at the last minute. According to the account, the meeting had been publicized "for a month" and was cancelled because of pressure from a local American Legion official and the Chicago branch of the Anti-Defamation League.[15]

Cancellation of hall rental agreements was something committee members came to expect. In Chicago, as in other meetings across the country, a second hall was rented. A car shuttle service ferried those who showed up at the first hall to the second.[16] The Chicago meeting went on as scheduled, with a crowd (estimated by the *Guardian*) of about 200. The rally was one of William Reuben's last public speaking appearances. He asked the crowd that night to refuse to let its own interests be dictated by "wealthy Jewish leaders." Reuben's jibe was directed at the political heart and soul of the mostly working-class audience. He hit upon a very sensitive issue that would cause great turmoil in the next year and a half. But still, the committee tried reaching any audience or group willing to listen. Eventually, debate over the Rosenbergs in the Jewish community would spill over into the mainstream press, but for now it was noted only in passing in the *Guardian*.

Ethel and Julius Rosenberg anxiously spent the morning of February 25, 1952, listening to radio news over the public address system in Sing-Sing. Late that morning, they heard that by a two-to-one decision the U.S. Court of Appeals, Second Circuit, had upheld their lower-court convictions and sentences. (The court also affirmed Morton Sobell's conviction).[17] The Rosenbergs' hopes had been particularly high because Judge Jerome Frank sat on the panel. Frank, whom some newspaper pundits thought a dangerous liberal, wrote the court's opinion. He said that because death sentences were involved, he and his colleagues had "scrutinized the record with extraordinary care."[18] He also said that the sentences were not unconstitutionally cruel and unusual punishment, though they marked the first time that American civilians would be executed for conspiracy to spy.[19]

Frank, however, did take the unusual step of hinting that the U.S. Supreme Court "may want to review" the issue of sentence reduction. (This suggestion ran counter to several generations of federal judicial procedure). Julius Rosenberg had entertained hopes that Frank would persuade his colleagues to set aside the convictions. The day after reading of Frank's majority opinion in the newspaper, Julius denounced the judge's deceit and sophistry."[20] In a letter to his wife, he sarcastically dismissed Frank as a "so-called 'liberal' and 'honorable man.' " Julius believed Frank's majority opinion was part of a frame-up engineered against them by the government. In fact, he was more convinced than ever that William Reuben was right. Sing-Sing's best known inmate said the latest judicial ruling was made with an eye for "keeping nonconformists in line."[21]

William Reuben went further than Julius Rosenberg in condemning Judge Frank's opinion. In a *National Guardian* front-page article, Reuben said the U.S. Court of Appeals had "drawn a forty-three page blueprint" for making fascism legal in the United States.[22]   "With the Appeals Court decision written into law, the number of Americans who can be jailed or executed for 'espionage' seemed limited only by the capacities of the machinery for arranging convictions."[23] Reuben said Americans could no longer depend on the Constitution as a guarantee of individual rights. In this doomsday paradigm, Senator Joseph McCarthy, Senator Pat McCarran (cosponsor of the Walter-McCarran Act), and President Truman now would decide the fate of citizens charged with national-security crimes.[24]

The *Guardian* and the *Daily Worker* could write to their hearts' content about conspiracies. Their messages were directed at relatively small, sympathetic audiences. The Rosenberg Committee had to find ways to spread itself throughout a continent among a population hostile to far-left politics. It could not content itself with providing news and opinions ordinarily not found in the mainstream press. It had to stress the fundamental unfairness of the trial and the contradictions in the trial transcript. That meant at least temporarily downplaying the conspiracy theory of the case.

For now, though, on the far left there was anger with the U.S. Court of Appeals and Jerome Frank. The *Daily Worker* seized news of Frank's opinion as an opportunity to comment on the case. Still, it was not prepared to affirm the Rosenbergs' claims with the same vigor as the *Guardian*. The *Worker*'s tone implied the embarrassment of a prodigal son explaining his absence from the latest family crisis. It said, "The court's ruling completely ignored opinions of leading nuclear scientists that there are no 'secrets' in the field of atomic science that are not known to scientists all over the world."[25]

Although the *Worker* did refer to a "frame-up" in a headline, the text of the article avoided the issue.

There are several possible explanations for the *Worker*'s reluctance to denounce the conspiracy earlier. The most obvious one is that the Rosenbergs (and Morton Sobell) had given up membership in the Communist Party to join a spy ring. Critics of the Rosenberg movement have pointed to the *Daily Worker*'s reluctance to defend the Rosenbergs sooner as a sign that the party feared they might confess. If that happened, supposedly the *Worker* and the party would look foolish as well as guilty. There probably is at least some truth to this explanation. In 1991, John Gates, of the *Daily Worker*, told the author he believed the Rosenbergs had been involved in Soviet espionage. In 1979, Gates told author Ronald Radosh that U.S. Communist Party cultural commissar V. J. Jerome had told him (in 1951) that "They're heros. They're going to their death and not saying anything."[26] Nevertheless, Gates denied in correspondence with the author that he had any evidence that the Rosenbergs were guilty.[27] Gates's successor at the *Daily Worker*, Max Gordon, also assumed the Rosenbergs were guilty. Gordon said he had turned down (on orders from top party officials) Manny Bloch's repeated requests for coverage of his clients' case. But Gordon also denied he had any knowledge of the Rosenbergs' complicity in a spy ring.[28]

Julius Rosenberg's view of the American judiciary in his letters was often jaundiced. But he frequently wrote to his wife of his confidence in the American public's judgment. It was with ordinary people that Julius thought he, his wife, and Morton Sobell would be vindicated. In an April 18 letter he told Ethel: "It's impossible to keep the truth and facts of our case hidden from the public . . . many people have already expressed to our lawyers and my family their sentiments and desire to help us."[29]

Even if expression of such support was confined to a small group, it likely struck the Rosenbergs as overwhelming. It cannot be said often enough that during the trial they had no public support. The *Guardian* series had changed that. Julius, especially, expected that as membership in the Rosenberg committee grew, there would be an editorial backlash of sorts from the American mainstream press. The day after he wrote about the Committee's modest success, he said, "The professional propagandists of hate are howling 'red' to frighten decent people. I expect to see their campaign of vilification grow in volume."[30]

By late 1952, the press, mostly syndicated columnists, began to discuss the Rosenberg case in depth. But in spring 1952, the Rosenberg Committee was still struggling to recruit volunteers. Until then only a series of articles on the case by International New Service (INS) columnist Bob Considine in late 1951 reminded newspaper readers of the Rosenbergs. In them, however, the Rosenberg Committee was not specifically discussed. Besides an occasional back-page squib in New York City newspapers, the Rosenberg movement was mostly ignored.[31] Nonetheless, the *Daily Worker* began defending the Rosenbergs in its columns with greater zeal. The May 2, 1952, *Worker* reported that U.S. Supreme Court Justice Robert H. Jackson had extended the time limit for defense lawyers to appeal their sentence to the court.[32] It described the trial as a "frame-up" and said "anti-Semitic war-hysteria was whipped up" there. Of course, it did not say that it neglected to cover the trial and provided no coverage of the movement until a year after the trial's end.

The first public reading of the Rosenberg letters was sponsored by the Communist Party. The correspondence was read by two actors at Yugoslav-American Hall in New York City.[33] Held in early May 1952, the event likely did not draw very well since the *Worker* did not mention crowd size. The Rosenberg Committee was not mentioned as a cosponsor, another sign of the "we'll go our way, you go yours" attitude that characterized relations between the Communist Party and the Rosenberg committee.[34]

Manny Bloch, no doubt, was willing to get publicity wherever he could. The fact that the Rosenberg Committee was wary of the party was nothing unusual. For two generations different union groups, political organizations, and social groups sometimes had to struggle to gain, retain, or wrest control of a movement from the U.S. Communist Party. This was true on the far left, where factions, splinter groups, liberal politicians, and intellectuals had long bickered with the party over issues, leadership, and objectives.[35] Now it was true in the Rosenberg-Sobell case. For their part, the Rosenbergs were happy to get backing from any political "progressives." Behind scenes of outward unanimity, though, fierce elbowing for position took place. The *Worker* never discussed William Reuben's series on the case. Then, too, the *National Guardian* frostily ignored the belated assistance of its older more doctrinaire cousin. Part of the tension between the papers had to do with the *National Guardian*'s reputation. A much better-written and better-edited paper, it was widely read and respected among leftists. The *Daily Worker* had never been read by more than half the Communist Party's membership at any time in its history. Its reputation was that of a soporific, humorless propaganda sheet one read, if at all, as an afterthought.

The *Daily Worker* heatedly rebutted Sterling North's review of *New York Post* reporter Oliver Pilat's book, *The Atom Spies*. In its May 30, 1952, issue, *Worker* reporter Robert Friedman declared Pilat's book an attempt to "confuse and demobilize" support for the Rosenbergs.[36] The *Worker* reporter reserved his greatest wrath for a review of Pilat's book by critic Sterling North in the *New York World-Telegram and Sun*. He dismissed it as "the language of Goebbels." Friedman also seized the occasion to support the *Guardian* view of the case, though he did not mention William Reuben or the higher-circulation newspaper.

> Millions of Americans still remember how another government framed another innocent victim for espionage, forging elaborate documents and utilizing the whole power of the state to convict him. The whole state still remembers the Dreyfus case as an example of depravity and monstrous duplicity of reaction. Now we have our own Dreyfus case. And one may confidently predict that tens of millions of people all over the world will clamor for justice for this American husband and wife as an earlier generation did to open gates for Alfred Dreyfus.[37]

The *Worker* had taken well over six months even to refer even indirectly to Reuben's series. By then the foundation for the Rosenberg campaign had been well established. The committee, the *Guardian*, and William Reuben thought it was too little, too late. The committee and the *Guardian* did not expect much help from the U.S. mainstream press.[38] But they privately expected more Rosenberg coverage than they had received from the *Daily Worker*.

Julius Rosenberg did not say what he expected of America's two most influential left-wing organs. As an inveterate newspaper reader, though, he spent a good deal of time following the case in the *New York Times* and also in the *New York Post, New York Herald Tribune,* and *New York Journal-American.* On May 29, 1952, he told his wife that he anxiously "scanned the newspapers" for news that the Korean War was ending. Rosenberg's melancholy pastime gave way to anger about the publicity surrounding Oliver Pilat's book.

> We have been clear, forthright, and outspoken as always because we have nothing to hide. It is our accusers and prosecutors who are in mortal fear of the truth. This can be the only explanation for the lies and smears they have had printed against us--an organized campaign to discredit and prevent people from examining the facts in the case, for they know they presented no evidence.[39]

Julius Rosenberg's analysis of the press and news media ranged from comparatively sophisticated to naively simple. Like many CCNY graduates of his generation, he split the press into "progressive" and "capitalist" camps. He also came to distrust liberal-press commentators such as Marquis Childs, Walter Lippmann, and Dorothy Thompson. After a column by the *Post's* Max Lerner, though, Julius Rosenberg reviled "the liberal press" as a conscienceless toady of the government. As the Rosenberg committee flourished, its difficulty in finding suitable rental halls increased. In a June letter to Ethel, Julius complained that the committee could not rent Madison Square Garden for a rally. He said the Brooklyn Academy of Music similarly "refused to accommodate" the committee.[40] At any rate, the committee finally rented the Biltmore hotel in Brooklyn for a rally. Max Lerner covered the affair for the *Post*, though normally he wrote a column. Lerner's piece appeared June 19, the day after the Brooklyn rally. Titled "Vulture and Victims," it was a strident condemnation of communist exploitation of "good people for an evil cause."[41]   As after Willie McGee's execution, Lerner deplored the "cynicism" of a publicity seeking "communist clique."

> The case of the atom spies Julius and Ethel Rosenberg is one of almost unrelieved ugliness and degradation: during the whole Flatbush meeting one listened in vain for a single hard fact that would cast a serious doubt on their guilt. The speakers stressed that those on whose testimony the Rosenbergs were convicted had betrayed the close ties of blood. It is a true fact and a shattering one. Yet it is a sword that cuts both ways. David Greenglass could not have sent his sister to her doom unless she had involved him in a real conspiracy to steal secrets for the Russians. . . . Albert Kahn made the collection speech. He read a message from the Rosenbergs and when he got to the pay-off sentence, his eyes filled and his words stuck in his throat. A heap of $5 and $10 and hundreds of dollar bills came to the platform.[42]

Lerner said the major objective of the rally was perpetuating the "legend" that the U.S. government had an anti-semitic plot against the Rosenbergs.   The *Post* columnist said he was "fed up" with communist attempts to manipulate the fears of American Jews. Lerner recalled a line that he had heard that night from each speaker. He said it was a quote from a Julius Rosenberg letter.   "We are as innocent of espionage as were our 6,000,000 brothers and sisters put to death in the death chambers of Europe."[43]

Lerner charged that was "a lie." He said the Rosenberg convictions and sentences "had nothing to do with their being Jewish."[44]   He denounced "half-pint Commissars," who exploited the sensibilities of working-class Jews in Brooklyn. He said the latter group "huddled together in anxiety," and listened to the "prize catch of the evening," an Orthodox Rabbi, Meyer Sharff.

Although he did refer to the campaign in behalf of the Rosenbergs, Lerner made no mention of William Reuben's *Guardian* series. At any rate, reaction to Lerner's column on the far left was interesting, to say the least. News of it set off an ideological brushfire of sorts in New York City. The *National Guardian* and the *Daily Worker* denounced the column in scathing terms. The *Worker's* Michael Vary did not mention Lerner but pointed to a similar "virulent attack" in the *Brooklyn Eagle*. Intriguingly, Vary's analysis of the rally was nearly diametrically opposite from Lerner's.

There was no shame in the tears that came when Mrs. Helen Sobell...walked to the microphone and brought a message from her husband. With deep emotion, she began: Morty said, "Tell them that, while I am buried in prison that they must be my eyes, my ears...Tell them that I want to walk free and proud again. Tell them I could never be a lying, crawling thing."[45]

Unlike Lerner, Vary quoted extensively from Helen Sobell's speech. Vary said she cautioned the crowd that the sentences given to the defendants were a "warning to each one of you." Her rhetoric was quite blunt, arguably demagogic. The *Worker* also quoted her as saying: "If we are the first who have been dragged into the chambers, will it be better for you if you are the second or the third? If we stay in prison, you move that much closer to prison. If we die at Sing-Sing, you move that much closer to death at Sing-Sing."[46]

Lerner's words also enraged the Rosenberg Committee. A syndicated columnist with a liberal cachet, he had a long-standing love-hate affair with the political left. His commentary on the Brooklyn rally, however, made him a despised figure among the "progressive" community. Most infuriated, though, was Julius Rosenberg. In a June 21 letter to his lawyer, he scalded the *Post* writer as a "so-called liberal" and "an apologist and hireling of the American Judenrat."[47] Rosenberg fairly seethed with contempt, saying Lerner had indulged in the "Goebbels technique of propaganda." Rosenberg said this technique involved attacking Jews and communists with hysteria manufactured to persecute "all things accused of communism. . . .You howled because you saw the visible evidence that the American people, the Jews of Flatbush who learned the lessons of Hitlerism, are rallying to support the committee in its fight to rectify this miscarriage of justice and are rejecting your poisonous propaganda."[48].

August and September were bittersweet months for the Rosenbergs. Both anxiously looked forward to vindication by the U.S. Supreme Court. Nonetheless, the late summer months had been fairly quiet. Even the *National Guardian* and the *Daily Worker* covered the pro-Rosenberg movement only sporadically. There really was not very much to report. The mainstream press had been preoccupied with the presidential conventions and the campaign. Then the *National Guardian* stirred controversy in late 1952 when it published names of U.S. prisoners of war in Korea. The *Guardian* had used nongovernment, back-channel sources to get the lists. The paper was roundly condemned by many newspapers, especially by editorials in the Hearst and Scripps-Howard chains. Still, Cedric Belfrage said the *Guardian* received hundreds of letters from grateful relatives of prisoners and missing-in-action soldiers.[49] The *Guardian* gained the mainstream news agenda by asking its readers to go to their local newspaper offices and ask editors why the names of American prisoners-of-war were not published in their local newspapers. Former *Guardian* reporter Leon Summit says the same agenda-setting, gate-crashing tactic was also used in the Trenton Six case.[50] It would soon be used in another case.

In a letter to Ethel, Julius said that "he had hoped to begin to hear of some favorable comment" from liberal columnists. Rosenberg's newspaper reading left him with a rather sober view of the country's political mood. "However, we must be realists. The political climate has not cleared up and a great fear is paralyzing many former liberals and progressives into silence. I'm still optimistic but I'm prepared for any eventuality."[51] Each morning Julius anxiously perused newspapers for news on the upcoming Supreme Court decision. (Actually it would be a decision on whether to review the case). On October 5 he correctly predicted October 13 as the date the Court would announce its decision. It would be a day both Ethel and Julius Rosenberg would remember with brutal disappointment.

The Court's decision was a terse statement denying review. A newspaper report said that husband and wife "did not appear to be upset over the news." The *New York Times* said both prisoners had taken outdoor exercise as usual. The Rosenbergs released a press statement through the Rosenberg Committee. The release made it sound as if they had been expecting the worst.

> Our pleas to the Supreme Court have been restricted by legal protocol, but before the bar of public opinion we cannot reassert often or emphatically enough our complete innocence of the charge. No matter what the result, we will continue in our determination to expose the political frameup against us by those who would silence by death, through spurious espionage accusations, opposition to the conspiracy to impose war abroad and a police state at home.[52]

To a reader of the *Daily Worker* or the *National Guardian* these words would not seem unusual. To mainstream newspaper reporters the statement probably would have been a surprise. A "frameup" of the Rosenbergs? When was this reported? A police state? What was Julius Rosenberg talking about? For most newspaper readers it was impossible to know for the Rosenbergs' press release was the first and only report the author knows of where a mainstream newspaper referred to the frame-up charge. (Max Lerner had spoken of the Rosenbergs' claims of innocence but omitted specifics).[53]

Chalmers Roberts of the *Washington Post* said that only an executive commutation "for giving American secrets to Russia" could save the couple. The report noted Manny Bloch's petition for a rehearing but also observed that such an action "hardly ever is successful."[54] The eight-to-one vote (with Justice Hugo Black dissenting) underscored Roberts's point. The *Herald Tribune* also said Bloch "might" petition for a new trial on the basis of "new evidence."[55] Bloch, however, declined to elaborate. Some newspaper accounts forgot to report that the Court had also refused to hear Morton Sobell's plea.[56]

The *Daily Worker* soon stepped up its coverage of the case. The Communist Party returned to the case with a somewhat renewed sense of purpose. In the *Worker*, the Rosenberg story moved from modest-length, inside-page coverage to front-page stature. Still, the *National Guardian* always would be the official journalistic sponsor of the case. But the *Worker* enjoyed one advantage the *Guardian* could not challenge. As a daily, it could handle late-breaking stories on the case. The *Worker* stole a march on the *Guardian* when it printed a letter from the Rosenbergs in its October 14, 1952, issue.

> We do not want to die. We are young and yearn for a long life. Yet, if the only alternative to death is the purchase of life at the cost of personal dignity and abandonment of the struggle for democracy and ethical standard, there is no future for us or any legacy we can leave our children or those who survive and follow us. For what is life without the right to live it? Death holds no horror as great as the horror of a sterile existence, devoid of social responsibility and the courage of one's convictions.[57]

The *Worker* followed the next day with a front-page plea, "They Must Not Die." Here it echoed historical allusions from William Reuben's 1951 *Guardian* exposé. "The Rosenberg case has no more to do with atom bomb espionage than the Mooney case with espionage, the Scottsboro case with rape, the Sacco-Vanzetti case with robbery, or the Mendel Beylis case of Czarist Russia with ritualistic murder."[58]

The *Worker* also publicized dates and places of the Rosenberg Committee's forthcoming rallies. That was coverage committee members were glad to get, but they also were under few illusions. The U.S. Communist Party would conduct itself as it saw fit in the case. Nonetheless, the final months of the Rosenbergs' lives would split the Jewish community in the United States, bring many liberals out of hibernation, and start a behind-the-scenes pas de deux for control of the case's news framing in national and international news markets. In Emily Arnow Alman's words, it would be a battle for "mainstream America's" attention and support.[59] Mainstream America was a solidly middle-class constituency. Americans were being asked to stand up for the Rosenbergs. It was one of the strangest clarion calls in U.S. political history.

9

France, the Rosenbergs, and Anti-Semitism

As I recall it, the foreign press just took up the Rosenberg case from us as important news, while the U.S. press never wanted it questioned that all was well on the justice front.[1]

Former National Guardian editor Cedric Belfrage in 1988 from a letter to the author

I was the Rosenberg attaché for God's sake. I mean, Jesus, almost all the [French] press was against us.[2]

Former Washington Post executive editor Benjamin C. Bradlee recalling his job as press attaché for the U.S. Embassy in France in 1952 and 1953 in a 1990 interview

In fall 1952, the U.S. press was riveted to a presidential election. However, the Rosenbergs were assured of at least several months of further legal appeals. The *National Guardian* and the *Daily Worker* certainly had not forgotten the case. Both newspapers gave a good deal of coverage to "clemency rallies." But more important, both had drifted far apart on the controversial subject of anti-Semitism and the Rosenbergs. In practical terms, this gap meant that the Rosenberg Committee and the U.S. Communist Party would not present a unified front. Both groups briefly would attend the same rallies-they had been planned for several weeks anyway. But Rosenberg Committee members knew the various liberal groups they sought to bring under their wing would be scared off by the vitriolic rhetoric of communists.

There certainly was some justification for that sentiment. The October 16 *Daily Worker* featured a front-page column by *Masses and Mainstream* editor Samuel Sillen. The article showed the *Worker*'s resolve to lay the Rosenbergs' convictions to long-standing political and religious hatred.

The whole judicial proceeding against them has been a terrible mockery.
They were tried by headlines and hysteria. The fight to save the
Rosenbergs is the fight to keep America free from Buchenwalds and
Dachaus. We must win this fight not only for the sake of the Rosenbergs,
but for the sake of our children. Snuffing out the lives of Ethel and Julius
Rosenberg would hasten the reign of the brute in America. A spinal cord
of decency would snap in the electric chair with them.[3]

Coincidentally, 1952 was the fiftieth anniversary of Emile Zola's
death.[4] The *Daily Worker*, which ignored William Reuben's references to
Zola in 1951, now reprised Zola's stirring "J Accuse" speech.[5] Sillen asked
American writers and artists to "take up the cudgels" of justice for the
Rosenbergs "in the thunderous accents of Emile Zola."

The death sentences eventually would elevate the Rosenberg case into
an international political obsession. For the time being, though, Rosenberg
supporters debated about how best to frame the case for public and media
consumption. Communist Party members in the United States also wanted to
continue demanding a new trial. The Rosenberg Committee also wanted a
new trial for the Rosenbergs, but its board members realized the chances of
staging a mass movement based solely on an appeal for a new trial were slim.
Instead, the committee decided on a two-pronged strategy. It would first
advocate a movement to save the Rosenbergs from death in the electric chair,
then promote a new trial. This decision was nicely tied to the Rosenberg legal
appeals, which would draw automatic coverage in the news media, especially
the press. Controversial executions usually command national news-media
attention. In this sense, the Rosenberg case was an agenda-setting Grand
Guignol: a double execution, which would leave the prisoners' children as
orphans. William Wolf, a Rosenberg Committee media-relations volunteer,
says the committee tried to peg its press releases to some aspect of the legal
appeals. "If you'd go to a paper and say, 'hey, look at this,' they'd be reluctant
to publish anything original. The attitude was well, 'if it's in court it would
legitimize it, otherwise it's propaganda.'"[6]

In one sense, the press was an ally of the committee. Newspapers
had to report the rescheduled execution dates, which were rescheduled from
appeal to appeal. That, more than provocative advertising copy or argu-
mentative press releases, would help attract volunteers. Still, no social or
political mass movement can exist indefinitely without news media coverage.
The Rosenberg Committee had to run an unusual gauntlet. On one side
awaited hostile press commentary and editorials; on the other was the cold
shoulder of no news media coverage. Nevertheless, the Rosenberg Committee
began as a grass-roots movement. It did not ask volunteers to believe the
Rosenbergs innocent.[7] The committee did, however, distribute copies of the
Rosenberg-Sobell trial transcript so doubters could draw their own
conclusions about the fairness of the trial. This crude marketing strategy was

quite effective. It helped raise badly needed revenue and reassured political liberals and moderates that nothing had been swept under the carpet. That strategy got the committee little if any mainstream press publicity, but it did succeed in proving that under certain conditions protest movements still could generate popular response without much news-media coverage. Still, a tremendous paradox surfaced: the closer the Rosenbergs were to execution, the better their chances for a news media investigation of their claims.

Suddenly, unexpectedly, the Rosenberg movement exploded in several directions in France and the United States. The case's popular appeal accelerated in both countries in different ways and for different reasons. Nonetheless, in Sing-Sing, Julius Rosenberg's irritation with the U.S. mainstream press had deepened. In a November 23, 1952, letter to Ethel Greenglass Rosenberg, he lashed out at the "hirelings of the Hearst press." Rosenberg accused an unnamed syndicated columnist of "spread[ing] forth some additional fabrications, products of whiskey-soaked brains, to hurt our fight." He condemned the news media of harboring the specter of a "phantom Goebbels."[8] Further, he bitterly accused "major newspapers" of promoting "neofascism" through an anticommmunist campaign. Rosenberg said this was done through the use of "distortions, professional stool pigeons, and constant repetition of big lies." A large movement in his name and that of his wife boosted his morale. By now, though, he was convinced that U.S. newspapers spoke in the same voice as the government.[9]

Around Thanksgiving 1952, the Rosenberg Committee's small office on Sixth Avenue regularly filled with walk-in volunteers. Phones rang constantly, from early in the morning until late at night. Sometimes the callers were anonymous financial patrons; others were visiting foreign journalists seeking quotes for feature stories on the case. By now more than forty Rosenberg Committees had been established nationwide. Small but well organized, they grew dramatically, sometimes exponentially, in a few weeks. What caused this sea of change in public sentiment? News reports that the Rosenbergs would be executed as early as January surely spurred interest.[10] But, then, the death sentences the Rosenbergs faced were conditional: they could save themselves from execution by confessing. No one, not even the Rosenbergs, had counted on a mass movement forming on their behalf. The Justice Department now faced a nasty, unyielding dilemma. There was no face-saving way to back out of the executions without appearing to cave in to communist propaganda. Mass-media scholars Maxwell E. McCombs and Donald L. Shaw note that the public learns not only what to think about from the media but the degree of importance to attach to an event or issue.[11] The U.S. press and news and other news media could ignore much of the Rosenberg movement, but they could not ignore the executions of two young parents. After the Supreme Court's decision not to review the case, the sentences became more than news dispatches. They became agenda-setting flags for a gruesome ritual known to generations of reporters as the death-house watch.

Former *Washington Post* executive editor Benjamin Bradlee remembers the Rosenberg case sweeping France like a Kansas prairie fire. At first, Bradlee, a young press attaché at the U.S. embassy in Paris, could only blink in amazement. In a matter of two weeks Bradlee says, the embassy was engulfed in controversy. The sudden, intense interest in the Rosenberg case had caught everyone in the diplomatic corps off guard. "We were starved for information about the case," he says. "But we didn't know anything about the case. You couldn't confront anybody or any argument if you didn't know the case. . . . With our information we didn't. . . . The American press wasn't covering it that well."[12]

The French press, which covers a broad spectrum of political opinion, was very much interested in the Rosenbergs. Until early October only the left-wing press, led by *L'Humanite*, newspaper of the French Communist Party, the far-left *Droit et Libérte* and left-leaning *Libération* took interest in the case. After the Supreme Court's decision in mid-October, *Le Monde* and *Le Figaro* ran editorials inveighing against the death sentences.[13] *Ce Soir* also raised questions about the wisdom of condemning to death the young American Jewish parents. Also, *Le Monde* assigned its well known columnist and American correspondent Henri Pierre to write a case analysis. Then *Le Combat*, a newspaper popular with liberals, radicals, artists, and cafe cognoscenti, forged links with the U.S. Rosenberg Committee. A French committee to save the Rosenbergs, "Comite Francais pour la Defense des Rosenbergs," was formed.[14] Also, Manny Bloch began correspondence with several French lawyers; an edited version of the trial transcript found its way to France. U.S. Ambassador C. Douglas Dillon and his staff had to scramble for information on the case. Bradlee recalls finding the little of what he could discover about the case in *Time* and *Newsweek*. The embassy did not have a newspaper library or clip file of American trials. Bradlee recalls that French journalists such as Henri Pierre and Maurice Fero "were beating us upside the face" on the death penalty. Further, delegations from throughout France daily visited the U.S. embassy, demanding to know why the Americans were being sent to their deaths when they had not been convicted of treason.[15]

In late November, the embassy staff sent a cable home requesting background information on the case. Bradlee waited for days without success. "At the end we must have sent a dozen cables to the State Department saying 'give us information about this case' so we can combat what was becoming, especially in France, very, very difficult."[16] Bradlee says about a half dozen requests to the State Department went unanswered. Nevertheless, the

Rosenberg case would not have united France as quickly as it did had it not been for American novelist and U.S. Communist Party member Howard Fast. Fast had written an article on the case that appeared in *L'Humanite*.[17] In his autobiography, *On Being Red*, Fast claims he and an American friend, Julie Turpin, "actually began the Rosenberg movement in the United States."[18] Although, at best, this is a forgetful exaggeration, Fast can plausibly claim some credit for the Rosenberg movement's quicksilver spread in France. Interestingly, Manny Bloch had approached Fast before he spoke with James Aronson of the *National Guardian*. Fast, an unpaid volunteer on the *Worker* staff, could do nothing for Bloch until mid-1952, when the U.S. Communist Party decided the case no longer posed a danger. On a trip to France that summer, Fast explained the case in some detail to the French Communist Party. In his words, French Communist Party chief Jacques Duclos agreed to "spearhead a worldwide movement" for the Rosenbergs.[19] Fast's article struck French radicals as an eerie reminder of the Dreyfus case. Unlike in the United States, the communist press in France exercised some influence on mainstream journalists. In a matter of weeks *Ce Soir*, *Le Figaro*, and *Le Monde* called for mercy for the Rosenbergs. It was cold war agenda-setting, Gallic style. Soon almost all France would be absorbed, bewildered, and agitated by "Le Cas Rosenberg." The mechanics of how the case grew from a single article to a national phenomenon illustrates the tremendous agenda setting and gatekeeping differences between the French and U.S. news media.

Sociologist Herbert Gans says mainstream American journalists in the twentieth century have avoided discussing political and ideological issues. Gans explains that public-opinion journals and periodicals in the United States have usually filled this role.[20] In 1952, though, the Rosenberg movement had to go begging for news coverage in Europe. In a sense, then, the French press was made for the Rosenberg case. As Ben Bradlee explains: "The French press generally is much more opinionated, and they use the press for political purposes in a way that the Americans don't or haven't since Hearst. . . It (the Rosenberg case) was like throwing raw meat to hungry dogs. The French loved it."[21] By early December, in Bradlee's words, "Almost all the press was against us."[22] *Libération* declared: "Watch out. America has the rabies. Cut all ties which bind us to her, otherwise, we in turn will be bitten and run mad."[23] Another leftist French periodical, *Les Temps Modernes*, declared the Rosenbergs innocent. "When one has read the transcript's 1,715 pages of the exchanges, of the pleadings, of the prosecutors and of the lawyers, doubt is no longer possible!"[24] On December 11, 1952, *Le Monde*'s Henri Pierre reached a less definite conclusion. He thought it impossible to determine clearly the Rosenbergs' guilt or innocence from reading the transcript.[25] Nevertheless, he did suspect anti-Semitism had played a major role the Rosenberg-Sobell trial. All this treatment suggested a much different news media conceptual framework, one quite close in tone to William Reuben's conspiracy thesis.

As far as most Americans in France were concerned, though, the Rosenberg case could not have come at a worse time. Anti-American sentiment had been running at high pitch anyway. Ben Bradlee was besieged by telephone calls from French reporters, some of whom were less than courteous. The pressure at the embassy had built to dangerous levels. Bradlee was furious that the State Department had ignored his many requests for information. Finally, Bradlee says, in early December 1952, he grew tired of not "knowing my ass from my elbow about the Rosenberg case."[26] He took his problem to William Tyler, director of the U.S. Information Agency. (Technically, Bradlee was a USIA employee). Bradlee suggested he take a brief trip back to the United States and read the official trial transcript at the Foley Square courthouse. His idea was to write a government position paper on the case to be distributed on his return to the French news media. Tyler liked the scheme and approved Bradlee's departure. But there was a major sticking point: no one in the embassy or the USIA. had funds for a round-trip plane ticket to the United States.[27]

The *National Guardian* announced in its Thanksgiving 1952 issue that only two avenues of appeal remained for the Rosenbergs. One was executive clemency; the other was a request for a reduction of sentence from Judge Kaufman.[28] The *Guardian's* Lawrence Emery said Rosenberg-Sobell defense lawyers were going to submit a petition to federal Judge Sylvester Ryan claiming that the defendants had been victims of pretrial and during-trial newspaper publicity in the New York City area. Emery stated that 30,000 column-inches of press reports on "atom-bomb" news stories had appeared in newspapers between Klaus Fuchs's arrest in February 1950 and the Rosenberg-Sobell trial in March 1951.[29] The petition said publicity had "inexorably preconditioned" the public mind to acceptance of the petitioner's guilt."[30] The *Guardian* included news about the petition on page 14 of the jump. It was a fairly strong indication that the issue was legal as well as a journalistic afterthought. Nonetheless, the *Guardian's* "Report to Readers" held high hopes for saving the Rosenbergs.[31]

The Rosenberg Committee announced it was starting a media campaign in the United States. With forty-plus chapters nationwide, Joseph Brainin and the Almans thought it time to move beyond living-room coffee klatches, letter campaigns, and an occasional rally. The *Guardian* said the committee's efforts would include newspaper advertisements and radio and television spots.[32] Until then, the Rosenberg Committee had to rely almost exclusively on the *National Guardian* and the *Daily Worker* for promoting and advertising rallies and protest meetings. The committee insisted its efforts would succeed if the "hundreds of thousands" of supporters rapidly multiplied.[33]

Time warned of a worldwide effort by communists to save the Rosenbergs from the electric chair. It conceded that U.S. civilian courts had never before meted out death sentences in peacetime;"but, then, never before [Korea] had the peacetime U.S. had its security jeopardized by one ring of spies. . . whose work probably shortened by years the Russians' efforts to build their own A-bomb." *Time* speculated that few of those Rosenberg protesters who signed clemency petitions or "cheered the public rallies" knew they were part of a communist-planned drive.

On December 1, 1952, the *New York Post* introduced a six-part Oliver Pilat series on the case. "The A-Spy Case: Moscow `Discovers' the Rosenbergs" was a hastily written postscript of his book, *The Atom Spies*, which had been published earlier in 1952. Pilat updated his story by noting that the case had been appropriated as international "Soviet propaganda."[34] He compared communist coverage on the Rosenberg case to a 1952 attempt by the communist press to make a case that U.S. forces had used germ warfare in Korea. Pilat said Julius Rosenberg's testimony was the stammering performance of a "six-year old who forgot to do his homework."

The *Post* reporter concluded that "All the stops were being pulled out now." Laborers in France, a large British trade council, and union members in Canada, Australia, and Japan had pledged themselves to save the Rosenbergs.[35] Pilat said the movement had succeeded because of a crude anti-U.S. strategy. The *New York Post* reporter said that "humanitarians" had been seduced into supporting the Rosenbergs. The *Post* backed Pilat's first article with an editorial, "Spies and Speech." It decried the "propaganda fraud" on the case contrived by the Cominform. As for the death sentences, the newspaper claimed that issue had been "fatally distorted." The editorial scorned the Rosenberg movement as a "monstrous example of communist doublethink."[36]

Pilat, Bob Considine, and the *Post's* Max Lerner were the only major mainstream American journalists to discuss the case in detail since the trial's end. In fact, there really had not been any analysis or commentary (independent of the FBI's and the prosecution's press releases and statements) on the case before or during the trial. As such, ironically, Pilat's series likely came as fresh news to many readers. The movement had succeeded internationally with almost no U.S. mainstream news coverage. The press finally had to respond, a case of agenda setting by international political pressure. It became a matter of ignoring the obvious, the news media's version of the emperor's clothes syndrome. In fact, there had been only a few references to the existence of the Rosenberg movement in the U.S. press. In truth, there was next to none. Now the very size and impact of the Rosenberg movement had compelled the editors of *Time* and the *Post* to open the gates and assign coverage and analysis. There was also the corollary issue of the clemency movement in Europe, which showed no signs of abating. Correspondents in foreign capitals could not cover a big story without editors at home assigning reporters to cover the same phenomenon. The movement broke through the limited terms of agenda setting, e.g., court coverage only, in the United States but at the expense of being labeled procommunist. But mainstream journalists in the United States widely assumed the Communist Party was the animating force behind the Rosenberg movement.

William Wolf, a Rosenberg media-relations volunteer, says this was far from being true. "Contrary to the myth that was going around that this was a communist conspiracy, a communist based movement on behalf of the Rosenbergs, the feeling around at the time was that the Communist Party leadership had to be dragged kicking and screaming to the case. . . The rank and file people of the party were not encouraged to join it. The initial reaction was that they [party officials] wanted to stay away from it."[37]   Wolf remembers that a few *Daily Worker* reporters at first wanted to give the case more coverage. But that did not happen in the *Worker*'s pages until mid-1952. Then, after the U.S. Supreme Court's refusal to review the decision, coverage stepped up noticeably. But the issue that Pilat had raised, a case backed almost exclusively by communists, would not go away. Instead, it would soon reappear after a leading Czechoslovakian Communist Party official was executed.

Julius Rosenberg had read Oliver Pilat's series. He made spirited, even hostile criticisms of it in a December 3, 1952, letter to Manny Bloch. Providing one of his most theoretically inspired criticisms of the American press, he declared:

> On this the fortieth day left to live, I want to talk about some of the servants of the abattoir, such as pen hirelings of big business. As you know, it takes large sums of money to own a newspaper and it depends on advertising and the revenue needed to keep on operating. Through control of the technical means in the newspaper business such as: newsprint, paper, the large news services, and by the very practical lever of paid advertisements, which is tantamount to a mortgage, the frat brothers control, and in the main, dominate the editorial and news slanting policies of the so called "free press."[38]

Julius's letter contained a lengthy, vitriolic questioning of the press's commitment to peace, justice, and social equality. He said, "practically the entire press" had worked on behalf of the "cartels," with the *New York Post* serving as a liberal apologist that printed "weasel philosophical excuses for the need to go along with the tide."[39] In the same letter he also broached the issue of anti-Semitism. Rosenberg was most upset with Oliver Pilat's charge that the Rosenberg Committee had used anti-Semitism as a propaganda smoke screen. "From the very beginning, starting with our arrest and going through the trial. . .and the various appeals, reading the trial record and all our letters and statements, it is crystal clear that we never said nor intimated that we were selected out and convicted because we were Jews."[40]

Julius insisted nothing could change the truth of his claim. He pointed to postsentencing editorials in the *Jewish Day* and *Jewish Daily Forward*. (Both newspapers had published editorials objecting to Judge Irving Kaufman's decision to sentence the Rosenbergs to death).[41]

In his letter to Bloch, Julius concluded that the Rosenberg Committee did not "create this issue" or claim anti-Semitism had an effect on the trial's outcome. "They only brought to public knowledge the existence of these statements and pointed out the appearance of anti-Semitic strikes and literature about the Rosenbergs as 'Jew-Communist-atom spy.'" Rosenberg said the committee feared the case would be used as an excuse for "eliminating liberties of the American people as a whole."[42]

Rudolph Slansky, former Marxist secretary general of the Czechoslovakia, and Vlado Clementis, Czech foreign minister, were hanged for treason in Prague, on December 3, 1952. Nine other Communist Party functionaries were also executed. Eight of the eleven victims were Jews who had been accused of "Zionist, Trotskyite" crimes against the state.[43] The trial had featured a rather lengthy attack on the alleged Zionist activities of the defendants.[44]

Slansky's execution caused the Rosenberg Committee and the Save-Rosenberg movement endless trouble. Although the two had no connection, critics of the Rosenberg movement alleged that communists had used the case to deflect attention from anti-Semitic purges in Eastern Europe. French Communist leader Jacques Duclos fueled this feeling when he denied the charge: "The conviction of U.S. atom spies Julius and Ethel Rosenberg was an example of anti-Semitism, but the execution of eight Jews in Czechoslovakia last week was not."[45]

Duclos's words were widely reported in newspapers throughout Western Europe and the United States. Columnists and editorialists some-times cited them in the final months of the case as an exemplar of Stalinist duplicity. In fact, there had been rumors of Soviet anti-Semitism in the Western news media even before the Rosenbergs' arrest. Did the Cominform seize the Rosenberg case as an international publicity diversion? Surely it did, to at least some extent. But, then again, the temptation to use the Rosenbergs for propaganda purposes must have been overwhelming.

The U.S. Rosenberg Committee had to deal with the fallout of a major propaganda disaster. Committee leaders now had to answer reporters' pointed questions about the "Slansky hangings." Obviously, the executions were an embarrassment to leftists everywhere in the West. But in the United States, they only encouraged the idea that the Rosenberg movement was communist controlled. Mainstream news-media editors, reporters, and commentators now had more reason to analyze the case from an anti-Stalinist paradigm. It was a familiar cold-war framework, particularly to the press, which looked for international events rich in political irony and symbolism.

The Save-Rosenberg movement had moved onto the American news agenda as an anticommunist story. This development was almost the reverse of events in Europe, especially in France. Julius Rosenberg was acutely aware of this international news-media role reversal. In a January 1, 1953, letter to Manny Bloch, he wrote:

> A holy crusade is on. The cry is 'Get the Rosenbergs.' Anything counts; all who wish to cleanse themselves of past sins (anything remotely progressive, that is, labeled pro-communist) can do so by joining the pack and throwing filthy lies, tales made of whole cloth, as long as it fits with the political propaganda of those in power. The truth, which cannot be created or destroyed, is perverted to suit their interests. Since they control the means of communication, the press, the radio, money and government, they feel secure that these terrible misdeeds will not be opposed."[46]

He also told Bloch that reading the latest issue of the *National Guardian* gave him "a wonderful feeling." As the "voice of progressive Americans," Julius said the weekly was responsible for "the great campaign that is being waged for justice in our case."[47] He described the *Guardian* as a newspaper that kept "the torch of liberty burning brightly." This endorsement implied that Julius had sided with the Rosenberg Committee in its dialectic battle with the Communist Party. Also, the fact that the *National Guardian* published the letter sent a strong signal to the party, the CRC, and the *Daily Worker*. The next week, Julius Rosenberg twice mentioned newspaper reports about the Save-the-Rosenbergs movement. In a December 4, 1952, letter to his wife, he complained of a "fabulous newspaper campaign" bearing "earmarks of desperation." A week later he observed: "It is indeed a tragedy how the lords of the press can mold public opinion by printing. . .blatant falsehoods. The pressure campaign is in high gear and many weak people will be scared off."[48] Clearly, knowing that newspaper readers in Europe were receiving a different perspective on the case upset Rosenberg.

The *National Guardian* and the *Daily Worker* could not indefinitely ignore the Slansky case. A week before Christmas, both newspapers carried news of the executions with their interpretation of events in Eastern Europe. Both stayed very close to the party line on the executions, something the

Worker always did and the *Guardian* sometimes did more out of solidarity than conviction. Still, the *Worker* accused the major news agencies and "commercial newspapers" of Great Britain and the United States of distorting the facts of the Slansky case.[49] Citing a London *Daily Worker* interview with the chief rabbi of Czechoslovakia, the *Worker* denied that the Slansky executions related to anti-Jewish policy.

The *Worker* said Reuters, the United Press, the Associated Press, and the International News Service had only diverted the newspaper-reading public's attention from "anti-Jewish and racist hysteria." It alleged that judges and witnesses, along with perjured testimony and "preconvictions by the press" had doomed the Rosenbergs.[50] (*Worker* editors obviously had not yet read Julius Rosenberg's comments on this issue). The *National Guardian's* James Aronson rather defensively agreed with the *Worker*. "The one possibility not even considered was that the defendants confessed because the evidence with which they were confronted . . . was conclusive and undeniable."[51] Moreover, Aronson argued that Western newspaper editors had been unable to give a rational explanation of why Slansky and his codefendants had confessed publicly.[52]

This rather unconvincing explanation was no help to the Rosenberg committee. The Slansky story was a painful thorn in the collective side of the Rosenberg movement. The executions in Prague collectively had rekindled memories of the Soviet purges of the 1930s. Rosenberg Committee leaders received many calls from reporters seeking reaction to the Slansky executions. Privately, many on the far left in the United States knew that Stalin really had been conducting an anti-Jewish purge. It was now an odd situation of one social movement in the United States having to explain (or refuse comment on) the behavior of disconnected events half a world away.

In a depressing Christmas story, the *National Guardian* ran a "Holiday Wish from the Death House." One of Ethel Rosenberg's few letters from Sing-Sing was a "Yuletide note" to Manny Bloch. "I see by the papers that the Holiday season is in full swing, and since 'justice' enjoins me from doing my shopping early, later or otherwise, it will have to be undertaken for me."[53]

Ben Bradlee would also have to do his Christmas shopping late. By the second week of December, he wanted to return to the United States to read the Rosenberg-Sobell trial record. He was going to write a "white paper" refuting claims of French critics and journalists that the Rosenbergs were victims of an unjust judicial system. Bradlee says he had trouble raising funds for the trip. However, the CIA station chief in France, Robert "Bobby" Thayer, was an old friend of Bradlee's family. French USIA chief Bill Tyler convinced Thayer to pay Bradlee's transatlantic ticket fare.[54]

Bradlee stayed only a few days in New York but spent most of that time in the basement of Foley Square "for what seemed like forever, taking notes."[55] Just then the CRC was making final preparations for its pre-Christmas clemency train to Sing-Sing. (Ironically, Bradlee recalls he was only vaguely aware of the Rosenberg movement in the United States). As far as he was concerned, though, he was only too aware of its considerable presence in France. "Most of the calls I got [in Paris] came from French journalists. They were typical; they didn't know the facts. They wanted to know 'why are you killing them?' They treated it as part of the McCarthy Red scare, and that it was American excess and everyone's scared of the commies. 'Why kill them?' 'Why kill Ethel?' Besides, they loved to beat up on the Americans."[56]

Bradlee remembers that he "holed up" for a couple of days in Foley Square trial library. After he was done taking notes, he spent a day dictating his report to two USIA secretaries in New York City. His white paper was then translated from English into French. Bradlee says reading the trial transcript persuaded him that the Rosenbergs had had a fair trial. But he was not as confident that the French press and other news media would be easy to convince.

Nevertheless, he left the United States with a thirty-six page, 7,000-word report. Back in France, the U.S. embassy quickly distributed the report to French journalists and news services. The paper also was sent to USIA branch offices in Cherbourg, Bordeaux, Lyons, Strasbourg, Lille, and Marseilles.

Bradlee says that within days there was a noticeable change in the French press on the Rosenberg case. Some columnists and reporters doubted that the American couple with the doe-eyed children were innocent. Then, again, Bradlee says most mainstream papers in France never claimed that the Rosenbergs were innocent. He insists the major controversy about the case was over the death penalty. His white paper was not written to persuade anyone in the French news media that the sentences were justified. For this reason, Bradlee says, he intentionally wrote the paper "sans spin." The experience was rather strange, from almost any propaganda perspective. The report, titled "Le Cas Rosenberg," was an instance of the U.S. government helping hostile journalists organize a big story into a coherent framework two years after it helped friendly, patriotic American journalists do the same thing. However, unlike the earlier efforts before and during the trial, this was a panicky, defensive attempt at news framing. Clearly, its major purpose was convincing the French news media that the Rosenbergs were not Alfred Dreyfus.

If you believe the *Daily Worker*, nearly 1,000 people showed up at Sing-Sing's gates on December 21, 1952. (The *New York Herald Tribune* put the figure at 800). Hundreds of multicolored umbrellas sprouted against a gray and black sky.   A steady rain fell on trainloads of disembarked commuters from New York and New Jersey. The *Worker* reported the streets of Ossining echoed with the refrain, "The Rosenbergs shall not Die."[57]

Warden Wilfred Denno did not permit the group to gather outside Sing-Sing's walls. The CRC-sponsored rally took place in a plaza downtown, near the train station.   About thirty reporters attended, including still photographers and newsreel cameramen.   It was a sometimes noisy but nonetheless peaceful gathering. Several speakers at the rally, including Howard Fast and Rosalie McGee (Willie McGee's widow), said the Rosenbergs were victims of an anti-Semitic government backlash.[58] Demonstrators carried a banner and sang the "Star Spangled Banner" and the "Battle Hymn of the Republic."[59]

The *Herald Tribune* report said Howard Fast charged the Truman administration with "terror, intimidation, and death." Reporter David Wise said Ossining police kept the clemency delegation a half mile from the prison to "prevent repetition of the 1949 riots at Peekskill, New York."[60] Wise described a near state of siege, as barricades and wooden horses lined the route to the prison. Two hundred police guarded the approaches to the Sing - Sing fortress.

A small CRC contingent was allowed to deliver holiday cards and a floral wreath just outside the prison. The wreath was left in the rain. Its sash had the message: "Greetings to Julius and Ethel Rosenberg from the People."[61]

10

The Courts and Clemency:
The Call of Death

Such a presentation required a perusal and analysis of every newspaper and magazine circulated in the metropolitan area. It was only the total picture that could persuade a responsible counsel that the character of publicity to which these petitioners were subjected rose to the level of legal and constitutional objectionability. This complete picture was unavailable to me from the date of my retainer up to and through the petitioners' trial . . . From the time I was retained by the petitioners I was so immersed in representing them . . . that I read the newspapers infrequently and was not cognizant of the many releases and press statements fed to the press by U.S. officials.[1]

Emanuel Bloch, in an affidavit submitted to a federal district court, December 1952

We enjoy a free press; neither the policies nor writings of the press may be censored or dictated by the state and government agencies.[2]

Federal District Judge Sylvester Ryan, commenting on Bloch's affidavit, in an opinion, December 10, 1952

Emanuel Bloch's petitions, affidavits, and exhibits are stored in old cardboard boxes at a military base in New Jersey. They are testament to the lonely task he had in representing the Rosenbergs. Although Bloch's 1952 appeal on prosecution-sponsored pretrial and trial publicity was tardy, it was not frivolous. In the United States, the topic of "fair trial and free press" has a legal history that dates at least to the late eighteenth century.[3] A detailed history of the Sixth Amendment is beyond the scope of this study, but as historian John Stevens notes, the twentieth century has staged many "trials of the century."[4] The 1920s also produced several trials that featured outrageous behavior by reporters, prosecutors, and defense attorneys. The Leopold-Loeb murder trial, plus the Hall-Mills and Gray-Synder trials, raised the issue of whether the news media had prejudged defendants with lurid publicity. The 1924 Leopold-Loeb case, a so-called thrill murder, left editors of the *Chicago Tribune* begging for more temperate journalistic practices.[5]

> Criminal justice is now a Roman holiday. The courts are in the Coliseum. The state's attorney office is an open torture room of human souls. Exposure of the processes of justice, originally a public safeguard, has been perverted into a public danger. The Franks' case (Bobby Franks was the murder victim) has been a three months' moral pestilence imposed upon our people before the trial. It is an aggravated instance of what has happened with increasing frequency before the trial. Newspaper trials before the case is called have become an abomination. The dangerous initiative that newspapers have taken in judging and convicting out of court is journalistic lynch law.[6]

The *Tribune's* hectoring editorial mostly fell on deaf ears. In 1927 a New York State crime commission report singled out Hearst newspapers for biased reporting of the Hall-Mills and Gray-Synder murder cases.[7] In 1933, the American Newspaper Guild (ANG) was formed and a newspaper code of ethics devised. One of the provisions sardonically asked reporters to "presume persons accused of a crime of being innocent . . . until they are convicted."[8] The code, however, was little more than public relations window dressing. Then the Lindbergh case exploded in an assault of noisy news media coverage, especially radio broadcasts.[9] The accused kidnapper and killer, Bruno Hauptmann, suffered what John Lofton describes as a "carnival atmosphere." Reporting before and during the trial was so biased it shocked even the most cynical of big city tabloid reporters.

The legacy of the Lindbergh case spawned an eighteen member Special Committee from the press, radio, and the bar. Then the American Society of Newspaper Editors (ASNE), the American Society of Newspaper Publishers (ASNP), and an American Bar Association (ABA) delegation suggested voluntary guidelines for news media coverage of trials. The committee urged broadcasters and reporters to stop commenting on evidence during a trial and to stop interviewing court officials, witnesses, and jurors. Committee guidelines also discouraged prosecution and defense attorneys from giving interviews, participating in vaudeville performances, or writing guest commentaries for newspapers. Publicity excesses of notorious trials of the 1920s and 1930s lessened somewhat after World War II. But it was not until the early 1950s that federal courts began seriously weighing the negative effects of news media publicity on a defendant's right to a fair trial.

Shortly after the Rosenberg-Sobell trial, the U.S. Supreme Court overturned a case involving several rape convictions by Florida courts. While the convictions were technically overturned on other grounds, two justices in

U.S. v. Shepherd condemned an Orlando newspaper for featuring a pretrial editorial demanding the death penalty for four African-American suspects.[10] In *Stroble v. California*, the Court heard a case involving the actions of a local district attorney. In this case, before the trial began, a local prosecutor leaked to the local news media details of a defendant's confession. The district attorney also told reporters he believed the defendant sane and guilty. The U.S. Supreme Court upheld the conviction but said there was a constitutional limit to the type and amount of publicity a prosecuting attorney could indulge before a trial."[11]

Only the year before, in *U.S. v. Dennis*,[12] the Court's majority agreed with Appeals Court Justice Learned Hand that "those who may have in fact committed a crime cannot secure immunity because it is possible that the jurors who try them may not be exempt from the general feelings prevalent in the society in which they live."[13] Early in 1952, the U.S. Supreme Court had upheld convictions of a defendant who was the subject of a prosecutor's press conference during his trial. Still, Justices Hugo Black's and William Douglas's dissents in *U.S. v. Leviton* portended a change in judicial philosophy regarding Sixth Amendment rights. Nevertheless, it did not come quite early enough to help the Rosenbergs or Morton Sobell.[14] Judge Sylvester Ryan ruled on December 10, 1952, that their constitutional right to a fair trial had not been obstructed by prejudicial publicity.[15] Instead, Ryan's opinion turned the claim of prejudicial publicity on its head. News reports said the federal district court judge defended newspaper publicity, saying it, "allay[ed] public anxiety and [gave] assurance that those charged with the protection of vital information were alert and diligent in the performance of their obligations."[16]

Defense lawyers immediately appealed Ryan's decision to the U.S. Court of Appeals. On December 31, that court upheld Ryan's holding. Nonetheless, the court's opinion said that the appeal was "obviously an afterthought inspired by the hope of securing a new trial after having exhausted all hope of reversing the verdict."[17] Judge Thomas Swan said if defense lawyers had thought their clients had suffered a miscarriage of justice, they would have complained about such publicity *before* the trial began.[18]

Swan referred to the defense's failure to request a mistrial the day after William Perl was arrested. (Perl's arrest came in the midst of the trial). Swan's rather blunt words obviously were directed at Emanuel Bloch. Nonetheless, it was Ethel Rosenberg who was stung and angered by Judge Swan's comments. In a New Year's day letter to Bloch, she delivered a spirited defense of her husband's lawyer-of-record.

> I am sick for the unconscionable sneering attitude, the snide insinuations you have had to suffer on our behalf. It is a shockingly deplorable level, indeed, to which morality has sunk when the public servants of such exalted position find entirely acceptable the questionable technique of slur

and the smear. With that extraordinary aplomb, your carefully organized, thoroughly documented, soberly stated arguments were dismissed.[19]

The *Daily Worker* and *National Guardian* also had strong opinions on the decision. Milton Howard of the *Worker* and the *Guardian's* Lawrence Emery alleged that several key sentences in Judge Swan's opinion were purposely omitted from mainstream newspaper reports. In fact, Swan had severely rebuked Irving Saypol for his timing of Perl's indictment and arrest. This is the passage from Swan's opinion that wire services and newspapers allegedly did not cite: "We must assume that the publication of the indictment was deliberately 'timed' and that the statement attributed to Mr. Saypol was made by him. Such tactics cannot be too severely condemned . . . such a statement to the press in the course of a trial was wholly reprehensible."[20] Howard and Emery probably were right. The author was not able to locate mention of Swan's quote in any of the four New York City mainstream daily newspapers he examined.[21] Whether the press was trying to minimize embarrassment for Irving Saypol (and itself) is hard to say. Nonetheless, overall, Swan's opinion did receive adequate, if somewhat bowdlerized, coverage.

The *National Guardian's* New Year's day issue rhetorically asked readers if they wanted to keep Michael and Robert Rosenberg from becoming orphans. The newspaper implored its readers to wire or write President Truman immediately. (A photo of an empty electric chair appeared on page 1). Nevertheless, for the Rosenbergs there was one very bright spot in the otherwise somber news. Nobel laureate and nuclear physicist Harold C. Urey announced that he had asked Judge Kaufman to grant the Rosenbergs judicial clemency.[22] Urey told the *Guardian* that he had also written a letter to the *New York Times*. "I wrote not as a scientist but as a citizen. I am not discussing the scientific evidence in particular. I am just not happy about the evidence in general."[23] Urey's brief statement was not exactly the modern-day equivalent of Emile Zola's "J Accuse." Still, it did come from a Nobel prize winner and an internationally respected figure. In fact, Urey was the first major scientific figure to intercede on behalf of the Rosenbergs.[24] The press had to report this development. Urey was no communist, no wild-eyed political radical. His announcement meant it would be much easier for the Rosenberg Committee to recruit well-known public figures. In practical terms, one Harold Urey was worth one hundred volunteers working a month from dawn to dusk.

Ben Bradlee's "white paper" helped defuse French suspicions that the Rosenbergs had been "railroaded." It did not, however, short-circuit the European Rosenberg movement. In late December, 5,000 attended a raucous Rosenberg rally in Paris at the Velodrome d'Hiver.[25] On the heels of the Velodrome d'Hiver rally, the leftist *Franc-Tireur*, moderate *Le Figaro*, and conservative *L'Aurora* urged President Truman to exercise mercy. On January 2, 1953, *Le Monde* featured an editorial that said while the Rosenbergs had received a fair trial, the evidence used to convict them was dubious.[26] *Le Monde* also observed that communist support of the case in France was "a diversion." By the New Year, however, Pablo Picasso's macabre black and yellow posters of the Rosenbergs sitting in electric chairs had made them the first topic of conversation in France.

    U.S. News and World Report's first article on the Rosenberg case sounded an ominous note. In its trademark telegraphese, the newsmagazine reported that no matter what happened in the case, "There is no evidence that the communists will quit trying to squeeze the last ounce of value from the Rosenbergs."[27] The report said if President-Elect Eisenhower granted clemency, then communists would boast of a successful international propaganda campaign. If the Americans were executed the magazine forecast the Rosenbergs could be reconfigured into "martyrs" for world peace.[28]

    There was some truth to that claim. The Slansky executions in Czechoslovakia had turned into a public-relations nightmare for communists, socialists, and political "fellow travelers" in the West. It was now evident beyond doubt that an anti-Semitic upheaval was sweeping Eastern bloc nations. For communists, "le cas Rosenberg" was simply too tempting not to use as a polemical and propaganda counterattack. It promised to be very ugly. The final stage on which the Rosenberg case appeared, the international news media, suggested a spectral clash that would haunt both sides in different ways. The international news media of 1953 had not yet achieved the global instantaneousness of satellite technology. The ideological tensions underlying the case made transcontinental communication doubly important. With passions aroused to a fever pitch, the news media of Western Europe and the United States could only hope not to be seared by the partisan heat of the messages they carried.

    Increasingly, small religious groups and individuals from various faiths joined the Rosenberg movement in the United States. Most did not join until after the U.S. Supreme Court had refused to review the Rosenberg-Sobell case. Relatedly, a Howard Rushmore story in the January 6, 1953, *New York Journal-American* reported "six outstanding Americans representing three religious faiths," had signed a statement claiming that the Rosenberg movement was exploited by communist propagandists.[29] Significantly, the statement was released by the Anti-Defamation League of B'nai Brith. The signers said they wished to fight "the impression that the Rosenbergs were doomed by a planned miscarriage of justice arising from anti-Semitic and other reprehensible influences." The signers, then, did not consider humanitarianism as grounds for participation in the Rosenberg movement.

Rosenberg sympathizers were said to have either "knowingly or unwillingly" assisted communist propaganda.

Fear that religion might serve as a communist mass media propaganda tool first was expressed in an American Jewish Committee memorandum in 1950. Shortly after Julius Rosenberg's arrest, AJC Executive John B. Slawson proposed a media-relations strategy to blunt a possible Anti-Semitic backlash to the "atom arrests" that year.[30] Slawson's memorandum, "Public Relations' Effects of Jewish Atom Spies," was designed to counter negative news media publicity with "propaganda-of-fact" tactics. He suggested the AJC try to place stories in the news media that stressed Soviet anti-Semitism and Jewish opposition to communism in the United States and Israel.[31]

Slawson's memorandum had little practical relevance until fall 1952. Until then, Rosenberg stories in mainstream newspapers tended to be firmly tied to judicial agenda-setting, i.e., court rulings on appeal. Now that was slowly changing. Oddly, the Rosenberg movement in Europe had again indirectly forced an issue onto the American news agenda. The January 6 *New York Herald Tribune* had a story on the State Department's efforts to "counter growing agitation" for the Rosenbergs in Europe. The Voice of America (VOA) had coordinated and carried out the campaign. Taking a cue from Ben Bradlee, the VOA distributed dozens of Rosenberg case background articles and "factual stories" to wire services and news-media outlets in Europe.

The *Herald Tribune* story reported that efforts to counteract the Rosenberg movement had been underway and "stepped up three months ago when reports from American public-affairs officers abroad indicated communist agitation appeared to be making headway among non-communists."[32] The article also said the propaganda campaign centered around a forty-page Justice Department paper on the Rosenberg-Sobell case. The Justice Department document was "rushed" to forty "countries on the continent." (This seems odd given that the U.S. embassy in Paris could get no information on the case from the State Department as late as mid-December 1952). The report probably was sent to Europe only after the Justice Department learned of Bradlee's unusual agenda-setting ingenuity. In any event, the *Herald Tribune* quoted an anonymous U.S. official, who said most French newspapers now had front-page coverage of the U.S. official stance on the case.[33]

The Slansky hangings had given the State Department some propaganda elbow room. Although the VOA did not compare the cases, their existence invited comparison. Nonetheless, several French newspaper commentators insisted that executing the Rosenbergs would play into the hands of Moscow's propagandists. Mindful of the showdown mentality of the cold war, French novelist Thierry Maulnier warned in a *Le Figaro* column:

"Don't give them their martyrs. Don't play their game."[34] *Franc-Tireur* told President Truman he would "do himself honor" by commuting the death sentences to life-in-prison terms before leaving office.[35]

Judge Kaufman granted a stay of execution on January 5, 1953. The delay gave Manny Bloch time to file a clemency petition with President Truman. Bloch hurriedly prepared a petition for U.S. Pardon Attorney Daniel Lyons.[36] Speculation in the press was that Truman would "pass" the petition to President-elect Eisenhower. Commenting on the case, the *New York Times'* Edward Ranzal said Manny Bloch had intentionally entangled the case "in a mesh of legalistic moves."[37] An editorial in the *Atlanta Constitution* said that while a stay was proper procedure, the defendants in the case would have been executed without a trial in Soviet Russia.

The *National Guardian* took the opposite stance. In an editorial, "Tell the President to Spare These Two Lives," the newsmagazine implied the American mainstream press was allied with the government. The *Guardian* claimed that attacks by the press against the Rosenberg movement had "immobilized thousands of people who in their hearts want the lives of Ethel and Julius Rosenberg spared."[38] In its frustration with the U.S. mainstream press, it said almost all French mainstream newspapers backed clemency. Comparing *Le Figaro* to the editorially moderate *New York Herald Tribune*, and "center-conservative" *Le Monde* with the *New York Times*, the Guardian wondered why those American newspapers couldn't follow the lead of their French brethren.[39]

Julius Rosenberg's implicit disavowal of the *Daily Worker*'s assertion of government anti-Semitism quickly found its mark. By early January 1953, the *Worker*'s anti-Semitic campaign was scaled back drastically. The *Worker* soon assumed the *Guardian*'s position and tone on the case. Also, *Worker* editors had stopped efforts to seek a new trial. "The fight now is for Presidential clemency, for commutation of the death sentence. On this, millions of men and women of goodwill agree."[40] The paper noted that a broad sampling of Americans, "conservative men, Catholic priests, top-flight scientists, Protestant ministers," now carried water for the movement. The *Daily Worker*'s shift in strategy and tactics was born of necessity. For the first time since Henry Wallace's 1948 presidential campaign, a variety of humanitarians and liberals had joined a far left-led group in significant numbers. Nevertheless, the Communist Party in the United States had trouble aplenty. Press historian Lauren Kessler's point that radical publications in the United States traditionally have tried to "strengthen the will of their comrades and convert those outside the movement"[41] makes sense when applied to this phase of the Rosenberg case. But the *Worker*'s circulation had sunk to a low ebb in 1952. Excluding the more popular *Sunday Worker*, at most its circulation was no more than 25,000. However, during this time the "pass-along" rate for both the Worker and *Guardian* likely increased as those who were afraid to openly buy or subscribe to these papers read their friend's copies. Also, liberals who sought to know more about the case than they could find in "commercial" newspapers discreetly acquired one or both newspapers. In addition, especially in New York City, reporters and editors at the big dailies kept an eye on the case this way.

While Manny Bloch prepared a clemency appeal, the Rosenberg movement grew abroad and in the United States. Picketing in front of American consulates and embassies overseas became commonplace. At home "constant pickets" circulated in front of the White House.[42] Despite these efforts, most U.S. news accounts of the case usually implied it was something happening elsewhere. The *New York Times* reported the case had "become a major topic in countries where communist propaganda finds a willing ear." The January 7, 1953, issue of the *Times* said French communists had taken to calling the Rosenbergs "American patriots" and the "American Dreyfus case." Celebrities and famous public figures lent their names and money to the clemency drive. Authors Bertholt Brecht, Ernest Hemingway, and Albert Camus joined Albert Einstein and Picasso in asking for mercy.

The movement had spread to the Scandinavian countries, where, the *Times* said, communists had distributed clemency petitions.[43] A large rally in East Berlin featured charges of anti-Semitism and war hysteria. The *Times* said excerpts from the Rosenbergs' letters were read to the crowd. Since the letters had never been quoted or reported in mainstream U.S. newspapers, this reference likely meant little to *Times'* readers. While the *Worker* had eased away from its no-holds barred anti-Semitic propaganda, it could not resist asking, "Is it not cause for wonder of the democratic peoples of the world that in so short a span of time, the citadel of Nazi genocide should now hear the weeping of Germans for a Jewish husband and wife?"[44]

Like the *Guardian*, the *Worker* delighted sometimes in dropping the names of artists, film stars, and writers who were joining the lengthening line of Rosenberg sympathizers. The *Worker* reported the support of Mexican painter David Siqueiros, existential philosopher Jean Paul Sartre, and French movie stars Simone Signoret and Yves Montand.[45] It is well to remember that a year before, no major public figure anywhere could be persuaded to lend his or her name to the movement. (Indeed as late as January 1952, the *Daily Worker* had ignored the Rosenbergs). Actually, the Rosenberg movement in the United States had attracted few notables from the arts and entertainment industry. Hollywood actors, big-name authors, and other celebrities had already undergone purges and blacklisting. The threat of a subpoena from HUAC or other congressional committees loomed behind a commitment to a left cause.[46] As a result, the Rosenberg movement in the United States lacked what Hollywood studios once called "star quality." Increasingly, though, major American religious and scientific persons signed petitions, attended rallies, and contributed money.[47]

Meanwhile, Scripps-Howard's Frederick Woltman said the Rosenberg movement "here and abroad, in capitals of Europe, Africa, and Asia . . . has reached a white heat."[48] Woltman explained that this phenomenon obtained because the trial record was "largely forgotten." He likely did not realize that a year and a half earlier William Reuben had based an extensive *National Guardian* exposé on the same transcript. George Sokolsky, a one-time left-wing partisan, was one of a half dozen conservative newspaper columnists who wrote rather vehement anti-Rosenberg essays. Sokolsky was convinced the movement to save the couple was cynical and manipulative. His angry comment that "freedom to steal" was not protected by the constitution soon reappeared in slightly different form in other commentaries. Sokolsky also said if the Rosenbergs wanted clemency they could confess and reveal what they allegedly knew of the spy plot.[49]

Like some columnists with a conservative reputation, Sokolsky enjoyed a good relationship with J. Edgar Hoover and other FBI officials. Sokolsky, Bob Considine, and Walter Winchell sometimes invoked the FBI's secret hope in their columns: that the Rosenbergs would weaken and confess. Sokolsky's voice was bitter, disgusted, and candidly vengeful. Forty years later, it is tempting to misclassify this attitude as cold-war reactionism that had only a lunatic fringe following. Such would not be true. Like some of his colleagues in the Hearst chain, Sokolsky spoke a harsh political idiom known as "Americanism." It was not the WASP-ish, well mannered, and polished "American Century" patriotism of Henry Luce.[50] It was the raspy, impatient hubris of the immigrant-descended urban working classes who had not left the city for suburban subdivisions. It was the voice heard in corner taverns, church bake sales, foundry lunchrooms, barber shops, banquet halls, and union meetings. But, ironically, the Rosenberg Committee had good success recruiting from essentially the same audience.

But the Rosenberg case was soon back in the news. On January 11, 1953, Bob Considine introduced a six-part series, "The Inside Story of the Rosenberg case." Like those of Oliver Pilat and Max Lerner, Considine's series alleged communist influence behind the "world wide" Rosenberg movement.[51] Considine had been the first American columnist to write a series on the case. In late 1951, he had reprised the Rosenberg-Sobell trial in a series of articles. The earlier series was a mainstream newspaper reporter's answer to William Reuben's exposé on the Rosenberg case. Now Considine updated his series on Rosenberg clemency efforts. "The once mute *Daily Worker* now seethes with grotesque panegyrics about the Rosenbergs, letters the unrepentant couple sent from the death house, sobbing features about the sons, and protests from communist fronts, left-wingers and fuzzy humanitarians all over the world."[52]   Several days later the *New York World-Telegram and Sun*'s James Daniel reiterated the same theme in a three-part series on the case. (One headline in his series read: "Mrs. Rosenberg was like a Red Spider").   Daniel asserted that the Rosenberg movement had two objectives: one, to embarrass the United States and, two, to flatter the couple with a propaganda campaign that would ensure their silence.[53]   Right or not, Daniel's and Considine's efforts suggested that the American press had embarked on a spontaneous "counterpropaganda" strategy.   Since Oliver Pilat's series in the *Post* in early December 1952, a growing number of American columnists and reporters had denounced the clemency-for-the Rosenbergs movement.   Unlike their French counterparts, however, many U.S. journalists advocated clemency for the Rosenbergs only as a *quid-pro quo* for confession.   Like Oliver Pilat, Bob Considine argued that the communists knew the Rosenbergs were guilty and willing to be executed.[54]   In language that would today be considered racist, he emphasized the success of the Rosenberg campaign in developing nations.

> Gullible areas of the world are captives of communist dominated countries and organizations have been repeatedly told, for example, that the Rosenbergs were condemned to death because they are Jewish.   This effort is to fan hatred of the United States and to help take the curse off the newly ordered wave of anti-Semitism in the USSR.   It blithely ignores the fact that Julius turned against his religion and his coreligionists to become a communist . . . The Russians have used the Rosenbergs to tell countless millions that the U.S. judicial system is corrupt.   Half clothed primitives in parts of darkest Africa today mull over reports, received from Red infiltrators, that American witnesses and such agencies as the FBI indulge in mass perjury.[55]

Julius Rosenberg's letters to Manny Bloch came to resemble a running indictment of the U.S. press.   In a January 12 letter to Bloch, he claimed, "the stupendous propaganda campaign against us is reaching unprecedented levels.   The sheer weight of newsprint staggers the imagination but it sets one thinking."[56]   Rosenberg accused New York City newspapers of only "presenting the prosecutor's side of the case."   Rosenberg described this as the "Goebbels' technique," that is, repeating a sensational falsehood often enough until it is believed.   Like his adversaries in the mainstream press, Julius Rosenberg believed he would be vindicated by the trial record.[57]   Still, Rosenberg's desire to counterattack the American press had taken new form. He asked his lawyer to prepare an "open letter" to editors of major U.S. newspapers.   The letter's purpose would be to refute "the lies and common misconceptions that the newspapers are feeding the public.[58]   Since they disseminate public information and news it is their duty to [present] and it is in the interests of fair play that they don't black out our side of the controversy and allow us the opportunity to place paid advertisements in their papers."[59]

Rosenberg thought such a venture was "worth a try." He also hinted that it might convince President Eisenhower to grant clemency.[60] Given Rosenberg's previous statements regarding the news media, his plan was somewhat out of character. While the Rosenberg Committee did step up attempts to secure paid advertisements in newspapers, the "open letter" was never written or published. Still, Julius Rosenberg's harsh judgment of the American press had at least some merit. As noted earlier, William Reuben's *National Guardian* exposé never was reported or discussed in any U.S. newspapers. This meant, of course, that the defects and contradictions in the prosecution's less than flawless case were never discussed, either. Why? Former Rosenberg Committee member William Wolf's explanation that the news media geared their news agenda on the case only to court decisions is a helpful partial answer. Nevertheless, American editors, columnists, and reporters had steadily ignored the claims of the *National Guardian* and the Rosenbergs for a year and a half. Why? Obviously because they lacked the sort of credibility necessary to trigger mainstream news reporting or investigation. Why they lacked credibility had much to do with the Rosenbergs' well-known radicalism, the *Guardian's* candidly socialist reputation, and the growing success of the Rosenberg movement.

The Rosenberg Committee had worked long and hard to acquire the support of Albert Einstein. The reclusive Princeton University professor decided in early January to join Harold Urey in recommending clemency for the Rosenbergs.[61] Einstein was a far better-known figure than Urey. The news gave a tremendous boost to the movement in the United States and abroad. The Rosenberg Committee had been established on the assumption it would receive little news-media attention. A burgeoning clemency movement in Europe plus a barely escaped execution date had changed that.

The day news of Einstein's clemency appeal appeared in the newspapers, a story broke in U.S. newspapers reporting that nine Jewish doctors in Moscow had been arrested on charges of "medical espionage."[62] The U.S. State Department claimed the doctors' arrests were part of a wave of official anti-Semitism in Eastern Europe. The next day Tass (the official Soviet news agency) charged that the doctors had tried to murder several top Soviet leaders. The physicians were declared "Anglo-American-Zionist agents." Moscow Radio said all nine doctors had confessed to charges. They were said to have accepted $1 million to be used for "espionage, diversion, and sabotage." *Izvestia*, (the official Soviet news organ), said the plot was "squelch[ed] as a loathsome reptile, along with its "filthy hirelings."[63]

What did the doctors' plot have to do with the Rosenberg case? On the face of it, nothing. At a symbolic level, however, it was directly linked to the sympathy expressed in Eastern and Western Europe for the condemned

Americans. Coming just five weeks after the Slansky executions, the plot strongly suggested anti-Semitism had been elevated to a semiofficial policy in the Soviet Union. Stalin was in the final months of his life. His hand unmistakably had appeared behind the recent purges of Jews in East Germany and Czechoslovakia.[64] For several weeks, Western newspaper correspondents, especially Americans, charged communist officials with seizing the Rosenberg movement as a convenient propaganda smokescreen. The doctors' plot lent at least some credence to this hypothesis. In any event, the timing for the Rosenberg Committee hardly could have been worse. Just as the members of the Slansky executions died in the news media, the doctors' plot rekindled the fire. William Wolf recalls that for weeks newspaper reporters wanted only to discuss the nine Soviet doctors. "Anytime there was any injustice over in Eastern Europe, the papers would call up the Committee and ask 'what do [you] have to say about that'? Usually we would not discuss these other issues. However, Joe Brainin, [a committee spokesperson] had very close ties to the Jewish communities and he issued a statement saying the doctors are innocent and as an individual he condemned such action."[65]

From a media-relations' perspective, the doctors' plot story had put the committee in a tight corner. Various communist officials and agencies in Eastern and Western Europe had done much to publicize the drive for clemency for the Rosenbergs. Condemning Marxists now might appear the height of ingratitude, at least to those on the far left. Wolf says, "Nobody wanted to criticize communists for fear of kicking them when they were down."[66] Nonetheless, a reluctance to condemn them was interpreted by many American journalists as merely "following the communist line." By now, even the CIA was concerned about the international campaign to save the Rosenbergs. In late 1952, a CIA agent prepared a memorandum on the propaganda possibilities the U.S. government might try in order to convert the Rosenbergs. He proposed a discussion of "Jewish persecution in the Soviet Union," and an aggressive publicity campaign to exploit reaction to the doctors' plot. Incredibly, he also recommended "a concerted effort to convince" the Rosenbergs that the Soviet Union had begun a campaign to exterminate Jews in Eastern Europe.[67] In this scenario, after the Rosenbergs had confessed, they would appeal through the news media to Jews worldwide to abandon communism. For this service presidential clemency would be granted.

Though obviously farfetched, the proposal had some attraction for FBI officials. Now that the Rosenberg movement had international impact, the temptation to stand it on its head was very tempting. "The importance of success in this venture can scarcely be overstated from a psychological standpoint. The communist parties throughout the world have built up the Rosenbergs as heros and martyrs to 'American anti-Semitism.' Their recantation would entail backfiring of the entire Soviet propaganda effort."

The CIA analyst argued that the Rosenbergs were "ideally suited" to split the Communist Party on the topic of the "Jewish issue." The author stated that any attempts by the Justice Department to trade confessions for death sentences would not work. Rather, he contended that the Rosenbergs would have to be convinced that the Soviet Union had "betrayed and is destroying their own people."[68] The memorandum outlined an audacious plan to recruit a "highly intelligent" American Jew to approach them with an offer. A rabbi, a representative of a Jewish organization, and a former communist were proposed as possible emissaries. Understandably, this strange counter-propaganda plan never got past the draft stage. Nevertheless, it demonstrated a growing concern within the government about international news-media coverage of the case.

By this time the Rosenbergs were a major topic of conversation in the United States. But the U.S. mainstream press analyzed the case as if the only issue were the Communist Party's backing of the clemency movement. Still, occasionally a newspaper or newsmagazine revealed that others besides communists had come forward for the Rosenbergs. In late January, *Newsweek* admitted that: "fellow travelers and many liberals" had joined those who "conceded the guilt of the Rosenbergs."[69]

More typical of the U.S. press was the *Washington Post's* criticism of *Le Monde's* Henri Pierre.[70] The *Post's* editorial, "*Le Monde* Buys a Hoax," said Pierre had been beguiled into joining an anti-American propaganda campaign. Pierre had earlier written in *Le Monde* that the "Rosenbergs are victims of a frightful police-plot hatched by the FBI and the American government with the view of intimidating the progressive movement."[71] Ironically, French newspaper readers now knew more about the alleged government conspiracy than did their American counterparts. Since American mainstream newspapers had never carried reports of William Reuben's exposé, readers of the *Post* likely puzzled over the phrase "police-plot." The *Post* claimed in December 1952 that Pierre had compared the trial of Rudolph Slansky with the Rosenberg-Sobell trial. In a letter to the *Post*, Pierre denied that he had made the statement. The fact that Pierre denied saying it was significant in that it implied few European journalists really believed the Rosenbergs innocent. Indeed, Ben Bradlee has long argued that the issue in France, as well as in Western Europe, always was the death sentences.[72] Still, in his *Post* letter, Pierre posed a question that cut to the heart of the clemency issue. "One must ask: why such severity? Is it not because they were communists as well as being guilty?"[73]

The *Washington Post* conceded that the issue of whether the death sentences were too severe was "an open question." The *Chicago Daily News* raised eyebrows when it came out for clemency in late January. (It was the only major mainstream American newspaper to advocate mercy). The *Daily News* said it realized "communist agitators" were behind the drive to commute the sentences. But it urged clemency in hope that the Rosenbergs would "give useful information."[74] The paper also noted that because communists were closely associated with the clemency movement, President Eisenhower might resist granting clemency for fear of surrendering to a "violent and irrational propaganda campaign."[75]

11

Eisenhower, the Pope, and the Console Table

In the death house at Sing-Sing, Julius and Ethel Rosenberg listened intently as the special news bulletin came in over the prison radio: President Eisenhower, after due deliberation, refused to commute the sentences.[1]

National Guardian, February 19, 1953

Furthermore, I am asked by the Holy See to inform the competent U.S. authorities that many more requests have been received by the Vatican asking the Holy Father to intercede for clemency for the Rosenbergs; and that left-wing newspapers continue to state that His Holiness has done nothing. I shall be most grateful to you if you will kindly notify the President of this."[2]

Letter from the Vatican's apostolic delegate to the U.S. to President Eisenhower, February 12, 1953

Dwight Eisenhower was sworn in as president under a bright blue January sky. He faced several very difficult problems, not the least of which was the war in Korea. Nevertheless, the General promised an honorable peace was forthcoming. The war would not end for six months, but politically it already was fading into history. Harry Truman was gone, and with him went the unending controversy surrounding his tenure as president. But Truman had left more than the Korean War for General Eisenhower. The outgoing President had left behind the most volatile political case since Sacco and Vanzetti; the Rosenberg case was even more sensitive and complex. Sacco and Vanzetti had began as a botched small-time robbery plus murder in a small Massachusetts town. It took years for it to outgrow its provincial origins and become a cause célèbre. The Rosenberg case, with newspaper headlines of "Atom Spies," was a complex, confusing international phenomenon from the day of Klaus Fuchs's arrest in England. Then the death sentences received by Julius Rosenberg and Ethel Greenglass Rosenberg tripped the light fantastic through a global campaign to save their lies.

Two days after President Eisenhower turned down the clemency bid, the pope entered the Rosenberg news-media frame through the White House back door by means of various supposed messages. The apostolic delegate to the United States, Reverend Amleto Giovanni Cicognani, said he had informed the U.S. Justice Department in December that Pope Pius XII "had received many requests to intercede for the Rosenbergs."[3] Cicognani explained that the Pope was informing the U.S. Government of this development "out of motives of charity." Still, presidential press secretary James C. Hagerty and Pardon Attorney Daniel Lyons said they could not find evidence that a papal message had been left for them.[4] A discomfitted James P. McGranery, Harry Truman's last U.S. attorney general, admitted he had received an "oral" message from the Vatican in December 1952 to the effect that the pope had gotten "numerous and urgent appeals" on behalf of the Rosenbergs. McGranery, however, had not seen fit to make this information known to the news media, or anyone else in government. Hagerty (somewhat misleadingly) said since Pope Pius XII had not expressed an opinion on clemency, there was "no reason to believe such a communication would have an effect on the President's decision."[5]

That probably was true, but a Vatican spokesperson had brought McGranery's oversight to the U.S. news media's attention. In early February, the Vatican's semiofficial newspaper, *L'Osservatore Romano*, reported the Pope's 1952 message to the Truman administration.[6] In New York, Manny Bloch quickly seized on the new development, making a statement to the news media. He claimed that the Pope's message was a request for executive clemency. Through their attorney, the Rosenbergs lashed out at the Truman and Eisenhower administrations for their "deliberate concealment of Pope Pius' sentiments." The couple alleged it "was dramatic confirmation of the fraud that has been practiced in our proceedings from the start."[7] The *National Guardian* condemned the "astounding disclosure of the Justice Department's suppression of a move for clemency."[8]

Manny Bloch and the Rosenbergs were right about the content of the papal message, though the Pope had declined to comment on the "merits of the case." Bloch and the Rosenbergs also were likely right about suppression of Pius XII's message. The Pope had urged "mercy," but McGranery denied the next day to the press that the pontiff had made an appeal for clemency. The press carried McGranery's denial, and for several months many Americans thought Pius's intercession a propaganda hoax.

Manny Bloch argued before the Second Circuit Court of Appeals that the trial verdict should be vacated because of Irving Saypol's arrest of William Perl during the trial. (District Judge Sylvester Ryan had earlier refused Bloch's motion for a new trial on the same motion). Now Bloch was trying to convince the court to overturn Ryan's ruling.[9] This effort made more sense than one might think. Six weeks earlier, Appeals Court Judge Thomas Swan had described Saypol's trial behavior as "reprehensible." At any rate, partly out of desperation, Bloch raised this point again. He reminded the judges of the publicity William Perl's arrest received.   According to a newspaper report, Bloch's comment triggered a colloquy between Judges Jerome Frank and Learned Hand.   Judge Frank said: "I don't see how something unknown to the jury could prejudice your clients."[10]   With that Judge Hand subtly disputed with his colleague. "There are some justices on the Supreme Court who may take a different view." Frank then conceded the Court might interpret the issue differently.[11] Hand had obliquely spoken to a troubling, old, and sometimes embarrassing judicial problem. The fact that a judge tells a juror not to follow the progress of a case in the news media does not ensure compliance. No one had asked any of the Rosenberg-Sobell trial jurors if they had followed Judge Kaufman's order. Some of them might have read a newspaper or heard a radio or television broadcast about the trial. If that had been the case, then a new trial might be granted. But at this stage, no one would ever know for sure.

Learned Hand's point was subtle but impressive. The Rosenbergs well might go to their deaths after a federal appeals' court judge had all but said they hadn't received a fair trial. Of course, if the Supreme Court decided to accept Bloch's petition, it would review the conviction and the Perl arrest. By now, Manny Bloch knew that possibility was quite unlikely.

Manny Bloch took the Rosenbergs' sons to visit their parents shortly after President Eisenhower declined to grant clemency. Michael Rosenberg wrote a letter about the visit to *National Guardian* readers in February 1953. "Manny Bloch took me and my brother Robby to see our parents in the death house Saturday. I had just been reading Ike's statement where he says "their deliberate betrayal of the entire nation could very well result in the death of many, many thousands of innocent citizens." The first thing I said was: "Are you innocent? Mommy said: "We are and we swear it on the bible. Do you think we would go through all this suffering if we were not?"[12] Until now, the *Guardian* had been relatively subdued in its coverage of the children. The step of using a letter written by a child (but earlier composed by an adult) was a rather drastic tactic. The *Guardian* would never have run the letter if it had not felt the need to pull out all the stops in its clemency campaign. It was a very chancy gambit, too. The Rosenberg Committee had risked a lot of bad publicity. But in an unusual way the U.S. press's cold-war gatekeeping had kept Michael Rosenberg's letter off the news agenda and, at least once, insulated the committee from negative commentary. In Europe, especially in East Germany, the letter was read to great effect at rallies and was widely reported in the news media. The *New York Times* noted that the "the plight of Michael and Robby" was tracked on a daily basis by East German network radio.[13] (The *Times*, however, did not refer to Michael's letter). To some extent the letter-writing incident was the propaganda equivalent of carrying coals to Newcastle. Stories on the Rosenberg children in the United States were usually confined to the *Daily Worker* and *National Guardian*.

Newspapers no longer said "if" the Rosenbergs are executed but "when" they would be electrocuted.[14] Nevertheless, there was growing sympathy for them in the United States. Enrollment in Rosenberg committees in most major cities had impressively grown in just several weeks. Still, sometimes local committees had strained relations with the news media. William Wolf recalls that people who headed local committees often had reputations for backing left-wing causes and activities. (Not surprisingly some were former Communist Party members).[15] Wolf says local press coverage often focused on the political backgrounds of the committee volunteers instead of on the Rosenbergs. "It was to malign the committee . . . to say that it was communist controlled. If you went around the country and spoke to newspaper editors they would always ask you 'well where are you getting your money from?' That was always one of the number-one questions. You'd say how the meetings were going but there was always the suspicion of it [communism]."[16] Nonetheless, Wolf says, he was often surprised by the willingness of editors to listen. They might not assign reporters to cover a rally or meeting, but no one threw Wolf out of his office, either. Wolf says some editors and reporters were even mildly sympathetic. Generally, though, getting the kind of press coverage the Rosenberg Committee sought, i.e., reasonably balanced, was impossible.

Emily Alman and her husband, David Alman, believed the key to saving the Rosenbergs resided with the American middle class. Emily Alman says she did not berate mainstream reporters who said committee rallies and vigils were communist orchestrated. "I don't think that any of us thought the press was anything but respectful and decent. We had a decent relationship with the press, but they did what they were paid to do. I think individually they were awfully good people. I don't think anyone was out to get us. You certainly didn't get baited by them, but they wrote the story from the point of view of the newspapers. You just didn't have the investigative reporting then."[17]

The Almans also knew that a major social and political movement exceeding the Sacco and Vanzetti and Scottsboro Boys cases had exploded in a few months from one small meeting. Moreover, it had happened with minimum and (from the committee's point of view) negative news-media coverage. The Almans also strongly suspected that the Communist Party's interest in the Rosenberg movement was something less than ingenuous. Early on the party had kept a cool distance from the case, especially the *Daily*

Worker. Now in 1953, the issue of communism was threatening to crowd out other topics. French Communist Party leader Jacques Duclos did not help matters any when he told the French press: "Those who accuse the Soviet Union of anti-Semitism should watch their words. We communists defend Ethel and Julius Rosenberg and they are Jews."[18] But Emily Alman especially felt contempt for the Civil Rights Congress, whose bellicose rally at Sing-Sing had turned into a press-relations fiasco. "Then they [the CRC] threw leaflets out of a window [in Manhattan] and we exploded. Our whole position was that you stand out on the street so you're not faceless."[19]

After President Eisenhower declined to grant clemency, news reports discussed the approaching executions. No relatives would be allowed to attend. Only three newspaper reporters, each from a major wire service, would witness the electrocutions and feed coverage to other news media outlets.[20]

Relatedly, *New York Post* columnist Leonard Lyons said Tessie Greenglass had visited Sing-Sing in an effort to convince her daughter to "save her life." Lyons also said U.S. Marshall William Carroll reported that the Rosenbergs did not want a rabbi at their executions.[21] According to Lyons, the couple believed rabbis were "tools of the capitalist state" and should not be allowed to preside at their executions. That came as news to Julius Rosenberg, who now read the *Post*, as well as most other New York City dailies. Rosenberg restated a theme he had invoked many times before: the press would distort the facts of the case whenever it had an opportunity. In a another letter to Manny Bloch, he heatedly protested: "This vicious lying must be stopped. There are a number of previous incidents that I brought to your attention. Here again, we have this complete fabrication with intent to poison the public mind against us and help the murder-plot against our lives."[22] Rosenberg also accused *New York Mirror* columnist Walter Winchell of repeating Lyons's story over network radio. He described Winchell's broadcast "as the latest twist in the campaign against us." Julius claimed Lyons's and Winchell's reports were part of a news-media conspiracy that promoted fraudulent reporting on the case.[23] "It is obvious to me that this is another desperate move sponsored by our enemies to stem the tide that is exposing this miscarriage of justice and demanding that we be saved. Naturally, it fits in nicely with the present hate-monger campaign to link-up communists with anti-Semitism and now, too, they add the Rosenbergs."[24]

From his Sing-Sing cell Rosenberg saw something in the trial transcript that caught his eye.[25] During the trial, David Greenglass had testified that his brother-in-law boasted of stealing a "proximity fuse" from Emerson Radio Corporation in 1945. (Rosenberg had briefly worked there at the end of World War II). In a letter to Manny Bloch, Rosenberg said that he could not have taken the proximity fuse in his briefcase, as David Greenglass testified, because the fuse, really part of a World War II bomb component, was too big to be concealed in a briefcase. He also said security precautions at Emerson would have made stealing the fuse improbably difficult.[26]

Julius Rosenberg asked his attorney to begin an investigation. The already overworked lawyer turned to *National Guardian* reporter Leon Summit for investigative help. Summit says he quickly learned that Rosenberg was right. The president of Emerson Radio, and other company officials, confirmed that a proximity fuse had not been stolen from Emerson during the war.[27] When Summit told Bloch of this confirmation, Bloch asked the president of Emerson, and others who had worked there with Rosenberg, to cooperate with Summit. In a 1990 interview, Summit says Bloch pleaded with the Emerson officials but none would give affidavits. Since he lacked subpoena power, Bloch couldn't force any of them to testify, either. Lacking affidavits, Summit said he and Bloch were stopped cold. Summit recalls that Bloch was convinced affidavits would have "blown the case wide open." While that is debatable, certainly affidavits indicating perjury by David Greenglass would have given the *National Guardian* a big story, possibly one the U.S. news media could not have ignored. Because the courts would have ruled on a new motion, the issue automatically would have appeared on the news agenda. But Bloch did not get the affidavits. Summit says, "[He] never did do anything about it . . . The question never came out."[28]

Not even the *Guardian* ran a story on the proximity fuse. Why not is unclear, but the frustration of having been close to a major break was a devastating setback to Bloch and Summit. In a February 25, 1953, letter to Manny Bloch, Julius Rosenberg stated that he and his wife were "incensed over the monstrous lies" about the Rosenberg movement in the U.S. press.[29] He also complained about recent "Red-baiting" statements about him by Assistant U.S. Attorney Myles Lane in the *New York Times*.[30]

Lately, Julius Rosenberg's grievances about the press had increased sharply. There was more coverage of the case, more discussion among syndicated columnists and high-ranking reporters. Nonetheless, most of the news reports about the Rosenbergs were routine stories on judicial rulings. True, there was more reportage and commentary on the case's phenomenal popularity in other parts of the world. But coverage of the Rosenberg movement in the United States was still quite sketchy. Articles by Oliver Pilat and Bob Considine had given a somewhat distorted picture of communist backing of the Rosenbergs. Then both columnists, as well as Max Lerner and other journalists, ignored noncommunists who had joined the movement or dismissed them as "dupes." But the U.S. press almost always positioned Rosenberg case news within a communist framework. Sometimes the result was absurd. In early March, the *New York Post* broke a story claiming the Save-the-Rosenbergs movement was supported by the Kremlin through funds in a bank account in Tangier.[31] More important, though, the story also reported that Acting Solicitor General Robert L. Stern had denied offering the Rosenbergs a chance to save themselves by confessing.

Emanuel Bloch denounced the rumored offer at an emergency press conference.   He described the alleged deal as "medieval barbarism" and scolded the *Post's* Robert S. Allen for "callousness toward human life."[32] (Allen had broken the story for the *Post*). Bloch, of course, disbelieved Stern, and his rebuff of the *Post* implied that Allen's scoop was the result of a Justice Department leak to see if the Rosenbergs would accept a back-channel clemency offer in exchange for full confession. Ironically, it was one of the few major Rosenberg news stories of 1953 that did not have communism at least as a minor theme.

Julius Rosenberg followed the case in the newspapers more closely than did his wife. His reaction to press reports and columns varied only in the intensity of his distrust and loathing. As he wrote to Ethel March 12, 1953, "Practically the entire press has embarked on a jingoistic campaign of open bellicose statements, editorials, and columns intensified among a welter of confusing and contradictory news reports."[33] No doubt, the mainstream press in the United States was leery about being used for propaganda in the clemency campaign.   No editorial ever called for an investigation into the *National Guardian's* charges of perjury, conspiracy, and prejudicial publicity. If anyone in the U.S. mainstream press thought the Rosenbergs innocent, he or she was not saying so in newsprint. To veteran newspaper reporters such as George Trow of the *New York Post*, the Rosenberg movement was mostly a political juggernaut, a front for political radicals seeking to exploit well-meaning liberals.[34] Conversely, to Rosenberg Committee volunteer William Wolf, the press was something you expected the worst of in hope that what appeared in newspapers the next morning would not seem half as bad.

While Ben Bradlee had tried to pull the plug on a high voltage propaganda campaign by communists in France, American reporters in foreign cities felt increasingly uneasy about the impending executions. In spring 1953, Russell Baker was a fresh-faced London correspondent for the *Baltimore Sun*. Like Bradlee, he privately opposed the death sentences.[35] But Baker also felt the Communist Party wanted the Rosenbergs to die.   For several reasons, the case had not excited the passion in Great Britain that it did in France. Still, as a young American newly arrived from the States, he sensed President Eisenhower was ignoring strong signals.[36] Moreover, it was obvious to Baker that the Rosenberg movement only was getting stronger. Whether on the Continent or in the United States, omnipresent newspaper and magazine photos of the couple had transformed the case from tabloid grist to a global postmodern case study in ideological and polemical conflict.   In Baker's words, "America wasn't handling things well and this proved it."[37]

Manny Bloch was not quick to trust people.   This reluctance sometimes made for friction between the attorney and the Rosenberg Committee.   Nevertheless, Bloch implicitly trusted *Guardian* reporter Leon Summit.   In February, when Bloch was frantically seeking new avenues of legal appeal, Summit discovered something that struck him as unusual in the trial transcript.   He says he was amazed to find seventy-nine pages of transcript devoted to a small table the Rosenbergs had in their apartment.[38] He knew the Greenglasses had said the table was a gift from the Russians to Julius Rosenberg.   He also knew it was supposed to contain a hollowed-out microfilming compartment.   "The thing that puzzled me was why didn't he [Bloch] introduce the Rosenbergs' table to support Julius Rosenberg's testimony? So I went to Manny Bloch to ask him."

Bloch told Summit that the prosecution had never physically produced the table at the trial.   Instead, several photos of "similar" Macy's tables were shown to the jury.   Further, Julius Rosenberg testified that none of the photos looked like his small drop-leaf table.

What happened to the real table? Bloch told Summit that he had told Julius Rosenberg's sister, Ethel Rosenberg Goldberg, to sell the condemned couple's furniture to a pushcart dealer in fall 1950.   Summit recalled that he checked out Bloch's story with Ethel Goldberg and learned that Bloch was right.   To his surprise and delight, Summit says he found that the small "console table" had never been sold.   Ethel Goldberg told him she had briefly stored the table, then had given it to her mother, Sophie Rosenberg.   Why neither one of them know they possessed material evidence? Summit says since neither had attended the trial or followed it in the press (Sophie Rosenberg was illiterate), the table meant nothing to them.[39]   Now it meant a great deal to the Rosenbergs.   Summit recalls that he hastened with a photographer to Sophie Rosenberg's Washington Heights apartment.   Once there, the two men found a small, unpretentious table in the living room. "She took off a telephone and a dresser scarf from the table.   We turned it over and photographed the markings on the underside of the table.   They looked like chalk markings."

Summit left the table at Sophie Rosenberg's apartment and rushed back to the *Guardian* offices.   When photos of the table were developed and printed, he took the subway to Macy's department store.   That afternoon a Macy's official verified that the code markings on the underside of the table corresponded to $20.37, including sales tax.[40]   Summit says the Macy's employee told him the table was probably sold around 1944.   The official, Joseph Fontana, eventually gave the defense an affidavit.   Once Julius Rosenberg found out about the table's reappearance, he asked Summit to check for drill holes on one of the legs.   Summit says he found several drill holes there, just as Julius Rosenberg had testified. (Author's note: Rosenberg said he had made an abortive attempt to repair the table). Summit says the Rosenbergs' former part-time maid, Evelyn Cox, identified the table for him, but then refused to provide an affidavit.[41] Cox had testified that Ethel Rosenberg told her the table was a gift from "a friend" of her husband's.

The *National Guardian* and the Rosenberg Committee were ecstatic over Summit's find. For a year and a half, critics had decried the *Guardian* as nothing more than a promotional outlet for communism. Here was something physical that strongly suggested Julius Rosenberg had told the truth. Manny Bloch and Gloria Agrin hurriedly prepared a new appeal.

The *National Guardian* broke the "console-table" story April 13, 1953. It matter of factly said it had discovered a crucial piece of trial evidence. "The facts are now available concerning the 'key evidence' by which the government attempted to link the Rosenbergs to 'atom spying' and provide new proof that witnesses David and Ruth Greenglass, whose testimony convicted their relatives, committed perjury on the witness stand."[42] *Guardian* editor John McManus and Leon Summit claimed they had "brought to light a sensational piece of evidence." That was a console table the prosecution was not able to locate for the trial.[43] According to David Greenglass's trial testimony, the table was a gift from the Russians to Julius Rosenberg and it was equipped with a microfilming compartment that Julius Rosenberg used for photographing classified documents. (Ruth Greenglass had testified that the table's underside contained a "hollowed out" section that was equipped with a light). The article said although the table had been "inventoried" by the FBI after the Rosenbergs' arrests, it never appeared at the trial. Julius Rosenberg had testified that he had bought the table at Macy's in 1944 or 1945. The *Guardian* said the table Leon Summit found did not have a hollowed-out microfilming compartment. Photos of the top and underside of the table, replete with retail code markings, appeared on pages 4 and 5 of the *Guardian*. McManus and Summit said the console table's recovery supported Julius Rosenberg's testimony and refuted a "major part of the case" that trial prosecutor Irving Saypol had built against the Rosenbergs. "The damning conclusion . . . is that the allegations about the table were not included in the original statements of the Greenglasses; . . . these were added long afterward . . . in uglier words, to make a frame stick."[44] Describing this addition as "sordidness plus," McManus predicted the discovery of the console table would form the basis of a new appeal. The *Guardian* used its aggressive agenda setting in an attempt to get the news into mainstream newspapers. "The *National Guardian* urges you to take this story and its accompanying pictures and documentation to the publisher and editor of your local paper. Ask them if they do not think this information warrants investigation by their staffs. The *Guardian* will cooperate to the fullest."[45] This attempt to use left-wing readers as a gate-crashing wedge was probably somewhat disingenuous.

In their 1978 memoir, James Aronson and Cedric Belfrage implied that they had already sent photos of the console, an affidavit from a Macy's official, and copies of the article to all New York mainstream newspapers and the wire services.

Nonetheless, the *Guardian* not only exceeded the traditional dissident goal of reporting news unavailable in the mainstream news media, it surpassed its previous attempts to gain access to the mainstream news agenda. To measure the receptiveness of the mainstream press to the *Guardian's* story, ten mainstream U.S. newspapers, two foreign newspapers, and three U.S. newsmagazines were examined for "week-after" coverage of the console table story. For the dates April 14 through 20, 1953 (the *Guardian* ran the story April 13), the *Chicago Tribune, Christian Science Monitor, Detroit News, New York Times, Louisville Courier-Journal, St. Louis Post-Dispatch, Times* (London) and *Winnipeg Free Press* did not report the story. The *Atlanta Constitution, New York Herald Tribune,* and *Washington Post* did report a Rosenberg appeal to the U.S. Supreme Court, but none reported the new development, either. Also, none of the three U.S. newsmagazines noted the *Guardian's* latest exposé.

In its April 20, 1953, issue the *National Guardian* claimed that the government had collaborated on a "blackout" conspiracy. "As this issue of the *Guardian* goes to press no other newspaper in the United States is known to have published a single reference to the discovery of the table, although copies of the *Guardian* were sent to all press services."[46]

Julius Rosenberg bitterly reproved the U.S. press for its lack of interest. "Is there any better proof of the complete bias of the press against us then by noting their complete silence on the exposé of the so-called Russian "gift" console table? Obviously, the kept press is corrupt and will not print the truth in this case."[47] Were the *Guardian* and Julius Rosenberg right? Did the U.S. news media shut the door on the console table story? American newspapers certainly had ignored this latest development. But why? The fact that the exposè originated in a radical newspaper was more than enough to keep it off the mainstream press agenda. Then, too, by now every editor in New York City knew the *National Guardian* was closely linked with the Rosenberg Committee. The Rosenberg Committee was reputed by several respected conservative newspaper columnists to have extensive communist backing. In most gatekeeping minds that likely suggested collaboration. The console table story was new, but to skeptical editors and reporters it was nothing more than a brazenly contrived propaganda stunt. Moreover, the console table was not yet part of the legal pleadings associated with the case. William Wolf's point about the issues being made legitimate for news media use by the courts is crucial. Logic and news gatekeeping would assure that when the courts ruled on the "new evidence," the news media would have to report on the *National Guardian's* latest story. Or would they?

In the 1920s, Walter Lippmann observed: "The facts we see depend on where we are placed, and the habits of our eyes."[48] In the United States, the Rosenberg story's conclusion would be rigidly reported from the point of view of placement, focus, and habit. It also would stand the notion of agenda setting on its head. Instead of the press influencing what readers thought about, readers (and various government agencies) influenced what reporters thought about the case's links to communism and to justice.

12

Confess or Die: A Test of Nerves

These two new elements are too important to be passed over in silence. It is up to American justice to evaluate them, check their accuracy, and decide in what measure they call for a new trial.[1]

Le Monde, April 20, 1953

My son said the papers print lies and he can't get justice! What chance have I got of getting mercy?[2]

Sophie Rosenberg to reporters, shortly before her son's death in the electric chair.

Sometime in February 1953 some documents disappeared from O. John Rogge's Lower East Side office. (Rogge was David Greenglass's lawyer). Rogge would not know that the documents, several pages of private interoffice memoranda, were missing until late April.

The identity of who took these documents is still unknown. Nonetheless, in early April 1953, Rosenberg committee spokesperson Joseph Brainin left for France by ship. Not long after he arrived, *Combat*, a Paris-based newspaper with connections to the French Communist Party, published a sensational story about the Rosenberg case.[3] On April 18, 1953, *Combat* printed photocopies of the Rogge memoranda and an accompanying article. The information reported in the documents was, by turns, captivating, bizarre, and comic. One memorandum, dictated after David Greenglass's arrest, quoted Ruth Printz Greenglass as saying her husband had a "tendency to hysteria"; that he sometimes suffered from deliriousness; and that once, when he had "the grippe," he ran naked through the hallway of a boarding house ranting about "elephants" and "lead pants."[4] *Combat* also quoted Ruth Greenglass as stating that her husband once had spoken of suicide. The newspaper further claimed that a handwritten statement by David Greenglass indicated that incidents he "couldn't remember" were invented by the FBI. Two days after *Combat* broke the story, *Le Humanité*, a politically left but noncommunist newspaper, featured a similar account. Then mainstream *Le Monde* discussed this new turn of events in "Le Cas Rosenberg." Three ideologically disparate French newspapers agreed that the memoranda indicated that the Greenglasses had given false testimony.[5] All three called for a thorough investigation. How the memoranda got to France has never been explained.[6] It does seem fairly evident, though, that the Rosenberg committee tried to gain access to the U.S. mainstream press by first making the agenda of the more politically diverse French press. The Rogge memoranda story made a salutary impression in France, where almost all newspapers opposed the death sentences. In the United States, events took a sharply divergent turn. Though the documents were pilfered from Rogge's office in New York City, no attempt was made to publish them in the United States. A report did not appear in the U.S. news media until May 4, 1953. That day the *New York Times* mentioned the "filched" papers, but only to note the FBI's interest in their transatlantic "wanderings."

The Rosenberg Committee disclosed the contents of the memoranda to the U.S. press at a clemency rally at New York City's Randall Island stadium.[7] The *National Guardian* estimated 10,000 attended the event, despite a steady drizzle and fog. The rally was staged to get as much publicity as possible out of the console table and the Rogge memoranda. For example, there was a theatrical presentation of the table to the crowd by *Guardian* editor Jack McManus.[8] Speaking in broken English, Sophie Rosenberg assured the crowd that until recently the table had been in her apartment. Joseph Brainin said he had documents to prove the "Greenglasses lied to the Government, to the Court, to the public, and to his family."[9] The *Guardian* reported that Brainin "declined to reveal the source" of his information. Whatever its exact origins, the Rogge memoranda story raised hopes among the Rosenberg supporters to new heights. But the U.S. news media were not interested in the story. Of the newspapers in the national sample (listed in this and earlier chapters) for May 4 through 10, 1953, only one, the *New York Times*, noted the existence of the interoffice memoranda.[10] The *Guardian* said it had notified the U.S. mainstream news media about its latest exposé, as well as the one on the console table. The May 11 *Guardian* denounced the silence of the New York City press on the console table.[11] Now that silence was followed by a near absence of reporting on the Rogge papers. But being ignored by the "big press" was just the beginning of trouble for the embattled socialist newspaper.

Amidst a blaze of television klieg lights and flashbulbs, *National Guardian* editor Cedric Belfrage appeared before the House Un-American

Activities Committee two days after the Randall Island rally.[12]   By coincidence, Belfrage testified the same day that Broadway choreographer Jerome Robbins did. Naturally, Robbins got the lion's share of headlines and coverage. While the latter spoke openly of his membership in the U.S. Communist Party, Belfrage declined to answer questions relating to his military activities in postwar Germany. He refused to reply to about twenty-five questions. Because he had worked as a press-control officer for Allied forces, he was suspected of helping install a procommunist newspaper editor at the *Frankfurter Rundschau.*[13]

During the hearings, acting HUAC chairperson Bernard W. Kearney threatened Belfrage with deportation. (Technically Belfrage had never applied for U.S. citizenship). For good measure, HUAC member Harold Velde described the *Guardian* as a "propaganda arm of the Soviet Union."[14] Coincidentally, the day after Belfrage's HUAC appearance, Murray Mardner of the *Washington Post* said Senator McCarthy had decided to turn his investigative spotlight on the U.S. news media.[15]   Mardner said McCarthy would try to uncover communists and fellow travelers in newspapers, magazines, and the broadcast industry. McCarthy and his Government Operations Subcommittee were assisted by one-time communists and some-time newspaper columnists Harvey Matusow and Louis F. Budenz.[16] The senator pulled no punches in his public instructions to his investigators. "I realize that this will be a monumental task . . . I will not set any date by which you are to complete it."

Matusow and Budenz were interesting choices for this reputedly daunting project. Matusow had been an FBI informant, and had once belonged to the American Newspaper Guild. Budenz formerly had served as editor of the New York *Daily Worker.* At any rate, Senator McCarthy denied he was "investigating the press." To some, his insistence that he was not focusing on the press for personal reasons rang a bit hollow. Only recently, for instance, the *New York Post* had published a series that was highly critical of McCarthy. Also, several other American newspapers had aggressively questioned the senator's methods and motives of investigation.[17]

McCarthy then had a celebrated skirmish with *New York Post* editor James A. Wechsler in late April 1953.[18] Few in the news media believed McCarthy's blunderbuss charges. Nonetheless, his words and actions were widely perceived as a signal to his antagonists in the news media that they had better be careful.[19] Historian David Caute explains that some mainstream journalists enjoyed no special immunity from the excesses of the McCarthy period. Though blacklisting in the U.S. news media was restrained, a number of respected newspapers conducted tacit inquiries into the political pasts of some of their reporters. At some major dailies, there were forced resignations and a handful of dismissals.[20]   It was a difficult time for the press, and especially for the broadcast industry. It would not get any easier, but now it was the *National Guardian*'s turn to face Senator McCarthy.

This time James Aronson joined Cedric Belfrage. On May 14, 1953, they appeared together in Washington, D.C., before Senator McCarthy's Subcommittee.[21] An "executive session," it was closed to the public and press. Aronson and Belfrage both declined to answer questions about whether they were communists. They also refused to respond to questions about their jobs as press-control officers in helping license newspapers in West Germany after World War II.[22]   (Some of the licenses evidently were awarded to communists). Senator McCarthy made plain he thought Belfrage should be deported to Great Britain, the latter's country of birth.

After the session, James Aronson told the *New York Times*'s C. P. Trussell that he and his colleague kept silent to defend their newspaper's readers. "We felt that if we had put into the record our identification with the *National Guardian* that would lead to demands for the lists of our subscribers and contributors and possibly result in the detraction of the organ's effectiveness."[23] Aronson also denied that the *Guardian* represented any political front.[24] By now both men were convinced that Belfrage's experience with HUAC, and their command performances before McCarthy's sub-committee, had been the result of the *Guardian*'s defense of the Rosenbergs and Morton Sobell.[25]   Both realized that already jittery newspaper editors would now be doubly reluctant to report on their exposés. That was unhappy news for the Rosenberg Committee. But not as unhappy as the news Cedric Belfrage got from the Immigration and Naturalization Service. On May 15, he was arrested in the *Guardian*'s Manhattan offices by U.S. Immigration officers. (Both editors had just returned from Washington.) The *Guardian*'s story of the arrest said the deportation order for Belfrage prohibited bail for the British-born editor. The article also said the order was personally signed by U.S. Attorney General Herbert Brownell, Jr.[26] The paper said that soon after Belfrage was jailed, cash contributions and support poured into its Manhattan offices. A "Belfrage Fight Back Fund" was hastily organized, though the *Guardian* said none of the expressions of solidarity came from the mainstream news media. "While the big press looked the other way, editors of many of the little press rallied to Belfrage's support."[27] The *Guardian*'s pique at being neglected likely involved more hyperbole than outrage. In truth, the mainstream news media in the United States rarely has come to the aid of its left-wing brethren. Defending radicals has been risky in the best of times and treacherous in politically troubled periods. To say the least, 1953 was a troubled time.

Rosenberg case authors Radosh and Milton describe the propaganda effect of the Rogge memoranda as "pure gold."[28] That certainly was true in

Europe, where the case enjoyed wide if uneven coverage. In the United States, though, the Rogge papers were the publicity equivalent of pure dross. The Rosenberg Committee simply was unable to reap any substantive press coverage from the memoranda. In late May, the *Guardian* hinted that the U.S. Supreme Court would rule against the Rosenberg's certiorari appeal.[29]

The *Guardian* sent out an urgent appeal for volunteers to work "day and night" to help publicize the existence of the "new evidence."[30] The *Guardian's* timing was prescient if anything. The day the newspaper asked for reinforcements for the clemency movement, the U.S. Supreme Court revealed it had turned down the Rosenbergs' bid for review.[31] It was the third time in seven months the Court had declined to review their convictions.

Before the Court's decision was made public, the Justice Department leaked a report to the press that said the Rosenbergs would not be executed if they provided a full disclosure of espionage activities."[32] It was a tacit admission by the government that the "lever" strategy had failed and that the Rosenbergs had been offered a "deal," at least through the news media. The war of nerves had been turned up a notch, and, as in Europe, the press was coopted into playing publicity agent.

Manny Bloch was enraged by the Justice Department's public maneuver. He bitterly dismissed the agenda-setting tactic as an "unethical and disgraceful thing to do." Bloch told reporters neither he nor his clients had been offered "any such proposition" by the Justice Department.[33] However, only two months earlier, Bloch had complained of a "barbarous offer," though, presumably, that was a trial balloon floated in the news media by the Justice Department. Bloch also said he would request another executive stay and a rehearing. "We have a lot of water to swim through before we're through in the courts."[34] He also hinted that a future appeal might be based on "new evidence," though he did not elaborate.

Judge Irving Kaufman had rescheduled the execution dates for the week of June 15, 1953. The Rosenberg Committee and the *National Guardian* feverishly sought more evidence. While demonstrators and vigils were planned, a feisty Los Angeles pamphleteer insisted to anyone who would listen that the *Guardian*, the Rosenberg Committee, and Manny Bloch were all wrong.[35] Irwin Edelman had been a member of the Los Angeles Committee until he was expelled for writing a pamphlet critical of Manny Bloch's decision to impound David Greenglass's "scientific" testimony at the trial. Edelman was upset enough to indulge the specialty of American radicals: writing fiery, intemperate tracts. He also had composed an advertisement about his experiences with the Los Angeles committee and tried having it published in the *National Guardian*. Fearing divisive internal debate, the New York based newspaper, however, promptly turned him down.[36]

Still, Edelman was undeterred by the *Guardian's* censorship. He circulated his pamphlet throughout the country at his expense. One came to the attention of Fyke Farmer, a Nashville lawyer. An advocate of international peace and world government, Farmer was intrigued by Edelman's argument. The lawyer did some research and came to the conclusion that the Justice Department had tried the Rosenbergs under the wrong statute.[37] Meanwhile the *National Guardian* angrily noted French and British newspaper coverage of its recent exposés on the Rogge memoranda and the console table.[38] It said that unlike in the United States, the news media in Europe were quite interested in "new evidence." In France, there was a strong feeling in the press that executing the Rosenbergs would be brutal, inexcusable behavior. U.S. embassy press attaché Ben Bradlee again had to scramble to control political damage. This time he did not have the option of returning to the United States. Like Russell Baker, Bradlee thought that the death sentences were heavy-handed and foolish. He also realized that *Le Monde's* Henri Pierre was right about at least one thing. By spring 1953, Bradlee says, he knew that executing the Rosenbergs would surely worsen an already bad diplomatic crisis.[39]

The June 8, 1953, *National Guardian* featured more information on the continuing episode of the Justice Department's confess-or-die deal. It said the couple had been "openly confronted with the final grisly stratagem of their government against them."[40] The *Guardian* said Federal Prisons' Director James Bennett had spoken separately with both Rosenbergs on behalf of Attorney General Brownell.[41] Because the meetings were private, no independent corroboration of the Rosenbergs' claims exists. Nevertheless, the couple was outraged enough to have Manny Bloch hold a press conference in order to reveal Bennett's reputed offer. The Rosenbergs also prepared a statement for the June 8, 1953, *National Guardian*.[42]

In the same issue, the *Guardian* also featured a letter by another Rosenberg, Michael. This one was written to President Eisenhower. Like in the earlier letter, it was obviously composed by an adult. The latest letter, however, had a keener political edge. In it, Michael referred to the recent release of Associated Press Correspondent William Oatis in Czechoslovakia.[43] (Oatis had been convicted there of espionage on trumped-up charges. He served two years of a ten-year sentence and was pardoned in spring 1953 by the president of Czechoslovakia). "My mommy and daddy are in prison in New York. My brother is six years old and his name is Robby. He misses them very much and I miss them, too. I got the idea to write to you from Mr. Oatis on television. Please let my mommy and daddy go and not let anything happen to them. If they come home Robby and I will be very happy, and will thank you very much."[44]

Whether the Rosenberg Committee wanted publicity value out of the letter is uncertain. In fact, the letter would be mentioned in some U.S. news accounts more than a week later. But by then Michael Rosenberg had written his third and final letter on behalf of his parents.

On June 4, the Rosenberg Committee claimed it had an affidavit indicating further proof of David Greenglass's perjury. The affidavit was signed by Greenglass's older brother, Bernard, who said that David admitted stealing a uranium sample from Los Alamos during World War II.[45] The *Guardian* said the affidavit "reveals deliberate perjury during the trial by David Greenglass and Ruth Greenglass with the knowledge of the prosecution."[46] The newspaper stressed that the affidavit "corroborates the testimony of Julius Rosenberg that his only involvement with David during his assignment at Los Alamos was to warn him through his wife against stealing government property."[47]

The console table, the Rogge papers, and the Bernard Greenglass affidavit suggested one of three things: (1) the Rosenberg Committee and the *National Guardian* had contrived "new evidence;" (2) everything happened as reported in the *Guardian* and the Rosenbergs were innocent; or (3) some of the Greenglasses' testimony was perjured, while some of the Rosenbergs' testimony was true.

Whatever the truth, the U.S. news media did not report on the *Guardian*'s new evidence. Part of the reason for this failure can be explained by the fact that Manny Bloch did not file this appeal until June 6, 1953. Obviously, the press was not going to report on it until the Rosenberg defense team sought judicial redress. Bloch's decisions later led a handful of his critics to conclude that he intentionally let the Rosenbergs go to their deaths. That surely was not true, but nonetheless, among some, suspicions mounted.[48]

Judge Kaufman refused to grant the Rosenbergs a new trial. The new evidence plea had not impressed him. An Associated Press report said the judge dismissed the motion as "too flimsy." Then, too, the prosecution had affidavits from Macy's officials that cast doubt on whether the table Leon Summit located was the same one Julius Rosenberg had purchased from Macy's.

After the Rosenbergs' deaths, the *Guardian* noted that Harold C. Urey had attended the June 8 hearing before Judge Kaufman and had given a stinging corridor lecture to a *New York Times* reporter who sought a quote from him.

Now that I've seen what goes in there [Judge Kaufman's courtroom], I see not Irving Kaufman, but McCarthy. I'm angry and alarmed at the terrible fear and hysteria that's sweeping all over America. What appalls me the most is the role the press is playing. The judge's bias is so obvious. I keep looking over at you newspapermen and there's not a flicker of indignation or concern. When are you going to stop acting like a bunch of scared sheep?[49]

The *Guardian* said Urey's quote did not appear in the next day's *Times*. Nevertheless, it prompts the question: How extensively did U.S. newspapers report on the new-evidence appeal? A week-after check of ten American and two foreign newspapers from June 9 through 15 reveals that the entire sample ran reports on the present legal status of the case. All newspapers in the sample reported the appeal, for a new trial had been denied by Judge Kaufman. However, only the agenda-setting *New York Times* and *Atlanta Constitution*[50] (using a *Times* news service article) reported the console table as a major basis of appeal-without explaining its significance. But even the *Times's* and *Constitution's* cryptic references likely meant nothing to their readers. Few wire service reports of the 1951 trial mentioned the so-called console-table testimony. Also, none of the U.S. or foreign newspapers or the three U.S newsmagazines discussed the Bernard Greenglass affidavit. Meanwhile, Cedric Belfrage was released on bail from Ellis Island detention.[51]

After more than two years of legal appeals, the last week of the Rosenbergs' lives happened in a surreal, fast-forward cinema-like montage.[52] There were a handful of days left now. Moreover, Julius Rosenberg thought it peculiar "that ever since the date was set, everybody [press and radio alike] has been harping on the same old theme of June 18th, as though nothing could possibly happen to upset the 'proper' functioning of the well-oiled machinery. Doesn't it help to pressure the Supreme Court into making a hasty decision because there's a 'deadline' to meet."[53]

On June 14, Michael Rosenberg, ten, his brother, Robert, six, and their grandmother, Sophie, hand-delivered a letter to the guard box at the northwest gate of the White House. This letter simply stated that Michael Rosenberg had sent an earlier letter to the president. The little boy told Eisenhower (who was out of town) that the earlier communication was important because "it is a letter about not letting anything happen to my mommy and daddy." The *New York Herald Tribune* said that when reporters asked Michael Rosenberg about the letter, he replied, "I wouldn't care to comment."[54] The pro-Rosenberg demonstration was very large for its time. Capital police reported it was the largest the city had seen in fifteen years.[55] Special trains brought streams of demonstrators for clemency from the New York City area. Pickets and marchers from around the country further swelled their ranks. The demonstration was clearly geared for news-media coverage. Photographers took many posed shots of the boys and their tiny grandmother. The boys were dressed in sport coats, dress shirts, and Brooklyn Dodger baseball caps. Television and newsreel cameras were also on hand for the event. The *Herald Tribune* said Sophie Rosenberg delivered an "impassioned and largely incoherent plea" beseeching the president to spare her son and daughter-in-law.[56]

The June 15, 1953, *National Guardian* said clemency trains from New York would take volunteers to Washington for an "eleventh-hour" fight. It quoted an excerpt from a *Laredo Times* editorial on Attorney General Brownell's bid to convince the Rosenbergs to confess. "This is a chapter in our history on the level of communist or fascist thinking. In our minds, under this type of thinking, it was impossible for the Rosenbergs to get a fair trial."[57] The *Times* was the only mainstream newspaper in the United States to hold this editorial position.

Manny Bloch took Michael and Robert Rosenberg to Sing-Sing the next day. The *New York World-Telegram and Sun* described it as a visit "for possibly the last time." In fact, it was the final visit. The approaching executions ensured full, dramatic front-page coverage. A United Press telephoto of the Rosenberg boys entering the prison with a bouquet of flowers made front pages of newspapers worldwide. The *Daily Worker*, however, said prison authorities would not allow flowers inside the prison. (It also said the boys presented report cards to their parents).[58] After a two-hour visit, Manny Bloch emerged from Sing-Sing with Michael and Robert Rosenberg. A swelling pool of reporters, photographers, and newsreel cameras recorded their departure. For two years, the Rosenberg children had been nearly invisible to the public. Now their every move became woven into the agenda-setting ritual of the last-minute death watch.

Manny Bloch displayed to the assembled crowd a ten-page clemency appeal from the Rosenbergs to President Eisenhower. Bloch readily shared its contents with reporters, who quoted its most memorable sentence: "We are asking you not to orphan our boys . . . hear the great and the humble for the sake of America."[59] The press corps wanted to know what had happened during the visit. Bloch told them that the boys had cried at the end of it. He assured them, however, that their parents "did not weep until after the children had left."[60]

It was an agonizing moment. But on another level, it was almost unreal. For the first time since their arrests, the Rosenbergs were shown by the news media as a complete family. Before then they had been the disembodied parts of a story too politically sensitive for the news media to present fully. Now with the end near, the characters were hastily assembled center-stage for the last tormented scenes of one of the most excruciating international news-media productions of modern times.

Manny Bloch hastened by car from Sing-Sing to La Guardia Airport. Then he flew to Washington. Even before he arrived in the capital, he likely knew the U.S. Supreme Court had denied another stay of execution.[61] Nonetheless, he met privately with Justice William O. Douglas and left a writ of habeas corpus with him. The press corps milled about outside, wondering whether Douglas would grant a stay. After Bloch emerged from the meeting, he told reporters: "He did not deny it. He did not grant it."[62]

In New York City, Judge Kaufman rejected an appeal by Fyke Farmer to obtain a stay of execution. The *New York Times* reported that Kaufman dismissed Farmer as an "intruder and interloper," acting without the Rosenbergs' consent.[63] What the *Times* or any other newspaper did not know (or report if they knew), was that Manny Bloch and his advisers were opposed to Fyke Farmer's writ. Nonetheless, the sudden appearance of a second Rosenberg legal contingent seemed purely academic. Monday June 15 was the final day the Court was in session for the 1953 term. Then it would recess until October.[64]

According to the *Times* of June 17,

> Reporters and cameramen kept a weary vigil throughout the day and Court officials were on duty overtime. Groups of tourists brightened up when they were told that behind the tall brass gates that close off the area containing the justice's chambers, Justice Douglas was wrestling alone with the problem of whether to give the spies a temporary reprieve.[65]

In late 1952 and early 1953, newspaper columnists analyzed the Rosenberg case almost exclusively within the framework of communist propaganda. Now in June it was something different, really quite new. Not surprisingly, the news media had little or nothing in their libraries and files to help them. The international clemency movement that had been ignored, then denounced by the news media in the United States, was about to explode. Something extraordinary was going to happen behind the drawn curtain of the U.S. Supreme Court. The climax of the Rosenberg case would be unlike any other political case in American history. Newspaper reporters who waited suspected something unusual was happening but were powerless to do anything but "keep a wearisome vigil."[66]

No one in the news media had expected that the case would take such a corkscrew turn. They were largely unprepared to report what was about to happen.

Justice Douglas first heard law professor Malcolm Sharp, volunteer civil rights' attorney John Finerty, and Gloria Agrin, then held a separate conference with Farmer and Los Angeles attorney, and yet another Rosenberg volunteer, Daniel Marshall. After the meetings, Douglas waited in his office well into the evening. His comings and goings were observed by reporters as if they had been those of an elusive movie star attending a Hollywood premier. After dining out, Douglas returned that evening for more research. At 10:30 P. M. the Supreme Court clerk told the news media clique that the justice had gone home without reaching a decision.[67] Reporters, photographers, newsreel cameras, and television crews went home. Justice Douglas had committed an unpardonable journalistic gaffe. He had failed to deliver his decision before the morning-edition deadline.

Justice Douglas's actions had caught the press unawares. Part of the reason was that Douglas had voted twice before to deny certiorari to the Rosenbergs.[68] Nevertheless, he stayed the Rosenberg executions on the morning of June 17. As the Court's clerk announced the stay, photographers took a picture of Manny Bloch and Fyke Farmer shaking hands. It was a staged scene. The reconciliation of Farmer and Bloch was temporary, empty, and forced. News of Douglas's decision, however, had hit the nation in the pit of the stomach. Georgia Congressional Representative W. M. Wheeler introduced a resolution that called for Douglas's impeachment.[69] The press hustled to get as much detail on the story as possible.

In any event, editorial comment on Douglas's stay was divided. While the *New York Times* did not take an editorial stand on his action, an FBI memorandum dated June 16, 1953, said a *Times* employee had recently called the FBI's New York office regarding news-media publicity the Rosenberg case had received. The memorandum reported that the *Times* reporter (or editor) had "informally discussed" with a caller "a campaign being waged by the Rosenbergs and the Communist Party for clemency or a stay of execution." The memorandum said the caller was worried that the clemency movement "had been making headway from a propaganda standpoint, and he wondered whether it was not possible for the government to hit back through the medium of newspapers."[70] Whoever had spoken with the FBI had evidently volunteered his services. He said he realized the Government would not be able to "carry the ball." The *Times* employee then offered the assistance of his newspaper.[71] The agent said that the *Times* would have to combat the clemency campaign [sic] "on their own."[72] He was concerned enough, however, to consult headquarters about "any slant we would want to give the *New York Times* for this purpose."[73] High ranking FBI official A. H. Belmont agreed with New York's Assistant Special Agent in Command Richard Whelan that "the Government should not be rushing into making any disclosures or comments counteracting this propaganda."[74] The *Times'* offer was politely declined.

13

The Supreme Court Reconvenes: Extra!

Julius and Ethel Rosenberg, their outward calm masking what must be an incredible agony of suspense, may not know until virtually the last minute whether they will die tonight-or tomorrow-or perhaps not for a long time. They were together twice yesterday-for a total of three hours, talking in low voices through a double mesh screen, with guards at elbows. It was their fourteenth wedding anniversary, the third time since they were sentenced to die-but they were allowed only to touch fingertips through the wire.[1]

New York Post, June 19, 1953

Justice William O. Douglas was checking into a motel in Uniontown, Pennsylvania, when he overheard a radio report that said the U.S. Supreme Court would meet in special session.[2] He immediately drove to Pittsburgh and took a plane back to Washington, D.C.

The news media would not know it, but the unprecedented session was the result of a meeting between Chief Justice Fred Vinson, Associate Justice Robert Jackson, and U.S. Attorney General Herbert Brownell. Amazingly, Vinson had decided before Douglas issued his stay to reconvene the Court if necessary.[3] All the Supreme Court justices but Hugo Black had consented to the hearing. While newspaper reports noted that Brownell had requested the session, no one in the press knew about the prearranged agreement. The closest the news media came to detecting the truth was a wire service report that said, soon after Douglas's stay was announced, that Brownell had received an urgent telephone call from President Eisenhower and that J. Edgar Hoover then hurried to Brownell's office.[4] Flourishing its trademark rhetoric, the *Daily Worker* alleged Brownell wanted the session to "get the charred bodies of the young people immediately."[5]

In Washington, a crowd of 2,000 clemency advocates shuttled between the Supreme Court building and the White House.[6] The Rosenberg defense teams' arguments before the U.S. Supreme Court was a difficult story for reporters to frame. First, there were now two teams. Second, the so-called special session was almost unprecedented-none had been held in modern times. Third, even veteran court reporters had difficulty keeping straight the case's pell-mell convergence of issues, personalities, and conflicts. Of course, the real framework was the life-or-death decision of the Court, one that could easily be compressed into familiar death-row coverage. Nonetheless, there was just enough suspense to keep everyone in the news media on guard.

The special session began at slightly past noon on June 18, 1953. The court's chamber-area rapidly filled with tourists, spectators, and Rosenberg sympathizers. Outside, the curious stood in long lines, hoping for a seat.[7] His voice barely audible to spectators and press, Acting Solicitor General Robert L. Stern argued on behalf of the Justice Department. He reasoned that the 1946 Atomic Energy Act could not be retroactively applied to overt acts committed in 1944 and 1945. Toward the end of his argument, Justice Jackson interrupted to say that if the Court found the Atomic Energy Act "covers this case, the whole case is out."[8] Jackson's sentence cut through the courtroom like a giant charge of static electricity.

Civil rights lawyer John Finerty spoke first for the Rosenbergs. In a testy mood, he claimed that the special session was an affront to Justice Douglas. The elderly, but still vigorous Finerty, then made several uncomplimentary remarks about Judge Kaufman and Irving Saypol. When Finerty said of the latter, "there never was a more crooked District Attorney in New York," Justice Tom Clark asked him to stick to the merits of the case.[9] Though no one in the press section noticed, Finerty likely missed a golden opportunity to explain why he thought Saypol was a crook. If so, Finerty had missed a chance to argue that the Rosenbergs had not received a fair trial because of state sponsored news-media publicity.

Daniel Marshall, like Finerty, said he was not yet prepared to argue the case. At that, Fyke Farmer shot out of his seat in the spectator's section and said, "I'm not contending that I'm not ready. I'm anxious to get up before the bar and argue."[10] Farmer sat down as a tremor of laughter rippled through the 400 and more spectators. Barely had Marshall resumed his argument when Justice Jackson asked him: "How did you get into the act?" Marshall explained that he had represented Irwin Edelman as a "friend of the court." Jackson asked Marshall if he had represented Edelman before the Court in a "vagrancy case" that had appeared before the Court the previous January. Newspaper accounts say the chamber then burst into embarrassed laughter. Marshall lost his temper and, incredibly, shook his finger at Jackson. "It was a free-speech case. I think this is shocking in a capital case where human lives are at stake." With that Chief Justice Vinson interrupted Marshall's tirade: "Don't let your temperature rise."[11]   An Associated Press report said Marshall slammed his hand against the speaker's lectern and, contradicting himself, insisted the session proceed in "an orderly manner."[12] But Marshall's time had ended before he could mount an effective presentation. Manny Bloch argued next; he immediately made the same complaint as Finerty and Marshall. Bloch said he had not had adequate time to prepare for the special session. "This Court cannot determine this issue in a matter of a few minutes or a few hours . . . I just don't know how to answer your questions."[13]   Bloch's courtroom behavior later became the subject of intense speculation. Fyke Farmer privately concluded that Bloch's heart was not in arguing the "interlopers" point of law.

Farmer wisely used his alloted time. Unlike his predecessors, he stuck closely to his script. He claimed the 1946 law could be imposed in espionage convictions only at the recommendation of a judge. He argued the crime in question had to be committed with intent to harm the United States national defense. (In fact, that charge was not in the wording of the Rosenberg-Sobell indictment).[14]   Farmer finished his presentation without noting the argument of "next friend" Irwin Edelman. Ironically, the issue of the impounded evidence was not brought to the Court's attention.[15] Nonetheless, it was Bloch, after all, who had made the impoundment request at the trial. By 1953, that incident was all but forgotten. Had Farmer raised the impoundment issue, newspaper reporters would have found in their clip files that Manny Bloch had requested that the news media and public be excluded from David Greenglass's "scientific testimony" in 1951. That request, no doubt, would have been deeply embarrassing to Bloch. But Farmer refrained from further alienating an already humiliated Bloch and said nothing.

The news media, Rosenberg demonstrators, millions of Americans, and the world had to wait nearly a day for the Court's decision. The next morning Chief Justice Vinson announced to a tense spectators' section that the Court had vacated the stay on a six-to-two vote.[16]   Justices Douglas and Black dissented, while Justice Felix Frankfurter reserved judgment. Speaking in a voice dulled by ponderous acoustics, Douglas said he knew he was right about the law. "The trial judge had no power to impose the death penalty."[17] In the end, Douglas said nothing about the trial prosecutor's conduct at the Rosenberg-Sobell trial. The Court's per curiam decision simply said, "The question is not substantial."

The U.S. Supreme Court's decision came as little surprise to the Rosenberg defense. It was even less of a surprise to the news media; indeed, the Court had already voted twice before not to review. Still, the Supreme Court's action gave an already sensational melodrama added publicity thrust.

Though the end was near, both sets of Rosenberg lawyers continued
efforts to gain another stay. The *New York Daily News* said Manny Bloch and
his assistants had filed several new motions. Because the executions had been
automatically rescheduled for 11 P.M. Friday, June 19, seven or eight hours
remained for last-minute efforts. Even before the Supreme Court's final
decision, two new motions were filed in district court in New York City.
Improbably, one was even mailed in by a Kansas lawyer.[18] Yet another
motion was introduced to the district court on Thursday, June 18.[19] The *New
York Herald Tribune* said a "similar appeal" had been rejected by Appeals
Judges Jerome Frank and Thomas Swan. However, Judge Irving Kaufman
saw merit in the point and said that he had spoken with Attorney General
Brownell about the matter. The *New York Times* said Kaufman then assured
last-minute Rosenberg lawyer Milton Friedman the executions "would not be
carried out on the Jewish Sabbath."[20]

However, neither Kaufman nor Friedman realized that Brownell had
decided to solve the dilemma by advancing the executions to 8 P.M. (The
Sabbath occurs at sundown, which began at 8:30 P. M. on June 19). The new
execution time created instant havoc at Sing-Sing. U.S. Marshall William
Carroll had hurriedly to locate the executioner to notify him of the adjustment.
Also, it meant reporters had to catch earlier trains to Ossining. The Rosenberg
executions would now compete with New York City's famous Friday evening
rush-hour exodus.

In Washington, Manny Bloch and Gloria Agrin composed a final
clemency plea directed to President Eisenhower. Bloch also had a highly
emotional letter from Ethel Rosenberg to the president.[21] At 6:45 he reached
the White House gates and left with guards the final clemency plea and
Ethel's letter. The next day a since famous newspaper photo appeared of
Bloch being turned away at the guard stand. Presently, Assistant Press
Secretary Murray Snyder said President Eisenhower had read the plea and the
letter and could find "no new issues."

When told the executions would take place three hours earlier than
planned, Bloch exploded: "It is my firm conviction that the action of President
Eisenhower indicates we are living under a military dictatorship garbed in
civilian clothes. I don't know what animals I am dealing with, but I am
dealing with animals."[22] Bloch's outburst, a product of exhaustion and fury,
also reinforced the radical image the news media had often given the
Rosenberg movement.

Meanwhile, Fyke Farmer drove with several others to Justice Black's
house in Virginia to try and obtain a stay. It was an errand in vain. Black
was not even home.

All roads to Sing-Sing prison were barricaded and guarded. Blue-
shirted prison guards and brown-uniformed state troopers defended it against

an expected "communist demonstration." On Friday afternoon, a CBS Television truck and a large generator arrived at the prison.[23] Like major battles, natural disasters, and political conventions, executions exact the best and worst instincts in the news media. Scores of reporters and broadcasters scurried to the prison administration building.

At 7:30 P. M. Judge Kaufman turned down Daniel Marshall's plea.[24] In Washington, Manny Bloch ran into a final wall. From his Statler Hotel room, he tearfully called Sing-Sing and left a final message for his clients. Inside a "condemned cell," Julius and Ethel Rosenberg skipped the traditional last meal to spend their remaining time together. Husband and wife had already been prepared for electrocution. At 8 P.M. Julius first entered the white, brightly lit death chamber accompanied by two guards and a rabbi. Three wire service reporters, Bob Considine, International News Service; Relman Morin, Associated Press; and Jack Wolilston, United Press; watched him enter. He was clad in a brown t-shirt, white pants, and slippers.[25] Reporters noticed that the prisoner's eyeglasses were missing and that his moustache had been shaved. They said Julius looked "impassive" but swayed slightly as he shuffled the last steps to the electric chair. Rabbi Irving Koslowe intoned the Twenty-third Psalm: "The Lord is my Shepherd, I shall not want." Rosenberg was strapped into the chair; a mask was secured over his face. At a signal from the warden, Wilfred Denno, executioner Joseph Francel pulled a knife switch. Two thousand volts of electricity, at eight to ten amperes, jolted the prisoner's body in two separate spurts. Julius Rosenberg was pronounced dead at six minutes past eight.[26] After her husband's body was placed on a gurney and removed, Ethel was escorted into the chamber at twelve past eight. She moved slowly and wore a dark green print dress. Rabbi Koslowe read the Fifteenth and Thirty-First psalms.

Ethel's "serene" expression surprised and discomfited even the veteran reporters. Before being strapped into the electric chair, she thrust out a hand at prison matron Helen Evans. Rosenberg pulled Evans toward her and kissed her on the cheek while being strapped into the chair. The switch was again thrown, and two jolts of electricity coursed through her body. Doctors George McCracken and H. W. Kipp hurriedly performed the postexecution exam. To their great surprise both physicians detected a heartbeat. They held a "whispered conference" and then informed the Warden that Ethel Rosenberg was still alive. Denno ordered two more surges of electricity be sent through the prisoner's body. Ethel Rosenberg was pronounced dead at about seventeen past eight. She was the first American woman to be electrocuted by federal order.[27]

Neither husband nor wife had left a final statement to the news media. Nonetheless, a posthumous final letter to their sons would be published in the *National Guardian*.

In Sing-Sing's parking lot, rumors circulated among reporters of big demonstrations in Paris, London, and New York's Union Square. Shortly before the executions, a large Rosenberg rally had convened at Seventeenth Street and Broadway, near Union Square. It was billed as a prayer meeting but also had heavy overtures of political rhetoric.[28] The gathering began with the national anthem and ended after police pulled the plug on the sound system.

In Washington, about 400 Rosenberg supporters had picketed the White House before the executions. After news reached the crowd that the executions were over, a storm of "cheers, catcalls and the blaring of automobile horns" drowned out the sobbing of clemency marchers. As in New York, though, there was no violence. A press photographer snapped a photo of Rosenberg pickets lined up single file, disconsolately heaping placards into piles.[29] Counterdemonstrators in Lafayette Park taunted their adversaries with signs that said: "Hang 'em and Ship Their Bodies COD to Russia" and "Two Fried Rosenburgers Coming Up."

By far the bloodiest reaction to the executions took place in Paris. Thousands of pro-Rosenberg demonstrators surged through streets chanting anti-U.S. slogans. Rioting in the Place de la Concorde left 1 dead; 400 were arrested.[30] The French riot had been brewing many months. In London, though, the story was much different. Wire service reports said about 1,000 Rosenberg demonstrators marched through Picadilly Circus shouting, "Save the Rosenbergs" and "Down with McCarthy."[31] In Rome, a swelling crowd noisily wound through streets and alleys, but the incident lacked the violence of the Paris demonstrations. Similarly loud but mostly peaceful protests took place in about twenty countries worldwide.

At the *Baltimore Sun's* London Bureau, Russell Baker recalls that a middle-aged British copy boy told him not to fret over the executions. "He said, 'don't have a bad conscience about it - the bloody buggers deserved it.'"[32] The remark struck Baker as crudely symbolic of the British approach to the case. Unlike in France, the Rosenberg case in Great Britain had not caught fire. Comment in the British press was almost nonexistent; what little criticism there was was muted. Baker said in a June 20, 1953, dispatch that most English citizens he interviewed blamed the American judicial system for bungling the case. "Few Englishmen seem to have swallowed-yet-the communist argument that the Rosenbergs were innocent. In Britain, everyone tells you pointedly, the condemned are executed with dispatch, generally within a few weeks of sentencing."[33]

To the cynical it might appear that the U.S. news media took an active interest in the Rosenberg sons only when it became apparent their parents would be executed. In suburban Toms River, New Jersey, reporters descended en masse on Ben and Sonia Bach's house. They asked Michael Rosenberg for his response to his parents' deaths. He was happy to oblige. "You can quote me. The judges of the future will look back at this case with great shame."[34] A *New York Daily News* photographer took a picture of the boys sitting on a front porch, obligingly reading a copy of the *Daily News*.

Michael found out his parents had been executed when a baseball telecast was interrupted by a special bulletin. News reports said the oldest Rosenberg son slumped in a chair and sobbed. "That's it. That's it. That's it. Goodbye, goodbye."[35]

As in June 1952, columnist Max Lerner questioned the wisdom of the executions. He wondered aloud in his *New York Post* column whether they were "necessary or wise." Depressed, he described the walk from Sing-Sing to the train station as if he were returning from an away college football game.

> The people along the road were out on their porches or on the sidewalk, clustered around their cars, listening to the radio, talking and laughing. I heard one child tell another she wished she could throw the switch. There were geraniums in the window boxes, trellises of roses, hedges adorned with lily paper cups discarded by the press.[36]

Some editorials in U.S. newspapers the next day appeared reconstituted from those published after Judge Kaufman passed sentence in 1951. The voice of Americanism had endured, but it was a strained, hoarse refrain, a defensive imitation of its prewar strength. The *Washington Post* said the Supreme Court had acted with "a high sense of responsibility." In a signed front-page editorial, *Atlanta Constitution* publisher Ralph McGill said he felt no remorse for "the atom spies whose traitorous chores cost the lives of thousands of American soldiers and placed in jeopardy the nation itself."[37] The *Detroit News* reasoned: "A front-line soldier is meted death for having let down his fellows. A citizen experiences a similar fate for having trafficked with the enemy."[38] The *Minneapolis Tribune* fretted that the Supreme Court's hasty decision in overturning Judge Douglas's stay had created "a great unanswered riddle."[39] The *Baltimore Sun* compared the Rosenbergs' fate to that of an East German man who had recently been charged, tried, convicted, and executed for rioting in two days' time. The *Sun* insisted the Rosenbergs had been justly treated. "In addition to thus invoking all legal tricks, their supporters have carried on an ever-expanding campaign to provide material for Moscow's campaign of hate against the United States."[40]

In their reports on the executions, *Newsweek*, *Time*, and *U.S. News and World Report* featured brisk cold-war editorial commentary. *Time* said the Rosenbergs were "fanatic to the end," using their plight to foment propaganda against the United States. "Though apostates of Judaism and sentenced by a Jewish judge, they helped to portray themselves as victims of anti-Semitism."[41]   *Newsweek* claimed the executions would be used by communists to "promote the cause they [the Rosenbergs] had served." *U.S. News and World Report* contended: "In Russia, conviction is the end, in U.S. the beginning.   It opens up a legal maze in which the crime is all but forgotten."[42]

Not surprisingly, the French press was unanimous in its condemnation of the executions, which it regarded as horrifying. *Franc-Tireur* commented that the electrocutions at Sing Sing were "without excuse . . . a blow delivered by America against herself, against the common cause of liberty."[43] *Le Monde* praised the Rosenbergs for their courage in turning down the "sordid deal offered them." *Le Monde*'s Henri Pierre described the Rosenbergs' deaths as "ritualized murder." *Le Figaro* characterized the executions as the "torture of hope." *Le Parisien Libére* said: "The republic of Jefferson, Lincoln, and Roosevelt has departed from its traditions."[44]   In a vitriolic essay, Jean Paul Sartre charged that the United States had "conducted a legal lynching which smears a whole nation."[45]

London's three afternoon dailies did not comment on the executions. However, the London *Daily Worker* ran a banner headline that read, "Murder!" Rome's *Giornale d' Italia* was one of the few European newspapers to sympathize with the Eisenhower administration. "We would wager that if American spies against Russia were involved, the communists would put an end to them without much ceremony."[46]   In a special Rosenberg-coverage edition, the *National Guardian* said it stood in "horror and shame" before the actions of its government.[47] The *Daily Worker* pronounced the outrage of the U.S. Communist Party's ruling body.[48] Poland's *Trybuna Ludu* claimed the Rosenbergs were executed "because they loved peace."   Agerpres, the Romanian news agency, said husband and wife died as "fighters for the cause of peace." U.S. wire services said Moscow Radio reported that the Rosenbergs were "honest American citizens guilty of no crime."[49]

Emily Alman pulled herself together after the executions for one task that everyone else had overlooked. "I claimed their bodies. I figured if I didn't do something right away, there'd be headlines about them lying there unclaimed and then there'd be a fight."[50]

The funeral was held in Brooklyn the day after the executions. Inside the I. J. Morris Funeral Chapel an honor guard of four stood over the caskets. An American flag hung nearby. Husband and wife lay in adjoining open coffins, dressed in traditional Jewish funeral robes. Two dozen police officers kept watch over the estimated 10,000 who filed past the biers. News reports said the Rosenberg sons were not present. Julius and Ethel Rosenberg were buried in Wellwood Cemetery on Long Island on Sunday. It was a steamy, sunny hot day with temperatures in the low nineties. The graveside service featured an angry oration by Emanuel Bloch.[51] Before the rough-hewn oak coffins were lowered into the ground, he alleged that the Rosenbergs were killed "by the face of Nazism." He cried: "I place the murder of the Rosenbergs at the door of President Eisenhower, Attorney General Brownell, and J. Edgar Hoover . . . This is not American justice . . . we must be angry."[52] There was also a long line of graveside speakers, including the African American civil rights advocate and scholar W. E. B. Dubois. Sophie Rosenberg wept over the graves of her son and daughter-in-law. A cantor chanted the Kaddish, the Jewish prayer of lamentation.[53]

Shortly after the funeral, Manny Bloch wrote an article on the Rosenbergs for the *National Guardian*. It was his only journalistic reflection on the case. In his brief essay, his harshest criticism was reserved for the U.S. news media. He claimed "a conspiracy of silence" had kept reporters from discovering the truth of the case." Our great newspapers, which during the trial, had seized eagerly upon every propaganda release of the prosecution, closed their pages to all news about the victims. From the Government's point of view, and the point of view of its ally the press, the Rosenbergs were as good as dead."[54]

National Guardian editor James Aronson unleashed a scalding attack on the mainstream press, first turning his wrath on the *New York Herald Tribune*. Aronson said the newspaper's editor refused to see a Rosenberg Committee delegation shortly before the executions. "The *Herald Tribune*, along with every other newspaper in New York, and most papers throughout the country, consistently spiked committee releases reporting that distinguished persons all over the country had urged clemency."[55] Blasting the U.S. press as "vultures in print," Aronson decried "poisoned serials" by the *New York Post* and the *New York World-Telegram and Sun*. He scored Max Lerner for making clemency calls for "victims of injustice twenty four hours after death."[56] The *Guardian* editor also said Walter Winchell generated enough hatred in his column and radio program to earn a "letter of recommendation from Heinrich Himmler." (Because Winchell was Jewish this was a particularly vituperative charge). "While the press abroad was clamoring for news and pictures and background, the American press for two years was silent, except for the sporadic snarls when an appeal was coming due."[57]

Aronson charged that a Rosenberg "blackout" among U.S. newspapers was so strong even that the Catholic press did not report Pope Pius XII's requests to President Eisenhower for clemency.[58] Although coverage of the case in the last week was "full and fair and sober," he thought the press was on the toboggan slide to fascism . . . The press whipped up atom-spy hysteria where there was disinterest. It created a Frankenstein monster of fear and hatred which it is perpetuating in its blind coverage of McCarthy . . . The press had it in its power to pen the monster. It chooses not to do so. There is access to the press . . . if you accept the debased morality of the keepers of the press."[59]

Epilogue

P.S. All my personal effects are in three cartons you can get from the warden.

All My Love, Julius

Ethel wants it known we are the first victims of American fascism.[1]

From Julius Rosenberg's last letter

Julius Rosenberg's last message (published in the *National Guardian*) was unusual, yet typical. He conflated several different messages: personal, political, and philosophical. Implicit in it, however, was the notion that the case would always be notorious. Julius Rosenberg was right, but in another way he was wrong. Soon after his execution, streets and monuments in Eastern European cities were named after the Rosenbergs. But it was a different story in the West. The *Christian Science Monitor's* Roland Sawyer correctly predicted the case would soon "be reduced to proper scale as other dramatic events roll across the world stage."[2] Sawyer was right, at least for about ten years. The Rosenberg case quickly faded from the news agenda of U.S. newspapers. It was, to paraphrase Ben Bradlee, a brief but violent blip on the international political radar screen. French journalists and government officials soon had their attention taken up by a land war in Vietnam. In July 1953, the Korean War came to an end. American soldiers returned to civilian life stateside, mostly bitter but uniformly silent.

Manny Bloch faced disbarment proceedings for his remarks about President Eisenhower.[3] Soon after, Bloch died of a heart attack in his New York City apartment.[4] Before his death, though, he announced that a trust fund had been set up for the benefit of the Rosenberg boys.[5] Even before

Bloch's death, Michael and Robert Rosenberg moved in with new foster parents, Abel and Anne Meeropol. A nasty, well-publicized custody dispute followed between the Meeropols and the New York City Department of Welfare.[6] The children were then temporarily awarded to Sophie Rosenberg. In 1957, the Meeropols adopted Michael and Robert Rosenberg and the boys' last name was legally changed to Meeropol.

The National Committee to Secure Justice in the Rosenberg Case became the Sobell Committee. Still, the case did not vanish altogether from news-media attention. The committee's finances and funding were investigated by Congress in the mid-1950s. Stories sporadically surfaced in the press about David Greenglass's life behind bars.[7] Bureau of prison documents from that era reveal that Greenglass feared retaliation from inmates because of "possible adverse newspaper criticisms." When he came up for parole in the late 1950s, his wife promised officials, "that we would not, under any circumstances, ever seek any notoriety or publicity."[8]

After the Soviet Union launched Sputnik in 1957, former Assistant U.S. Attorney Myles Lane told reporters the Rosenberg spy ring had given "satellite secrets" to Russia. Lane's remarks caused a stir and the case was resurrected in headlines briefly. David Greenglass and Harry Gold again were questioned by Senate investigators but revealed nothing new.[9] Without hard evidence to support Lane's charges, the news media quickly lost interest.[10]

Nonetheless, the case periodically found a way back to the news agenda. Klaus Fuchs was released from Wakefield prison in July 1959, and immediately left for East Germany, where he took up residence. David Greenglass was paroled from Lewisburg penitentiary in November 1960. His release was something of a modern paradox in news-media relations. After his release, his attorney, O. John Rogge, held a press conference to say his client "wanted to be forgotten."[11] Harry Gold served fifteen years of his sentence and was paroled from Lewisburg in April 1966. Morton Sobell was the last freed of the Rosenberg case defendants. In 1969, he was ordered released from the Atlanta penitentiary by the U.S. Court of Appeals.[12]

Sobell also held a press conference after his release. After eighteen years in prison, there had been enormous political and cultural change in the United States. Like other institutions, the news media had changed too. Television was the news communication's master, the press a humbled and increasingly embattled medium. The *New York Journal-American, New York World-Telegram and Sun, New York Herald Tribune,* and *New York Mirror* had all died while Sobell was in prison. Many other newspapers had failed or had merged with other newspapers across the United States. Another, better educated, more aggressive generation of journalists had emerged from colleges and universities. Many of the younger reporters were too young to remember clearly the old passions and phobias of the domestic cold war.

William Wolf attended the Sobell press conference and recalls that younger reporters mostly asked polite questions.[13] By 1969, "atomic espionage" was as far removed from the news-media consciousness as polio vaccinations and bomb shelters.

But was the news media engaged in a "conspiracy of silence"? On this issue Julius Rosenberg, Harold Urey, Emanuel Bloch, and the *National Guardian* were at least half right. Although there was silence, there was no conspiracy, at least not in the classic sense of a cover-up or covert plan. There was no need for one; the political mechanics of agenda setting, i.e., gatekeeping, had long ago excluded from mainstream publications exposés and press releases from radical sources and newspapers. If there was a conspiracy in the news media regarding the Rosenberg-Sobell case, it was one of patriotic bias and political prejudice. In the final stages of the case, the news media simply averted their heads. That was unfortunate, if for no other reason than that the press might have uncovered unknown facts about the Rosenbergs if it had bothered to dig beneath the government's explanations of the case. Instead, the press allowed cold-war agenda setting, e.g., what government institutions, the general public, and news media consumers thought about communism to dictate the limits of Rosenberg case news coverage and analysis.

In this sense, then, agenda setting was effectively turned on its head.[14] Instead of the press strongly influencing what people thought about, the public and government strongly influenced how the news media reported on left-wing radicals and political dissidents. In a sense, the FBI and the Justice Department had framed the Rosenberg case for the news media before Julius Rosenberg was arrested. The arrests of Klaus Fuchs, Harry Gold, and David Greenglass ensured that each new arrest in the chain reinforced the news media impact of the next. If news framing provides a "window on the world," then the view of the Rosenberg case was arranged almost exclusively by the FBI and the Justice Department. This situation exemplified James Reston's term "news management."[15] That, of course, was not unusual or unprecedented. The government has "managed" the news for many generations. But the rise of the national security state and the onset of the cold war had accelerated dependence on news management. Government agencies and institutions could frame news stories just as they always had but with less chance of the news media questioning their policies and views.[16]

Of course, the Rosenberg case became more than a legal case. It became a cause célèbre that dwarfed other American social and political movements and causes. As such, it became Dwight Eisenhower's first major domestic crisis. Brigitte Lebens Nacos rightly asserts, "Crises represent the most fateful and crucial time for a nation and its presidents."[17] The Eisenhower administration's attempts to persuade Julius Rosenberg to "talk" backfired, leading to an international confrontation that played out on the front pages of newspapers throughout the world. President Eisenhower had the editorial support of the U.S. press but the scorn of much of the international news media in pursuit of his resolution of the Rosenberg crisis.

The Rosenberg case is not the only one in U.S. history where the press accepted the government's version of an issue without investigating the opposition's claims. The news media's reporting of the war in Vietnam until 1968 was mainly a record of unquestioning acceptance of government assertions. But the death sentences made the news media's lack of interest in the *National Guardian's* government conspiracy claims even more unusual.

Forty years later, debate continues as to whether the Rosenbergs were really guilty. Evidence in the 1970s revealed that the FBI and the Justice Department had arrested Ethel Rosenberg as a means for getting her husband to talk. That, of course, was not known by any one in the news media or press. Still, there were several clues to suggest it was a strong possibility. For example, the timing and circumstances of Ethel's arrest, Ruth Greenglass's unindicted status, and the Greenglasses' eleventh-hour story changes in February 1951, stand out as several obvious irregularities in the case. In the end, no one in the mainstream news media probed the *Guardian's* claim of conspiracy. This might have been understandable in 1951. Though intriguing, William Reuben's series lacked supporting evidence. But in spring 1953, after interoffice documents and alleged physical evidence were uncovered, the press had no good reason not to investigate the Rosenbergs' protestations of innocence.

The day after the Rosenbergs were buried, Justice Felix Frankfurter released a ten-page dissent on the case.[18] Ironically, Frankfurter took the same position as John Finerty, Daniel Marshall, and Manny Bloch: he had not had enough time to consider the new legal point. In a Hamletesque phrase, he said he realized his dissent "had an appearance of pathetic futility . . . But history also has its claims."

What (if any) lessons did the Rosenberg case impart to the news media? That is very difficult to determine. The case is too indiosyncratic, too rooted in cold-war passions to have left any clearly defined answers. Still, historians and other scholars well might consider the influence of politics and ideology more closely when they analyze the news media in wartime. It is all too easy to assert that left-wing radicals never again will face the crushing prejudices from the government and the press that they did in the 1920s and 1950s. It is well to remember that the news media have no foolproof filtration system for the elimination of government bias, distortion, manipulation, or propaganda. Today there certainly is no shortage of citizens who claim they have been treated unfairly by the press. Some say there is a disconcerting habit in the United States to admit that certain groups and individuals have not received fair treatment by the news media only long after their trials, causes, and cases have passed from notoriety. Perhaps "history too has its claims," but that is cold comfort to those looking in from the political outside.

Notes

PREFACE

1. George Sokolsky, "About Rosenberg Plea for Clemency," *New York Journal-American*, Jan. 9, 1953, p. 20.

2. Perry Miller, *The New England Mind: From Colony to Promise* (Cambridge: Harvard University Press, 1953), p. 238.

3. Robert J. Donovan, *The Tumultuous Years: The Presidency of Harry S Truman, 1949-1953* (New York: W.W. Norton and Co., 1982), p. 107.

4. Gregg Herken, *The Winning Weapon: The Atomic Bomb in the Cold War, 1945-1950* (New York: Alfred A. Knopf, 1980), p. 303n.

CHAPTER 1

1. "Results of Experiment: Steel Tower Vaporized, Fireball at 40,000 Feet," *San Francisco Chronicle*, Aug. 7, 1945, p. 1. The announcement of the July 17 test near Alamogordo was delayed until after the first bomb was dropped on Hiroshima on August 6, 1945. See "First Atomic Bomb Dropped on Japan," *New York Times*, Aug. 7, 1945, p. 1. For a multi-perspective analysis of Truman's decision to drop the bomb after the successful Alamogordo test see James West Davidson and Mark Hamilton Lytle, "The Decision to Drop the Bomb" in *After the Fact: The Art of Historical Detection* (New York: Alfred A. Knopf, 1982), pp. 320-55.

2. Arthur Miller, *Timebends: A Life* (New York: Grove Press, 1987), p. 387. In a somewhat Pecksniffian understatement, *New York Times* drama critic Brooks Atkinson said in his review of *The Crucible* that "Neither Mr. Miller nor his audience are unaware of certain similarities of justice then and now." *New York Times*, Jan. 22, 1953, C., p. 15.

3. Miller, *Timebends*, p. 387.

4. For example, the following texts and books that discuss the United States cold-war period refer only in passing to the case or do not talk about it at all. Carl M. Degler, *Affluence and Anxiety, 1945 Present* (Glencoe, Il.: Scott, Foresman and Co., 1968), p. 40; Walter Johnson, *Sixteen Hundred Pennsylvania Avenue: Presidents and People, 1929-59* (Boston: Little, Brown and Co., 1960); John Brooks, *The Great Leap: The Past Twenty-Five Years in America* (New York: Harper and Row, 1966); Eric F. Goldman, *The Crucial Decade and After: America, 1945-60* (New York: Vintage Books, 1960), p. 245; William E. Leuchtenberg, *A Troubled Feast: American Society Since 1945* (Boston: Little, Brown and Co., 1979), p. 29. Nevertheless, the case is discussed in some detail in an essay in David W. Noble's and Peter N. Carroll's, *Twentieth Century Limited*, (Boston: Houghton Mifflin Co., 1980), pp. 379-84.

5. For a record of the trial see a microfilm record of the transcript and case related briefs-available in most university law libraries. *U.S. v. Rosenberg* (microform) prepared by the Fund for the Republic, New York City (James P. Kilsheimer III, an assistant U.S. attorney who helped prosecute the Rosenbergs, assisted in the preparation, Wilmington, Del). M. Glazier (1978.) "The record of the trial in which Julius and Ethel Rosenberg were convicted for conspiracy to commit espionage and proceedings after convictions in the U.S. District Court and the Court of Appeals for the Second Circuit. Briefs in the Court of Appeals." Box title: "Conspiracy Trials in America, 1919-1953, *U.S. v. Rosenberg.*" The transcript and case motions and appeals and other case- related documents are also on file at the Federal Records Center (FRC) in Bayonne, N.J. (*U.S. v. Rosenberg, Sobell, Yakovlev, and Greenglass* [Cr. No. 134-245]. (Hereafter referred to as trial transcript). See accession nos. 021.88.124 and 021.-59A149, agency box nos. 1 2 3 4 34102, FRC location, So. 520616-701238A. *Rosenberg et al. v. U.S. S.D.N.Y.* (1951) aff'd F. 2d 583, (2d Cir. 1952); *U.S. v. Rosenberg*, 108 F.Supp 798 (S.D.N.Y. 1952); *Rosenberg v. U.S.*, cert. denied, 344 U.S. 838 (1952), reh'g denied, 344 (U.S. 889 (1952); *U.S. v. Rosenberg*, 195 U.S. F. 2d 583, 2nd Cir. (1953); *Rosenberg v. U.S.* 345 U.S. 965 (1953); *Rosenberg v. U.S.* 346 U.S. 273 (1953); *U.S. v. Rosenberg*, 200 U.S. 666, (2d Cir. (1952); *Rosenberg v. U.S.*, 204 F. 2nd 688 (2d Cir. 1953).

6. Robert J. Lamphere and Tom Shachtman, *The FBI-KGB War: A Special Agent's Story* (New York: Random House, 1986), pp. 91, 93. An FBI counterintelligence agent, Lamphere gave information regarding Barr to the CIA where it remained undeveloped until about 1950, p. 94. Also see John Lewis Gaddis, "Intelligence, Espionage, and Cold War Origins," *Diplomatic History* 13 (spring 1988); Alan Moorehead, *The Traitors* (New York: Charles Scribner's Sons, 1952); Norman Moss, *The Man Who Stole the Atom Bomb* (New York: St. Martin's Press, 1987).

7. Ronald Radosh and Joyce Milton, *The Rosenberg File: A Search for the Truth* (New York: Holt, Rinehart and Winston, 1983), p. 9; also, generally see Ralph DeToledano, *The Greatest Plot in History* (New York: Duell, Sloan and Pearce, 1963); and H. Montgomery Hyde, *The Atom Spies* (New York: Athenaeum, 1980).

8. Moorehead, *The Traitors*, p. 134.

9. Virginia Gardner, *The Rosenberg Story* (New York: Masses and Mainstream, 1954), p. 39.

10. Ibid., p. 39.

11. Louis Nizer, *The Implosion Conspiracy* (Garden City, N.Y.: Doubleday, 1973), p. 18.

12. Gardner, *The Rosenberg Story*, pp. 18, 25.

13. Ibid., p. 19.

14. Ibid., p. 21.

15. Nizer, *The Implosion Conspiracy*, p. 16.

16. Ibid., p. 17.

17. Gardner, *The Rosenberg Story*, pp. 52-3; also, see *Death House Letters of Ethel and Julius Rosenberg* (New York: Jero Publishing Co., 1953), pp. 116-17.

18. Gardner, *The Rosenberg Story*, p.53.

19. Jonathan Root, *The Betrayers: The Rosenberg Case-A Reappraisal of an American Crisis* (New York: Coward-McCann, 1963), p. 354.

20. Ibid., p. 75.

21. Ibid.

22. Ibid.

23. Gardner, *The Rosenberg Story*, p. 58.

24. Root, *The Betrayers*, p. 80.

25. Ibid.

26. Ibid.

27. Michael Meeropol and Robert Meeropol, *We Are Your Sons: The Legacy of Ethel and Julius Rosenberg*, 2nd ed. (Champaign-Urbana, Il.: University of Illinois Press, 1986), p. 8. The Meeropols, sons of Julius and Ethel Rosenberg, cite a letter from their parents dated July 24, 1950, in which Julius urges Ethel to sell the shop but not in haste. When Ethel was arrested, however, this chore fell to Emanuel Bloch, Julius Rosenberg's lawyer-of-record.

28. Ibid., p. 25; "Rosenbergs Executed as Atom Spies After Supreme Court Vacates Stay; Last-Minute Plea to President Fails," *New York Times*, June 19, 1953, p. 1.

29. Robert R. Byrnes, *Anti-Semitism in Modern France: The Prologue to the Dreyfus Affair*, vol. 1 (Rutgers University Press, 1950); Jean-Denis Bredin, *The Affair: The Case of Alfred Dreyfus* (New York: George Braziller, Inc., 1986), pp. 55-7, 96-7, 144; Robert L. Hoffmann, *More Than a Trial: The*

Struggle over Captain Dreyfus (New York: Free Press, 1980); Jacques Kayser, *The Dreyfus Affair* (New York: Covici, Friede Publishers, 1931).

30. See the Sacco and Vanzetti Case, *Transcript of the Record of the Trial of Nicola Sacco and Bartolomeo Vanzetti: In the Courts of Massachusetts and Subsequent Proceedings, 1920-27*, 5 vols. (New York: Henry Holt and Co., 1928); Francis Russell, *Tragedy in Dedham: The Story of the Sacco-Vanzetti Case* (New York: McGraw Hill Book Co., 1962); Felix Frankfurter, *The Case of Sacco and Vanzetti: A Critical Analysis for Lawyers and Laymen* (Boston: Little, Brown and Co., 1929); Louis G. Joughin and Edmund M. Morgan, *The Legacy of Sacco and Vanzetti* (New York: Harcourt, Brace and Co., 1948); Ben Bagdikian, *The Media Monopoly* (Boston: Beacon Press, 1983), pp. viii-ix; John Dos Passos, *The Best Times: An Informal Memoir* (New York: New American Library, 1966), pp. 166ff; *Facing the Chair: The Story of the Americanization of Two Foreignborn Workmen* (New York: De Capo Press, 1970); Daniel Aaron, ed., *Writers on the Left* (New York: Harcourt, Brace and World), pp. 170, 172-74.

31. Dan T. Carter, *Scottsboro: A Tragedy of the American South* (Baton Rouge: Louisiana State University Press, 1969), pp. 4-5; Haywood Patterson and Earl Conrad, *Scottsboro Boys* (Garden City, N.Y.: Doubleday and Co., 1950).

32. Henry Weihoffen, "Legislative Pardon," *California Law Review* 27: pp. 381- 86; G. Edward White, *Earl Warren: A Public Life* (New York: Oxford University Press, 1982), p. 58; Richard H. Frost, *The Mooney Case* (Stanford, Calif.: Stanford University Press, 1968); John Lofton, *Justice and the Press* (Boston: Beacon Press, 1966), p. 89.

33. John Chabot Smith, *Alger Hiss: The True Story* (New York: Holt, Rinehart, and Winston, 1976); Meyer A. Zeligs, *Friendship and Fratricide: An Analysis of Whittaker Chambers and Alger Hiss* (New York: Viking Press, 1967); also, see Allen Weinstein, *Purjury: The Hiss Chambers Case* (New York: Alfred A. Knopf, 1978).

CHAPTER 2

1. *New York Times'* columnist James Reston in Joseph Kraft, "Washington's Most Powerful Reporter," *Esquire*, November 1958, pp. 123-26.

2. The following represent some of the major works written on the Rosenberg case: Jonathan Root, *The Betrayers*; S. Anhill Fineberg, *The Rosenberg Case: Fact and Fiction* (New York: Oceana Publication, 1953); Oliver Pilat, *The Atom Spies* (New York: Van Rees Press, 1952); Radosh and Milton, *The Rosenberg File*, 1983); Walter Schneir and Miriam Schneir, *Invitation to an Inquest*, 4th ed. (New York: Pantheon Books, 1983); John

Wexley, *The Judgment of Julius and Ethel Rosenberg* (New York: Cameron and Kahn, 1955); William A. Reuben, *The Atom Spy Hoax* (New York: Action Books, 1955); Meeropol and Meeropol, *We Are Your Sons.* (University of Illinois Press, 1986).

3. The author relies on Lauren Kessler's description of the radical press. That is defined here as a newspaper or periodical published regularly with a professed socialist, communist, anarchic, or populist position. See Kessler, *The Dissident Press: Alternative Journalism in American History* (Beverly Hills, Calif.: Sage, 1984), p. 111. According to Earl Babbie, the best way to guarantee content reliability and validity is to code manifest and latent content of communication. (Babbie, *Research Methods in the Social Sciences* [Belmont, Calif.: Wadsworth, 1980], p. 240). Manifest content refers to material that can be objectively categorized and quantified; latent content analysis requires a more subjective response. Babbie says manifest analysis is the superior method; but latent analysis is better designed for thematic analysis. Because research in this book involves thematic analysis, latent content analysis is used exclusively.

4. Editorialized reporting is defined as the taking of a position by a reporter in the course of a news story. "Day-after" coverage actually includes two days after an event or incident occurs.

5. See Maxwell E. McCombs and Donald L. Shaw, "Structuring the Unseen Community," *Journal of Communication* 26 (spring 1976): 18-22; McCombs and Shaw, "The Agenda-Setting Function of Mass Media," *Public Opinion Quarterly* 36 (summer 1972): 176-87; McCombs and Shaw with the assistance of Lee E. Becker, *The Emergence of American Political Issues: The Agenda-Setting Function of the Press* (St. Paul, Minn.: West Publishing Co., 1977); Kurt Lang and Gladys Engel Lang, "The Mass Media and Voting" in Reader in *Public Opinion and Communication,* 2nd ed., edited by Bernard Berelson and Morris Janowitz, (New York: Free Press, 1966); For a more recent retrospective on agenda setting see McCombs, "Explorers and Surveyors: Expanding Strategies for Agenda-Setting Research," *Journalism Quarterly* 69 (winter 1992): 813-24; Marilyn S. Roberts, "Predicting Voting Behavior via the Agenda-Setting Tradition," Journalism Quarterly 69 (winter 1992): 878- 92; Donald L. Shaw and Shannon E. Martin, "The Function of Mass Media Agenda Setting," *Journalism Quarterly* 69 (winter 1992): 902-20.

6. Bernard C. Cohen, *The Press and Foreign Policy* (Princeton: Princeton University Press, 1963), p. 13.

7. Ibid.

8. See Shearon Lowery and Melvin De Fleur, *Milestones in Mass Communication Research: Media Effects* (New York: Longman, 1983), pp. 380-81.

9. Todd Gitlin, *The Whole World Is Watching: Mass Media in the Making and Unmaking of the New Left* (Berkeley, Calif: University of California Press, 1980), p. 7.

10. Gaye Tuchman, *Making News: A Study in the Construction of Reality* (New York: Free Press, 1978), p. 49.

11. Bagdikian, *The Media Monopoly*, pp. viii-ix.

12. Ben Bagdikian, *The Effete Conspiracy and Other Crimes of the Press* (New York: Harper and Row, 1972), pp. 40ff.

13. See U.S. House Subcommittee of the Committee on Government Operations, *Availability of Information From Federal Departments and Agencies,* Hearings before a Subcommittee of the Committee on Government Operations, 84th Cong. 1st sess., Nov. 7, 1955, pp. 25-27, (hereafter referred to as Hearings).

14. James Reston, "U.S. Suppression of News Charged," *New York Times*, Nov. 8, 1955, p. 25.

15. Herbert J. Gans, *Deciding What's News: A Study of CBS Evening News, NBC Nightly News, Newsweek, and Time* (New York: Pantheon, 1979), pp. 190ff.

16. Michael Schudson, *Discovering the News: A Social History of American Newspapers* (New York: Basic Books, 1978), p. 167.

17. Kessler, *The Dissident Press,* pp. 12-15; Margaret Blanchard, "Americans First, Newspapermen Second: The Conflict between Patriotism and Freedom of Press During the Cold War, 1946-52," Ph.D. diss., University of North Carolina, Chapel Hill, 1981.

CHAPTER 3

1. Bob Considine, "Pinks and Liberals are Mute Since Spy Arrests," *New York Journal-American,* June 21, 1950, p. 31.

2. See Robert J. Donovan, *The Tumultuous Years,* p. 193; also, *see Foreign Relations of the United States,* June 25, 1950, vol. 7, pp. 125-6; Merle Miller, *Plain Speaking: An Oral Biography of Harry S Truman* (New York: G.P. Putnam's Sons, 1973), p. 269; Max Hastings, *The Korean War* (New York: Simon and Schuster, 1987); Burton I. Kaufman, *The Korean War: Challenges in Crisis, Credibility and Command* (Temple University Press, 1986).

3. "Hearing Deferred in Espionage Case," *New York Times,* June 24, 1950, p. 2.

4. W.A. Gamson, "News as Framing," *American Behavioral Scientist* 33 (1989-90): 157.

5. Todd Gitlin, *The Whole World is Watching,* p. 7.

6. Richard Hofstadter, "The Paranoid Style in American Politics," *Harper's* (November 1964): 77-86. Hofstadter says: "Style has more to do with the way in which ideas are believed and advocated than with the truth or falsity of their content." p. 77; also, see Raymond J. Moley, *The American Legion Story* (New York: Duell, Sloan and Pearce, 1966); Merle Curti, *The Roots of American Loyalty* (Columbia University Press, 1946); Earl Hunter, *A Sociological Analysis of Certain Types of Patriotism* (New York: 1932).

7. Drew Pearson, "Gigantic Faces in Mount Rushmore," *San Francisco Chronicle*, June 26, 1950, p. 18.

8. "Caught in the Dragnet," *Newsweek*, June 26, 1950, p. 18.

9. "U.S. Should Execute All Communists as Its Foes," *New York Journal-American*, June 29, 1950, p. 3.

10. Ibid., p. 3.

11. Ibid. Weeks later, Hearst's *New York Journal-American* supported Pegler in an editorial: "Quite different and more dangerous is an enemy that lurks behind the lines, an enemy that assists the alien foe with stratagems of trickery and treason; an INTERNAL ENEMY that seeks to contrive defeat by sabotoging means of victory." "Intern the Reds," *Journal-American*, July 13, 1950, p. 1.

12. "Atomic Spy Wins Delay, Hint He's Ready to Talk," *New York Mirror*, July 13, 1950, p. 17; Walter Schneir and Miriam Schneir, *Invitation to an Inquest*, pp. 78- 9.

13. *New York Mirror*, July 13, 1950, p.17.

14. FBI file (JR), Headquarters (herein referred to as HQ), File no: 65-58236, ser: 151, July 17, 1950, p. 12. This report is a summary of David and Ruth Greenglasses' statements to the FBI in mid-July.

15. For this incident see A. H. Belmont to D. M. Ladd, FBI file, (JR), HQ, memorandum, File no: 65-58236, ser. 97, July 17, 1950.

16. See James C. Clark, "Robert Henry Best: The Path to Treason, 1921-1945," *Journalism Quarterly*, 67:4 (Winter 1990): 1015-61.

17. For a photocopy of the Hoover-McGrath press release see Department of Justice press release, proceedings under Section 2255, Title 28, U.S.C., Nov. 24 and 25, 1952, exhibit three. This document may be obtained at the Federal Records Center, Bayonne, N.J. (Herein referred to as FRC). [Cr. 134-245], accession no. 021-88.124, agency box nos. 1,2,3; FRC loc. So 520476. For books on Hoover's career and life see Richard Gid Powers, *Secrecy and Power: The Life of J. Edgar Hoover* (New York: The Free Press, 1987); Athan G. Theoharis and John Stuart Cox, *The Boss: J. Edgar Hoover and Great American Inquisition* (Temple University Press, 1988); also, see Frank J. Donner, *The Age of Surveillance: The Aims and Methods of America's Political Intelligence System* (New York: Alfred A. Knopf, 1980); Fred J. Cook, *The FBI Nobody Knows* (New York: MacMillan Co., 1964); Sanford Ungar, *FBI* (Boston: Little, Brown and Co., 1975); Donald F.

Whitehead, *The FBI Story: A Report to the People* (New York: Random House, 1956); Ovid Demaris, *An Oral Biography of J. Edgar Hoover* (New York: Harper Magazine Press, 1975); Max Lowenthal, *The Federal Bureau of Investigation* (New York: William Sloane Associates, Inc., 1950); Hank Messick, *An Inquiry into the Life and Times of John Edgar Hoover and his Relationship to the Continuing Partnership of Crime, Business and Politics* (New York: McKay Co., 1972); Curt Gentry, *J. Edgar Hoover: the Man and His Secrets* (New York: W. W. Norton and Co., 1991); Kenneth O'Reilly, *Hoover and the UnAmericans: the FBI, HUAC and the Red Menace* (Temple University Press, 1983.)

18. FRC, Hoover-McGrath press release.

19. "Fourth American Held as Atom Spy," *New York Times*, July 18, 1950, p. 1.

20. FRC, Hoover-McGrath press release.

21. *New York Times*, July 18, 1950, p. 8.

22. "New York Engineer Held as Paymaster in U.S. for Fuchs A-Spy Ring," *New York Post*, July 18, 1950, p. 2.

23. *New York Journal-American*, July 18, 1950, p. 9.

24. "New Yorker Held by FBI as Link in Spy Ring," *St. Louis Post-Dispatch*, July 18, 1950, p. 5 (UP report).

25. *New York Journal-American*, July 18, 1950, p. 9.

26. Ibid.

27. Ibid.

28. "Spy Suspect Knew Time Would Come," *New York Mirror*, July 19, 1950, p. 5.

29. *New York Post*, July 18, 1950, p. 1.

30. *New York Journal-American*, July 18, 1950, p. 9.

CHAPTER 4

1. Ted Morgan, "The Rosenberg Jury," *Esquire*, 83 May 1975, p.105.

2. Trial transcript, roll three, pp. 34ff.

3. Ibid., pp. 50-51.

4. Ibid., pp. 64-5; *New York Herald Tribune*, July 18, 1950, p. 1; *New York Daily News*, July 18, 1950, p. 1.; *New York Mirror*, July 18, 1950, p. 1.

5. The remaining headlines in the sample are "Fourth American Held as Atom Spy," *New York Times*; July 18, 1950, p.1; "Another Spy Arrest-Fourth Important Link in the Soviet Atomic Spy Network," *San Francisco Chronicle*,July 18,1950, p. 7; "FBI Seizes manufacturer as Soviet Spy," *Louisville Courier-Journal*, July 18, 1950, p. 1. *Time*, the only newsmagazine to report Julius Rosenberg's arrest, did not have a headline.

6. Black's Law Dictionary, *Definitions of the Terms and Phrases of American and English Jurisprudence, Ancient and Modern*, 5th ed. (St. Paul, Minn.: West Publishing Co., 1979), p. 280.

7. See Hoover-McGrath press release, FRC.

8. *St. Louis Post-Dispatch*, July 18, 1950, p. 1.

9. *Time*, July 31, 1950, pp. 12-3.

10. For a discussion of the rise of objectivity in American news reporting see Dan Schiller, *Objectivity and the News: The Public Rise of Commercical Journalism* (Philadelphia: University of Pennsylvania Press, 1981); Schudson, *Discovering the News*, pp. 22-23, 155-56; Ronald Shilen, "The Concept of Objectivity in Journalism in the U.S.," Ph.D. diss., New York University, 1955.

11. *New York Times*, July 18, 1950, p. 1.

12. *Time*, July 31, pp. 12-3.

13. Edwin R. Bayley, *Joe McCarthy and the Press* (University of Wisconsin Press, 1981), p. 20; also, see: Earl Latham, *The Communist Conspiracy in Washington: From the New Deal to McCarthy* (Cambridge: Harvard University Press, 1966), pp. 284- 96.

14. "A-Spy Suspects Shop Did Jobs for U.S., City," *New York Daily News*, July 19, 1950, p. 6.

15. Ibid., p. 6.

16. Ibid.

17. *New York Herald Tribune*, July 20, 1950, p. 10.

18. Ibid.

19. Ibid.

20. "President Warns U.S. of Spy Peril, Calls on All to Report Subversion," *New York Times*, July 17, 1950, p. 1.

21. "New Spy Round-up Brings 2 Arrests, Others Due Soon," *New York Times*, July 30, 1950, p. 1.

22. Ibid.

23. Ibid.

24. Ibid.

25. See J. Edgar Hoover to Attoreny General J. Howard McGrath, FBI file, JR) (HQ,) File no. 65-58236, ser. 97, July 19, 1950; also, see See D. M. Ladd to A. H. Belmont, JR, (HQ), memorandum, file no. 65-58236, ser. 188, July 17, 1950.

26. Ibid.

27. Schneir and Schneir, *Invitation to an Inquest*, p. 150.

28. "Plot to Have G.I. Give Bomb Data to Soviet Is Laid to His Sister Here," *New York Times*, Aug. 12, 1950, p. 1; "Mother of Two Seized as Atom Spy Ring Link," *New York Herald-Tribune*, Aug. 12, 1950, p. 5. Also, see Elaine Tyler May, *Homeward Bound: American Families in the Cold War* (New York: Basic Books Inc., 1988), pp. 93ff.

29. *Times*, Aug. 12, 1950, p. 30.

30. This does not mean that the FBI or Justice Department thought that Ethel was an innocent bystander in the ring's business. Robert Lamphere describes deciphered KGB cables from the 1940s that mention an American woman code named "Ethel," who was aware of her husband's espionage activities. However, critics of the Rosenberg-Sobell prosecution would point out that intelligence operatives are never referred to by their real names. Soviet espionage scholar David J. Dallin asserts that agents would not be given their real first name as a code name, but he nonetheless identifies the Rosenbergs as members of the Soviet GRU, formerly the chief intelligence administration of the Soviet government. See Dallin, *Soviet Espionage* (New Haven: Yale University Press, 1955), pp. 5, 9. Dallin, however, on this issue cites Elizabeth Bentley as his bibliographic source.

31. The remaining headlines are: "Mother of Two Hold in Atom Spy Case;" *Washington Post*; "Mother of Two Seized as Atom Spy Link;" *New York Herald Tribune*; "Atom Arrest Number Eight," *Newsweek*. Nonetheless, "Plot to have G.I. Give Data to a Soviet is Laid to Sister Here," *New York Times* and "Wife of Accused Spy Arrested for Conspiracy," *Louisville-Courier Journal*.

32. See "Hearings;" Allen Drury, "U.S. Suppression of News Charged," *New York Times*, Nov. 8, 1955, p. 25.

33. "Hearings," p. 25.

34. Tuchman, *Making News*, pp. 1ff; also, see Leon V. Sigal, *Reporters and Officials:The Organization and Politics of Newsmaking* (Lexington, Mass.: D.C. Heath and Co., 1973).

35. "Here's the Stark Story If A-Bomb Strikes," *New York Post*, Aug. 13, 1950, p. 1 (UP report).

36. See Morton Sobell, *On Doing Time*, (New York: Charles Scribner's Sons, 1974), pp. 3-22.

37. Ibid., p. 84.

38. Helen Sobell, letter to author, April 23, 1991.

39. Sobell, *On Doing Time*, p. 17.

40. "Engineer Is Seized at Laredo as Spy for Russian Ring," *New York Times*, Aug. 19, 1950, p. 1; "FBI Seizes Ex-D.C. Man as a Red Spy," *Washington Post*, Aug. 19, 1950, p. 1; however, a Mexican "government official" did confirm Sobell's arrest; see *Chicago Tribune*, Aug. 19, 1950, p. 16 (AP report); "Ex-Russian Agent is Indicted as Spy," *New York Times*, Aug. 18, 1950, p. 7.

41. *New York Times*, Aug. 18, 1950, p. 1.

42. "New York Radar Expert Held; Is 8th in Red Atom Spy Ring," *New York Herald Tribune*, Aug. 19, 1950, p. 18.

43. *New York Times*, Aug. 19, 1950, p. 1.

44. *New York Herald Tribune*, Aug. 19, 1950, p.18; the remaining headlines in the sample for the Sobell arrest are "Former Civilian Engineer in Navy Arrested as Spy," *St. Louis Post-Dispatach*, Aug. 19, 1950; "Radar Man Held in Fuchs Spy Ring," *San Francisco Chronicle*, Aug. 19, 1950; "Spy Suspect Held; Knows Top Secrets," *Atlanta Constitution*, Aug. 19, 1950; "Mexico Hands Spy Suspect To FBI at Border," *Chicago Tribune*, Aug. 19, 1950; "Atom Arrest Number Eight," *Newsweek*, Aug. 28, 1950; "Detour," Aug. 28, 1950, *Time.*

45. "Atom Arrest Number Eight," *Newsweek*, Aug. 28, 1950, p. 30.

CHAPTER 5

1. Teletype, FBI file, JR, (HQ), New York to Washington, file no. 65-58236, ser. 813, Feb. 26, 1951.

2. Of the three defendants only Julius Rosenberg had ever before been jailed. Apparently he was jailed briefly in 1936 after a strike action against a department store in New York City. See Ilene Philipson, *Ethel Rosenberg: Beyond the Myths* (New York: Franklin Watts, 1988), p. 91f.

3. Lewis Schaeffer wrote three articles for the *Jewish Daily Forward* on the Greenglasses. See "At the Home of David Greenglass-A Talk with His Wife," Aug. 20, 1950, p. 4; "Mrs. Greenglass' Husband Was Misled by His Brother-in-Law," Aug. 30, 1950, p. 4; "My Husband Was Misled but He Is Not a Traitor," Says Ruth Greenglass, Sept. 2, 1950, p. 6. The *Forward*'s articles on the Greenglasses also symbolized that paper's shift from the far left. Founded in 1897 by Abraham Cahan as a Socialist Yiddish-language weekly, the *Forward* was read for generations in Lower-East Side homes. Nevertheless, by 1950 the paper was stiffly anti-communist.

4. See Radosh and Milton, The *Rosenberg File*, p. 519n.

5. Meeropol and Meeropol, *We Are Your Sons*, pp. 25ff.

6. Sobell, *On Doing Time*, p. 100.

7. "Rosenbergs Demand Espionage Case Data," *New York Times*, Sept. 15, 1950, p. 22.

8. "Slack Pleads Guilty as Red Spy; Transmitted Explosive Secrets," *New York Herald Tribune*, Sept. 19, 1950, p. 13 (AP report).

9. "Slack, Spy, Gets 15 Years," *New York Times*, Sept. 23, 1950, p. 32.

10. "Rosenbergs Lose Plea to See A-Bomb Data," *New York World-Telegram and Sun*, Oct. 6, 1950, p. 16.

11. "Ex-Army Man Pleads Guilty as Spy for Russia," *New York Herald Tribune*, Oct. 19, 1950, p. 1.

12. Ibid.

13. See Daniel Hallin, *The Uncensored War: The Media and Vietnam* (New York: Oxford University press, 1986), p.70; also, see: Phillip Knightley,

The First Casualty: From the Crimea to Vietnam: the War Correspondent as Hero, Propagandist, and Myth Maker (New York: Harcourt, Brace Jovanovich, 1975; John Morton Blum, *V was for Victory: Politics and American Culture During World War II* (New York: Harcourt, Brace Jovanovich, 1976).

14. "Gold Prepares to Testify Against 2 in Atom Spy Ring," *New York Daily News*, Nov. 8, 1950, p. 5.

15. Ibid., p. 10.

16. "Miss Bentley Calls Engineer a Red Contact," *Chicago Tribune*, Nov. 15, 1950, p. 19. However, on cross-examination, Bentley admitted she did not understand the blueprints. Also, see: Cook, *The FBI Nobody Knows*, pp. 283-7; "Red Ring Bared by Blond Spy Queen," *New York World-Telegram and Sun*, July 21, 1948, p. 1, *New York World-Telegram and Sun*, July 22, 1948, p. 1.

17. "Semenov His Boss As Spy," *New York Times*, Nov. 16, 1950, p. 1; "Gold Testified Brothman Was in Spy Ring," *New York Herald Tribune*, Nov. 16, 1950, p. 12.

18. "Chemist, Woman Aide Guilty, Espionage Jury Here Finds," *New York Times*, Nov. 23, 1950, p. 1; "Gold Got Hug For Telling FBI a Phony Story," *New York World-Telegram and Sun*, Nov. 17, 1950, p. 3; "Soviet Gratitude to Spies Depicted," *New York Times*, Nov. 17, 1950, p. 1.

19. Schneir and Schneir, *Invitation to an Inquest*, p. 105.

20. "Two in Spy Case Get Maximum Penalty," *New York Times*, Nov. 29, 1950, p. 25.

21. "Gold Atom Spy, Gets 30 Year Maximum for Aiding Red Spy Ring," *New York Times*, Dec. 10, 1950, p. 1. The severity of the sentence even surprised reporters and spectators in court. Attorney General McGrath had personally recommended a twenty-five-year term. The *New York Times* pointedly reminded readers that Gold's punishment was more than double Klaus Fuchs's fourteen-year sentence.

22. Schneir and Schneir, *Invitation to An Inquest*, p. 462.

23. FBI file, HG (NY), file no. 65-15324, ser. 599, Dec. 28, 1950.

24. Ibid.

25. FBI file, HG, (HQ), file no. 65-57449, ser. 799, March 5, 1953, p. 3.

26. FBI file, JR (HQ), file no. 65-58236, ser. 813, Feb. 26, 1951.

27. See Sol Stern and Ronald Radosh, "The Hidden Rosenberg Case," *New Republic*, June 23, 1979, pp. 20-21.

28. *New Republic*, June 23, 1970, p. 21.

29. Ibid., p. 24.

30. FBI file, JR (HQ), confidential report to FBI Director, file no: 65-58236, Ser. 130, July 17, 1950.

31. Stern and Radosh, "The Hidden Rosenberg Case," p. 21.

32. See Edwin Emery and Michael Emery, *The Press and America: An Interpretive History of the Mass Media* (Englewood Cliffs, N.J.: Prentice Hall, 1988), pp. 363-4; also, see Bernard Roscho, *Newsmaking* (University of Chicago Press, 1975), p. 18; generally, see Curtis MacDougal, *Interpretive Reporting* (New York: Macmillan, 1938). For an early path-breaking history of objectivity in U.S. journalism see Ronald Shilen, "The Concept of Objectivity." Generally, see Schudson, *Discovering the News*, pp. 156-57; Hallin, *The Uncensored War*, pp. 62-75.

33. See FBI file, JR, (HQ), file no. 65-58236, ser. 663, Jan. 24, 1951. In this file, an FBI teletype, David Greenglass is reported as saying that "about May 1945" he was chosen as one of the Los Alamos soldiers to be sent to an island in the Pacific "to assemble the atom bomb." He said his group leader, John P. Fitzpatrick, would not let him go because Ruth Greenglass still was recovering from a miscarriage. Fitzpatrick, an AEC employee in 1951 at the Argonne National Laboratory in Chicago, was interviewed by FBI agents on January 25. They reported the next day that Fitzpatrick "advised no recollection Greenglass selected to assemble atom bomb in Pacific." See FBI file, JR, (HQ), teletype, file no. 65-58236, ser. 660, Jan. 26, 1951; lastly, Fitzpatrick told Chicago field agents that Greenglass had no special skills that would have earned him consideration for the task of assembling the atomic bomb. See FBI file, JR, (HQ), file no. 65-58236, ser. 696, Feb. 2, 1951. Generally, for for a discussion of the credibility of declassified government files as credible historical sources see Frank Donner, *The Age of Surveillance*, p. 23f; David Garrow, *The FBI and Martin Luther King, Jr.*, (New York: W.W. Norton and Co., 1981), p. 13. For an analysis of the credibility of FBI files in the Rosenberg case see Radosh and Milton, *The Rosenberg File*, pp. 471-2; Walter Schneir and Miriam Schneir, *Invitation to an Inquest*, pp. 426-30.

34. "Espionage Trial of 3 To Open on March 6," *New York Times*, Feb. 14, 1951, p. 13.

35. "Spy Trial to Hear 3 Atom Scientists," *New York Times*, March 1, 1951, p. 14; "FBI Head Alerts Nation on Security," *New York Times*, Feb. 28, 1951, p. 5.

36. "Spy Trial," p. 14.

CHAPTER 6

1. "Rosenbergs Sentenced to Die, Sobell Gets 30 Years as Soviet Atom Spy," *New York Mirror*, April 6, 1951, p. 3.

2. For a *New Yorker*-inspired discussion of journalism in New York City in this and an earlier era, see A .J. Liebling, *The Press*, 2nd ed. (New York: Ballantine Books, 1973).

3. "Three Go on Trial as Atom Spies: War Crimes Guilt Can Mean Death," *New York Times*, March 7, 1951, p. 1; "Jurors Chosen to Try 3 as Atom Spies," *New York World-Telegram and Sun*, March 6, 1951, p. 31.

4. "Theft of Atom Bomb Secrets in War Stressed at Trial," *New York Times*, March 8, 1951, p. 1.

5. Ibid.

6. The *San Francisco Chronicle* and *Washington Post* used UP reports while the *Chicago Tribune* relied on different wire services. The *New York Times* and *New York Herald Tribune* used staff reports.

7. The *Atlanta Constitution* relied on a *New York Times* report. News editing can account for differences in stories. *Newsweek* and *U.S. News & World Report* did not cover the trial.

8. The remaining headlines for the sample are: "Prosecution Opens Atom Spy Trial," *San Francisco Chronicle;* "Sketch of A-Bomb Taken, U.S. Charges," *Washington Post,* "Jury Selected for Trial of Three as Atom Bomb Secrets Spies," *St. Louis Post-Dispatch.* All dates are from March 8, 1951, except the *Post-Dispatch*, which has a March 7, 1951 date. The *Louisville Courier-Journal* did not carry a story for this date.

9. Gaye Tuchman, "Objectivity as a Strategic Ritual: An Examination of Newsman's Notions of Objectivity," *American Journal of Sociology* 77, no. 4 (November 1972): 660-69.

10. Cohen, *The Press and Foreign Policy*, p. 13.

11. "Costello Back under Lights for Grilling on Mysterious Parley with O'Dwyer," *New York Post*, March 14, 1951, p. 3.

12. "Costello's Hands Scream Their Secret Story on TV, " *New York Post*, March 14, 1951, p. 3.

13. Morton Sobell, telephone interview by author, Dec. 16, 1990.

14. Everett M. Rogers, James W. Dearing, and Soonbum Chang, "Aids in the 1980s: the Agenda-Setting Process for a Public Issue," *Journalism Monographs* 26 (April 1991): 2, 3.

15. See Gamson, "News as Framing."

16. Trial transcript, p. 261.

17. Ibid.; years later declassifed FBI documents on the Rosenberg-Sobell case revealed that Elitcher had been followed to the Sobells' house, but surveillance then ended there. See Max Elitcher (HQ), file no. 100-215, ser. 60, Oct. 15, 1948.

18. "War Secrets In D.C. Jury Told," *Washington Post*, March 9, 1951, p. 12.

19. The *Louisville Courier-Journal* and *Washington Post* both used AP stories dated March 9, 1951. The *New York Times* report came from a staff reporter.

20. The *New York Herald Tribune* used a staff report while the *Atlanta Constitution* relied on a *New York Times* account. The *San Francisco*

Chronicle used a UP story and the *St. Louis Post-Dispatch* used an AP report. The *Chicago Tribune* did not carry a story on the trial that day.

21. Trial transcript, p. 276.

22. Ibid., p. 499.

23. Ibid., p. 502.

24. Bloch made his "grandstand" comment in a conversation with Irwin Edelman in Los Angeles in December 1953. Edelman described the encounter in a tract on the case, "Religion, the Left, and the Rosenberg Case." This undated work was likely published sometime in the mid-1950s, available in records of the National Committee to Reopen the Rosenberg case, State Historical Society of Wisconsin, Madison (hereafter refered to as SHSW). For Judge Kaufman's remark about "good judgment" see: trial transcript, pp. 508-09.

25. Radosh and Milton, *The Rosenberg File*, p. 189; also, see Gerald E. Markowitz and Michael Meeropol, "The Crime of the Century Revisited: David Greenglass's Scientific Evidence in the Rosenberg Case," *Science and Society* 44 (spring 1988): 1-26; Roger M. Anders, "The Rosenberg Case Revisited: The Greenglasses' Testimony and the Protection of Atomic Secrets," *American Historical Review* 83 (April 1978): 388-400.

26. Trial transcript, p. 509.

27. "Space ship Spying Bared; Witness Says Pal Told Him Scheme," *Chicago Tribune*, March 13, 1951; "Spies Got New A-Bomb Plans, Jury Hears," *Washington Post*, March 13, 1951, p. 1 (AP report); Greenglass's admission that he made the freehand sketch of the lens mold the day before his testimony appears on p. 463 of the trial transcript; the sketch he made of the cross-section of the atomic bomb was made slightly earlier. See "Spy's Idea of A-Bomb Partly Right and Partly Wrong, Bared at Trial," *St. Louis Post-Dispatch*, March 13, 1951, p. 2 (AP report). In his analysis, AP science writer Howard Blakeslee took a compromise position on the scientific value of the former army sergeant's testimony: "The Greenglass bomb is partly Rube Goldberg stuff and partly real. Its disclosure is enough to tell any atom-bomb maker how to overcome some of his most serious difficulties." Later, *Life* magazine and the *Bulletin of Atomic Scientists* would cast further doubt on Greenglass's account. See "Spy's Version of A-Bomb," *Life*, March 26, 1951, p. 51.

28. All but the *St. Louis Post-Dispatch* had reports in the March 15, 1951, edition. The *Post-Dispatch*'s report on Ruth Greenglass's testimony appeared in that paper's late-city edition, March 14, 1951.

29. William R. Conklin, "Greenglass' Wife Backs His Testimony on Theft of Atom Bomb Secrets," *New York Times*, March 15, 1951, p. 1.

30. Trial transcript, p. 775.

31. "Columbia Teacher Arrested, Linked to Two on Trial as Spies," *New York Times*, March 15, 1951, p. 1; "Columbia Professor Held for Trial as Spy Link," *New York World-Telegram and Sun*, March 15, 1951, p. 1.

32. *New York Times*, March 15, 1951, p. 1.

33. "Columbia Law Professor Held," p. 1; however, Perl's attorney, Raymond L. Wise, told a *New York Times* reporter his client had been "approached" by the Manhattan U.S. Attorney's Office. Wise said Perl was told "it was believed" he had committed perjury during grand jury testimony. He implied his client had refused to be intimidated into testifying for the prosecution in the Rosenberg-Sobell trial. Wise also said Perl had applied not for a new passport but had applied for renewal of an old one. He explained that his client had been considering a "summer vacation abroad."

34. The incident is recounted in detail in Sobell's memoir, *On Doing Time*, pp. 189-91.

35. Radosh and Milton, *The Rosenberg File*, pp. 204-05.

36. Both stories appeared above the fold on page 1 of the March 15, 1951, *New York Times*.

37. Trial transcript, roll 1, pp. 756-67.

38. "Admitted Spy is Star U.S. Witness; Details Aid to Russia and His Dealing with Fuchs and Others at Trial of Three, " *New York Times*, March 16, 1951, p. 8.

39. Generally see Louis Nizer, *The Implosion Conspiracy*.

40. "Defense Allows Story of Spies to Stand," *New York Herald Tribune*, March 17, 1951, p. 22.

41. "Real Life Cloaks and Daggers," *New York Daily News*, March 17, 1951, p. 15.

42. Ibid.

43. Gold's testimony began on March 15, 1951. Of the three news-magazines, only *Time*, in its March 19, 1951, issue, devoted coverage to the Rosenberg-Sobell trial.

44. Trial transcript, p. 987; "Miss Bentley Helps Forge Red Network Link," *New York World-Telegram and Sun*, March 21, 1951, p. 11.

45. Wexley, *The Judgment*, p. 243.

46. Ibid.

47. Ibid.

48. However, the *Louisville Courier-Journal* did not feature a story on the trial on March 21 or 22.

49. *Time's* March 26, 1951, issue had an article on the trial, "My Friend Yakovlev," but no indication that either of the Rosenbergs had testified. Also, see "Spies in U.S. Told Russia All," *U.S. News and World Report*, April 6, 1953, pp. 13-15. This report, published after the convictions but before the sentencings, marked *U.S. News'* s first extensive report on the case since the Rosenbergs' arrests.

50. "The Faceless Men," *Time*, March 19, 1951 p. 27.

51. *Time*, March 26, 1951, p. 27.

52. "Rosenberg's Wife Shies at Red Query," *New York Times*, March 27, 1951, p. 21.

53. Schneir and Schneir, *Invitation to an Inquest*, p. 150; Radosh and Milton, *The Rosenberg File*, pp. 261-63.

54. Trial transcript, p. 1, 396.

55. *New York Times*, March 27, 1951, p. 21.

56. Trial transcript, pp. 1, 371-79.

57. Sobell interview.

58. Radosh and Milton, *The Rosenberg File*, p. 260.

59. "Spy Case Against 3 Goes to Jury Today," *New York Times*, March 28, 1951, p. 18.

60. Trial transcript, pp. 1, 431-32.

61. Ibid., pp. 1, 452-53.

62. Ibid., p. 1, 453.

63. Ibid., p. 1, 486.

64. "Spy Jury Put off for Night, Out Seven and 1/2 Hours," *New York Herald Tribune*, March 29, 1951, p. 1.

65. Trial transcript, p. 1, 517.

66. Trial transcript, p. 1, 582.

67. "All Three Convicted as Atom Spies: May Get Death for Aiding Russia," *New York Herald Tribune*, March 30, 1951, p. 1.

68. "Doomed A-Spies Sing in Cell," *New York Mirror*, April 6, 1951, p. 1.

69. "Spy Couple Sentenced to Die: Aide Gets 30 Years," *New York Times*, April 6, 1951, p. 1.

70. "Death of Rosenbergs Decreed for Giving A-Secrets to Russia," *Washington Post*, April 6, 1951, p. 1 (AP report).

71. Ibid.

72. Ibid.

73. "Doomed A-Spies Sing," April 6, 1951, p. 3.

74. Ibid., p. 30.

75. "Spy Couple Sentenced."

76. *New York Post*, April 6, 1951, p. 48. This was from the "Lyons' Den" column. Lyons also claimed Julius Rosenberg sometimes acted condescendingly towards another federal prisoner, Eugene (Gene) Dennis, U.S. Communist Party leader. The columnist said Julius's high-handed attitude was that of an espionage agent patronizing a political functionary.

77. "Death Sentence for Traitors," *Atlanta Constitution*, April 6, 1951, p. 22.

78. "Death for the Atomic Spies," *St. Louis Post-Dispatch*, April 6, 1951, p. 1.

79. *Jewish Day*, April 6 and 8, 1951.

80. *Jewish Daily Forward*, April 6, 1951, p. 1.

81. "Rosenbergs Sentenced to Death, Made Scapegoats for Korean War," *Daily Worker*, April 6, 1951, p. 2. Further, if FBI documents are an accurate source of information Judge Kaufman was moved to convey his editorial gratitude to FBI Director Hoover. According to declassified files, the same afternoon that Kaufman sentenced the Rosenbergs, he contacted Edward Scheidt, head of the Manhattan FBI office. The memo says Kaufman told Scheidt to convey to Hoover his congratulations on a "fabulous job, an outstanding job." Apparently, Hoover returned the compliment the next day. He informed the judge that "the communist underground ranks . . . have been stunned by your forthright action." This file is quoted in Radosh and Milton, *The Rosenberg File*, p. 285. For more of Judge Kaufman's role in the Rosenberg-Sobell case, see U.S. *House Subcommittee on Criminal Justice of the Committee on the Judiciary*, 97th Cong., 1st and 2nd sess., serial no. 132, pt. 3, app. 2., "The Death Penalty" (Rosenberg Case), Dec. 16, 1982, pp. 2, 337-2,403. The Kaufman papers may be obtained from the records of the National Committee to Reopen the Rosenberg Case, SHSW. The FBI files relating to Kaufman appear in these documents; also, see Vern Countryman, "Out Damned Spot," *New Republic*, Oct. 7, 1977, p. 15.

82. "Greenglass Gets 15 Years; Judge Recognizes Spy's Aid," *New York Times*, April 7, 1951, p. 1.

83. "Atom Spy Greenglass Given 15 Years," *New York Mirror*, April 7, 1951, p. 2.

CHAPTER 7

1. Julius Rosenberg to Ethel from prison correspondence, October 1951. See *Death House Letters*, p. 66. For other references on the prison letters, see: *The Testament of Ethel and Julius Rosenberg* (New York: Cameron and Kahn, 1954); Andrew Ross, ed., "Reading the Rosenberg Letters," in *No Respect: Intellectuals and Popular Culture* (New York: Routledge, 1989); Meeropol and Meeropol, *We Are Your Sons*.

2. "Truman Relieves M'Arthur of All His Posts," *New York Times*, April 11, 1951, p.1; "Truman fires M'Arthur," *Washington Post*, April 11, 1951, p. 1; "MacArthur Agrees to Address Congress," *Washington Evening Star*, April 12, 1951, p. 1 (AP report).

3. Dorothy Thompson, "What Constitutes Treason?" *Evening Star*, April 12, 1951, p. 23-A.

4. Ibid.

5. Ibid.

6. Sobell, *On Doing Time*, p. 256.

7. "Why Willie McGee was Murdered," *Daily Worker*, May 9, 1951, p. 1.

8. Ibid.

9. *Testament*, p. 27.

10. Max Lerner, "The Just and the Unjust," *New York Post*, May 8, 1951, p. 30.

11. "Four Negro Rapists Are Electrocuted," *San Francisco Chronicle*, Feb. 3, 1951, p. 7 (AP report).

12. *National Guardian*, May 16, 1951, p. 5; "News Source Held Without Privilege," *New York Times*, May 8, 1951, p. 33.

13. *National Guardian*, May 16, 1951, p. 5.

14. "Atom Spy Going to Sing Sing," *New York Times*, May 15, 1951, p. 27.

15. "Trial of Trenton Six Turns into Low Comedy," *National Guardian*, May 2, 1951, p. 1; "Victory, 4 of Trenton 6 Free," *National Guardian*, June 6, 1951, p. 1; "Judge Rules Out Three of Trenton Six Confessions," *National Guardian*, June 6, 1951, p. 1.

16. "Victory," *National Guardian*, June 6, 1951, p. 1.

17. James Aronson and Cedric Belfrage, *Something to Guard: The Stormy Life of the National Guardian* (New York: Columbia University Press, 1978), pp. 169-71; also, see Aronson, *The Press and the Cold War* (Indianapolis: Bobbs-Merrill, 1970), p. 59.

18. William Reuben, interview by author, Sept. 26, 1990.

19. FBI, Emanuel H. Bloch, File no. 100-99876, ser. 124, p. 3. Nov. 5, 1953.

20. John Gates, interview by author, Feb. 5, 1991; in a 1978 interview with Radosh and Milton, Max Gordon said when he became editor of the *Worker* (after Gates went to prison), he was held to a "hands-off" policy on the Rosenberg-Sobell case. Radosh and Milton, *The Rosenberg File*, p. 332.

21. Aronson and Belfrage, *Something to Guard*, pp. 170-71.

22. Reuben, interview.

23. Ibid.

24. Ibid.

25. Aronson and Belfrage, *Something to Guard*, pp. 9-10.

26. David Armstrong, *A Trumpet to Arms: Alternative Media in America* (Boston: South End Press, 1981), p. 40.

27. Aronson and Belfrage, *Something to Guard*, pp. 9-10.

28. "Daddy When Are You and Mommy Coming Home,?" *National Guardian*, Aug. 8, 1951, p. 1.

29. "Is This the Dreyfus Case of Cold War America?" *National Guardian*, Aug. 15, 1951, p. 1.

30. Ibid.

31. Ibid., p. 4.

32. Ibid., p. 1.

33. Ibid., p. 4.

34. Ibid., p. 1.

35. Kessler, *The Dissident Press*, p. 113.   However, historically newspapers and periodicals of a left-wing character rarely have made distinctions between news and editorial functions.   News reporting and analysis and political and ideological dogma have tended to be integrated indiscriminately in the reporting of radical papers, journals, and magazines. For example, Seymour Lutzky observes in a Ph.D. dissertation on the nineteenth-century reform press that radical and reform editors typically pursued dual purposes: educating readers on economic and social issues while attacking political systems and their leaders.   See Seymour Lutzky, "The Reform Editors and Their Press," Ph.D. diss., State University of Iowa, 1951; also, see Jean Folkerts, "Functions of the Reform Press," *Journalism History* 2:1 (spring 1985); in contrast, political, and ideological positions in twentieth-century mainstream publications ordinarily (at least in theory) are confined to the opinion/editorial page.   See Herbert J. Gans, *Deciding What's News*, pp. 190ff.   Also see: Joseph Conlin, ed., *The American Radical Press*, vols. 1 and 2 (Westport, Ct.. Greenwood Press, 1974); Aaron, *Writers on the Left*.

36. *National Guardian*, Aug. 15, 1951, p. 1.   Actually, *Guardian* editors wrote the introductory series article.

37. William Reuben, "Did the FBI Buy Political Scapegoats with Mercy for a Spy? " *National Guardian*, Aug. 22, 1951, p. 3.

38. Ibid.

39. Ibid.

40. William Reuben, "Did the FBI Lie to Launch a Frame-up? " *National Guardian*, Aug. 29, 1951, p. 1.

41. Ibid., p. 3.   A review of the exposé to this date appears on this page.

42. Ibid.

43. Ibid,. p. 1.

44. *New York Mirror*, July 13, 1950, p. 1.

45. Wlliam Reuben, "How the FBI Got a Witness and a New Scapegoat Too," *National Guardian*, Sept. 5, 1951, p. 5.

46. Ibid.   A review of the series to this date appears on this page in a lined, four-column box.

47. Ibid., p. 6.

48. Ibid., p. 5.

49. William Reuben, "The Trial: The Question Seemed Not to Be Guilt or Innocence, but Whether They'd Die," *National Guardian*, Sept. 12, 1951, p. 5.

50. Ibid.; also, see "Not One Shred of Evidence Presented by U.S. to Back Its Charges," *National Guardian*, Sept. 19, 1951, p. 5.

51. Testament, p. 63.

52. William Reuben, "Did the Court Prejudice Jury Against Defendants?" *National Guardian*, Sept. 26, 1951, p. 5.

53. Ibid.

54. William Reuben, "Death Sentence 'Too Cruel and Too Horrible-Unprecedented and Illegal in the Bargain," *National Guardian*, Oct. 3, 1951, p. 5.

55. Ibid.

56. Ibid.

57. "The Letters of Ethel and Julius Rosenberg," *National Guardian*, Oct. 10, 1951, p. 3.

58. Ibid.

59. Reuben, interview.; see *National Guardian*, Oct. 17, 1951, p. 4. Reuben said a committee was being organized "in response to a flood of inquiries from all over America." In this issue, the *Guardian* continued its coverage of the Rosenbergs' correspondence. See: "Oh, How Indescribably Bitter It Is to Be Separated from One's Children-Yet I Must Curb My Longing.," Oct. 17, 1951, p. 4.

CHAPTER 8

1. "Doomed Atom Spies Lose in High Court," *Washington Post*, Oct. 14, 1952, p. 1.

2. "Court Dooms Rosenbergs: Urge Appeals to Truman," *Daily Worker*, Oct. 14, 1952, p. 1.

3. William Reuben, "A Christmas for Two Kids," *National Guardian*, Dec. 19, 1951 p. 2.

4. Ibid.

5. Meeropol and Meeropol, *We Are Your Sons*, p. 224f.

6. Reuben, interview.

7. Ibid.

8. David A. Shannon, *The Decline of American Communism: A History of the Communist Party Since 1945* (New York: Harcourt Brace and Co., 1959), p. 221.

9. "A Mother Writes from the Death House," *National Guardian*, Jan. 16, 1953, p. 3.

10. *National Guardian*, Jan. 16, 1952, p. 3.

11. Shannon, *The Decline of American Communism*, p. 221.

12. Reuben, interview.

13. Emily Arnow Alman, interview by author, Oct. 4, 1990.

14. "Rosenberg Case Rally Held [Despite] Cancelled Hall," *National Guardian*, Feb. 13, 1952, p. 1.

15. Ibid., p. 4.

16. Ibid.

17. "Spy Death Sentences: Rosenbergs Should Be Executed, Circuit Court of Appeals Rules," *San Francisco Chronicle*, Feb. 26, 1952, p. 4 (UP report).

18. "Rosenbergs' Guilt as A-Bomb Spies Upheld on Appeal," *New York Times*, Feb. 26 1952, p. 1.

19. Ibid., p. 14.

20. *Testament*, p. 86.

21. Ibid.

22. William Reuben, "Whole Population of U.S. Will Be Adversely Affected," *National Guardian*, March 5, 1952, p. 1.

23. Ibid.

24. Ibid.

25. "Court Upholds Death in Rosenberg Frameup," *Daily Worker*, Feb. 26, 1952, p. 1.

26. Radosh and Milton, *The Rosenberg File*, p. 328.

27. John Gates, letter to author, Dec. 9, 1990. Gates said that he "concluded they [the Rosenbergs] were guilty from the atmosphere in top circles of the communist party which reported the Rosenbergs as heroic, presumably because they went to their deaths without revealing their involvement in espionage. I felt that if they were in fact innocent, what was heroic about saying they were?"

28. Radosh and Milton, *The Rosenberg File*, p. 328; but Gordon said in letters to *In These Times* (Nov. 16-22, 1983) and *New York Review of Books* (Nov. 10, 1983) that he had no specific knowledge of the Rosenbergs' participation in spying.

29. *Testament*, p. 92.

30. Ibid., p. 92.

31. *Daily Worker*, April 29, 1952, p. 4. Here in its "Press Round-Up," the *Worker* complained that *New York Post* columnist Leo Lyons "writes gaily of the impending legal murder" of the Rosenbergs.

32. "Rosenbergs Get until June 7 to File Supreme Court Appeal," *Daily Worker*, May 5, 1952, p. 3.

33. "Rossenberg Letters Read at AS Preview," *Daily Worker*, May 7, 1952, p. 7.

34. Ibid.

35. See William L. O' Neill, *A Better World: The Great Schism: Stalinism and the American Intellectuals* (New York: Simon and Schuster, 1982.); John Earl Haynes, *Communism and anti-Semitism in the U.S.: An Annotated Guide to Historical Writings* (New York: Garland Publishing, 1987); Walter Goldwater, ed., *Radical Periodicals in America, 1890-1950: A Bibliography with Brief Notes* (New Haven: Yale University Press, 1966); Irving Howe and Lewis Coser, *The American Communist Party: A Critical History* (New York: Praeger, 1962); Theodore Draper, *Tke Roots of American*

Communism (New York: Viking Press, 1957); M. J. Heale, *American Anticommunism: Combatting the Enemy Within, 1830-1970* (Baltimore: Johns Hopkins University Press, 1990). For the memoir of a former party member during this period see Dorothy Healey and Maurice Isserman, *Dorothy Healey Remembers: A Life in the American Communist Party* (New York: Oxford University Press, 1990). For the autobiographies of three former members of the U.S. Communist Party who sometimes used the press as a means for revealing their "underground" lives in the party, see Elizabeth Bentley, *Out of Bondage* (New York: Devin-Adair, Cox, 1951); Whittaker Chambers, *Witness* (New York: Random House, 1952; Herbert Philbrick, *I Led Three Lives: Citizen, Communist, Counterspy* (New York: McGraw-Hill, 1952).

36. Robert Friedman, "Oliver Pilat Does His Bit for the Anti-Semitic Frameup of Rosenbergs," *Daily Worker*, May 30, 1952, p. 7. Meanwhile, William Reuben attacked Pilat for personally contacting "mainline" Jewish organizations to warn them that the Rosenberg Committee was a communnist front group. See "Behind the Attack on the Rosenberg Defense," *National Guardian*, May 22, 1952, p. 8.

37. Friedman, "Oliver Pilate Does His Bit."

38. Emily Alman, interview.

39. *Testament*, p. 93. The excerpt in this letter is dated May 25, 1952.

40. *Testament*, p. 96.

41. Max Lerner, "Vultures and Victims," *New York Post*, June 19, 1952, p. 22.

42. Ibid.

43. Ibid.

44. Ibid.

45. Michael Vary, "One Thousand at Overflow Brooklyn Rally Pledge Fight for Rosenbergs," *Daily Worker*, June 19, 1952, p. 3.

46. Ibid.

47. Quoted in Meeropol and Meeropol, *We Are Your Sons*, pp. 131-32.

48. Ibid., p. 132. Julius also said he had read Howard Rushmore's "loud braying" in the flagship Hearst newspaper, the *New York Journal-American*. Rushmore was a former communist and one of several Hearst writers who often wrote about communism. Julius Rosenberg said "he could tell" the *Journal-American* reporter was trying to retard the committee's newfound success.

49. See Aronson and Belfrage, *Something to Guard*, p. 112. Belfrage said that originally the names of POWs appeared in the *China Monthly Review*, which was published in Shanghai by U.S. citizen John W. Powell, Jr. He said Powell first sent "advance proofs of his lists" to U.S. news-media outlets but initially only the *Guardian* printed them.

50. Leon Summit, interview by author, Nov. 23, 1990.

51. *Testament*, p. 107. This letter was dated Oct. 2, 1952.

52. "High Court Rejects Atom Spies Appeal of Death Sentence," *New York Times*, Oct. 14, 1952, p. 1.

53. Lerner, "Vultures and Victims."

54. Chalmers Roberts, "Doomed Atom Spies Lose in High Court," *Washington Post*, Oct. 14, 1952, p. 1.

55. *New York Herald Tribune*, Oct. 14, 1952, p. 1.

56. "Top Court Paves 'Last Mile' For Rosenbergs," *Atlanta Constitution*, Oct. 14, 1952, p. 1 (AP report).

57. "Ethel and Julius Rosenberg Appeal from Death House," *Daily Worker*, Oct. 14, 1952, p. 1.

58. "They Must Not Die," *Daily Worker*, Oct. 15, 1952, p. 1.

59. Emily Alman, interview.

CHAPTER 9

1. Cedric Belfrage, letter to author, Oct. 30, 1988. Belfrage lived the final years of his life in Cuernavaca, Mexico, where he worked as an essayist, author, and literary translator. He died in July 1990.

2. Benjamin C. Bradlee, July 20, 1990, telephone interview by author.

3. "Samuel Sillen Assails Plot to Electrocute the Rosenbergs," *Daily Worker*, Oct. 16, 1952, p. 1.

4. "Zola's Fight in Dreyfus Case Can Inspire Fight to Save Rosenbergs," *Daily Worker*, Oct. 23, 1952, p. 7.

5. Ibid.

6. William Wolf, interview with author, Oct. 14, 1990.

7. Alman, interview .

8. See Meeropol and Meeropol, *We Are Your Sons*, pp. 156-57.

9. Ibid.

10. "Rosenberg Deaths Set for January," *New York Times*, Nov. 22, 1952, p. 7.

11. McCombs and Shaw, "Structuring the Unseen Environment," p. 18.

12. Bradlee, interview.

13. See Robert B. Glynn, "L´ Affaire Rosenberg in France," *Political Science Quarterly* 70 (December 1955): 498-521.

14. Ibid., p. 503.

15. Bradlee, interview.

16. Ibid.

17. The Fast article on the Rosenberg case appeared in *L'Humanite* on Nov. 14 1952; also, see Howard Fast, *On Being Red* (Boston: Houghton Mifflin Co., 1990), p. 278.

18. Fast, *On Being Red*, p. 278.

19. Ibid.

20. See Gans, *Deciding What's News*, pp. 190ff.

21. Bradlee, interview.

22. Ibid.

23. Glynn, "L' Affaire Rosenberg in France," p. 510.

24. Ibid.

25. Ibid.

26. Benjamin C. Bradlee, letter to author, March 7, 1991.

27. Ibid.

28. "Top Scientists Tear Holes in Greenglass's Trial Story," *National Guardian*, Nov. 27, 1952, p. 1.

29. Ibid., p. 4.

30. Ibid., p. 14.

31. "Thanksgiving, the Trenton Six, the Rosenbergs, You and Us," *National Guardian*, Nov. 27, 1952, p. 2.

32. Ibid.

33. Ibid.

34. Oliver Pilat, "The A-Spy Couple, Moscow 'Discovers' the Rosenbergs," *New York Post*, Dec. 1, 1952, p. 4.

35. Ibid.

36. "Spies and Speech," *New York Post*, Dec. 1, 1952, p. 25.

37. Wolf, interview.

38. Meeropol and Meeropol, *We Are Your Sons*, p. 161.

39. Ibid., p. 163.

40. Ibid.

41. Ibid., p. 164.

42. Ibid.

43. "Prague Hangs 11 as Plotters," *Baltimore Sun*, Dec. 4, 1952, p. 23. (AP report).

44. Ibid.

45. Glynn, "L`Affaire Rosenberg in France," p. 509.

46. "Letter from the Death House," *National Guardian*, Jan. 1, 1953.

47. Meeropol and Meeropol, *We Are Your Sons*, p. 161.

48. Schneir and Schneir, *Invitation to an Inquest*, pp. 228-29.

49. "They Lie about Prague Trials to Cover Anti-Jewish Acts Here," *Daily Worker*, Dec. 17, 1952, p. 4.

50. Ibid.

51. "James Aronson, The Facts on the Prague Treason Trials," *National Guardian*, Dec. 18, 1952, p. 3.

52. Ibid.

53. "A Holiday Wish from the Death House," *National Guardian*, Dec. 18, 1952, p. 1.

54. Bradlee, letter.

55. Ibid.

56. Bradlee, interview.

57. "One Thousand at Prison Wall Demand Clemency for the Rosenbergs," *Daily Worker*, Dec. 22, 1952, p. 1.

58. Ibid.

59. Ibid.

60. "Sing Sing Rally for Rosenbergs Balked," *New York Herald Tribune*, Dec. 22, 1952, p. 1.

61. "A Great Mound of Flowers Lined the Prison Wall," *Daily Worker*, Dec. 26, 1952, p. 2.

CHAPTER 10

1. See Proceeding Under Section 225, Title 28, U.S.C.-CR No. 134-245, FRC, exhibit 10, p. 3.

2. "Rosenbergs Move Step Closer to Chair," *New York Times*, Dec. 11, 1952, p. 26.

3. See Donald Gillmor, *Free Press and Fair Trial* (Washington, D.C.: Public Affairs Press, 1966); Alfred W. Friendly and Ronald Goldfarb, *Crime and Publicity: The Impact of News and the Adminstration of Justice* (New York Twentieth Century fund, 1967); Lofton, *Justice and the Press*.

4. John Stevens, *Sensationalism and the New York Press* (New York: Columbia University Press, 1991).

5. "Justice and Publicity,"*Chicago Tribune*, July 23,1924, p. 8.

6. Ibid.

7. Gillmor, *Free Press*, pp. 44-45.

8. Lofton, *Justice*, P. 122.

9. Gillmor, *Free Press*, p. 44; also, author interview with Gillmor, Oct. 5, 1990.

10. *Shepherd v. Florida*, 341 U.S. 50 (1951).

11. *Stroble v. California*, 243 U.S. 181 (1952).

12. *Dennis v. U.S.*, 341 U.S. 494 (1951).

13. *U.S. v. Dennis*, 183 F. 2d 201 (2d Cir., 1950).

14. For a record of Morton Sobell's separate appeal on these charges see U.S.C. 134-245, exhibit 14. Attorney Howard Meyer represented Sobell in his appeals.

15. For a record of Ryan's opinion see *U.S. v. Rosenberg,* 108 F. Supp. 798 (S.D.N.Y.).

16. *New York Times*, Dec. 11, 1952, p. 26.

17. "Rosenbergs Lose in Appeals Court," *New York Times*, Jan. 1, 1953, p. 11; *U.S. v. Rosenberg*, 200 F. 2d 666 (2d Cir., 1952).

18. *New York Times*, Jan. 11, 1953, p. 11.

19. See Meeropol and Meeropol, *We Are Your Sons,* p. 176.

20. *U.S. v. Rosenberg,* 200 F. 2d 666, 670 (2d Cir., 1952); "Rosenbergs Get Brief Stay; President Is the Last Hope," *National Guardian,* Jan 8, 1953, p. 1; "Court Admits Rosenbergs Had No Fair Trial, But OKs Doom," *Daily Worker,* Jan. 5, 1953, p. 1.

21. *New York Times, New York World-Telegram and Sun, New York Herald Tribune,* and *New York Post* for Jan. 1, 1953.

22. "Top Atom Scientist Urges Judge Kaufman to Grant Clemency to Rosenbergs," *Daily Worker,* Dec. 31, 1952, p. 1.

23. "Atomic Scientist Urey Voices 'Doubt' on Rosenberg Verdict," *National Guardian,* Jan. 1, 1953, p. 1.

24. Ibid.

25. See Glynn, "L' Affaire Rosenberg in France," p. 505.

26. Ibid.

27. "The Story of Two Spies; Communists Seek to Make Martyrs of the Rosenbergs, " *U.S. News and World Report,* Jan. 9, 1953, pp. 42-43.

28. Ibid., p. 43.

29. "Three Faith Leaders Hit A-Spy Plea," *New York Journal-American,* Jan. 5, 1953, p. 3. A joint statement was signed by former General Electric President Charles Wilson; Rev. Daniel A. Poling, editor of the *Christian Herald;* Rev. Joseph N. Moody of Cathedral College; Clarence E. Manion, former dean of Notre Dame Law School; and two well-known rabbis, Samuel Rosenman and William P. Rosenblum.

30. John Slawson's memorandum is available in the archives of the American Jewish Committee (AJC) Institute of Human Relations, New York City; parts of the memorandum are cited in Radosh and Milton, *The Rosenberg File,* pp. 353-55.

31. Slawson memorandum, AJC, July 31, 1950.

32. "Voice' Fights Red Agitation on Rosenbergs," *New York Herald Tribune,* Jan. 7, 1953, p. 3.

33. Ibid.

34. "Term Cut Refused Sobell, Atom Spy," *New York Times,* Jan. 10, 1953, p. 4.

35. Ibid.

36. "Stay of Execution Given Rosenbergs," *New York Times,* Jan. 6, 1953, p. 1.

37. Ibid.

38. "Tell the President Today to Spare Their Lives," *National Guardian,* Jan. 8, 1953, p. 2.

39. Ibid.

40. "You and the Rosenberg Case," *Daily Worker,* Jan. 7, 1953, p. 5.

41. Lauren Kessler, *The Dissident Press,* p. 113.

42. "Pickets Keep Up Rosenberg Pleas," *New York Times*, Dec. 29, 1952, p. 8 (UP report).

43. "Rosenbergs Agree on Plea to Truman," *New York Times*, Jan. 7, 1953, p. 3.

44. "Democratic Germany's Plea," *Daily Worker*, Jan. 8, 1953, p. 5.

45. Ibid.

46. See Victor Navasky, *Naming Names* (New York: Viking, 1980).

47. Emily Alman, interview.

48. Frederick Woltman, "Rosenberg Atomic Spy Plot Stretches Back Over Years," *New York World-Telegram and Sun*, Jan. 10, 1953, p. 2.

49. George Sokolsky, "About Rosenberg Plea for Clemency," *New York Journal-American*, Jan. 9, 1953, p. 20.

50. Henry R. Luce, *The American Century* (New York: Farrar and Rinehart, 1941); James Baughman, *Henry R. Luce and the Rise of the American News Media* (Boston: Twayne, 1987); John Kobler, *Luce: His Time, Life, and Fortune* (New York: Doubleday and Co., 1968); W. A. Swanberg, *Luce and His Empire* (New York: Charles Scribner's Sons, 1972).

51. Bob Considine, "The Inside Story of Two A-Spies," *New York Journal-American*, Jan. 11, 1953, p. 1. (Considine's series was distributed through the International News Service.

52. Ibid.

53. James Daniel, "Why Did the Rosenbergs Betray Our Country?" *New York World-Telegram and Sun*, Jan. 14, 1953, p. 1; "Mrs. Rosenberg Was like a Red Spider," *New York World-Telegram and Sun*, Jan. 15, 1953, p. 18; "Anti-Semitic Cry a Lie in Case of Rosenbergs," *New York World-Telegram and Sun*, Jan. 16, 1953, p. 26.

54. Bob Considine, "Rosenbergs Worked Hard to Become Red A-Spies," *New York Journal-American*, Jan. 12, 1953, p. 5; for the remaining articles in this series see "Rosenbergs' Kin Was Spy," Jan. 13, p. 13; "How Rosenbergs Planned to Flee," Jan. 14, 1953, p. 12; "Fallacies in Red Spy Pleas," Jan. 15, 1953, p. 4; "Judge Put Duty above Feelings," Jan. 16, 1953, p. 17.

55. Considine, "The Inside Story."

56. Meeropol and Meeropol, *We Are Your Sons*, p. 179.

57. Ibid.

58. Ibid., p. 180.

59. Ibid.

60. Ibid.

61. "Einstein Supports Rosenberg Appeal," *New York Times*, Jan. 13, 1953, p. 5.

62. "State Department Blasts Soviet Arrest of MD's," *New York Journal-American*, Jan. 13, 1953, p. 9. (INS report).

63. "Reds Purging Jewish MD's," *Journal-American*, Jan. 13, 1953., p. 1.

64. Ibid.

65. Ibid.

66. Wolf, interview.

67. Ibid.

68. This CIA memorandum appears in the "Kaufman Papers," see *Hearings*, the "Death Penalty," pp. 2, 327ff.

69. Ibid., p. 2, 328.

70. "Payment Deferred," *Newsweek*, Jan. 26, 1953, p. 42.

71. "Le Monde Justice," *Washington Post*, Jan. 23, 1953, p. 20. The *National Guardian* featured a translation of Pierre's earlier *Le Monde* column. See "Atomic Age Drama; the Rosenberg Case," *National Guardian*, Dec. 25, 1952, p. 5.

72. "*Le Monde* Justice."

73. Bradlee, interview

74. "*Le Monde* Justice."

75. "Befogged Issue," *Chicago Daily News*, Jan 22, 1953, p. 12.

76. Ibid.

CHAPTER 11

1. The letter was hand delivered to Sherman Adams, then assistant to President Eisenhower. The incident is recounted in "The Vatican and the Rosenberg Case," papers of the National Committee to Secure Justice in the Rosenberg Case, SHSW. This pamphlet features a partial reprint of Pope Pius XII's plea for the Rosenbergs in the Feb. 13, 1953 issue of *L'Osservatore Romano*.

2. FBI file, (JR), Memorandum, SAC New York City to HQ. File no: 65-15348, ser: 2188, Feb. 19, 1953.

3. Robert J. Donovan, "Pleas by Pope Made in '52 for Rosenbergs," *New York Herald Tribune*, Feb. 14, 1953, p. 1.

4. Ibid.

5. Ibid.

6. Ibid.

7. "Pope Made No Plea to Aid Rosenbergs," *New York Times*, Feb. 15, 1953, p. 24.

8. "Brownell Urged Ike to Spare Rosenbergs," *National Guardian*, Feb. 15, 1953, p. 1; also, see Nancy L. Roberts, *Dorothy Day and the Catholic Worker* (Albany: State University of New York Press, 1984), p. 142f; "Meditation on the Death of the Rosenbergs" from the *Catholic Worker*, July-

Aug. 1953 in *By Little and By Little; The Selected Writings of Dorothy Day*, Robert Ellsberg, ed. (New York: Knopf, 1983).

9. "Rosenbergs Preparing New Appeal; Lawyers Base Plea on Unfair Trial," *New York Post*, Feb. 18, 1953, p. 5.

10. "Rosenbergs Get New Death Stay for Last Plea to Supreme court," *New York Herald Tribune*, Feb. 18, 1953, p. 6.

11. *Herald Tribune*, Feb. 18, 1953, p. 1.

12. "We are Innocent-We Swear It," *National Guardian*, Feb. 19, 1953, p. 3; Robert Meeropol was too young at the time to read newspapers or remember the role the news media played in his parent's case. Since then, he has concluded that the U.S. news media was reluctant to provide coverage of he and his brother, more out of "fear of evoking sympathy for my parents than out of respect for our privacy." Meeropol says he was told that after 1954 President Eisenhower "played an active role in ensuring that no stories were published about us, and I believe that his motives were essentially good." Letter from Robert Meeropol to author, May 27, 1992.

13. "Rosenbergs Used in Hate U.S. Drive," *New York Times*, Feb. 18, 1953, p. 1.

14. *New York Times*, Feb. 17, 1953, p. 1.

15. Author interview with William Wolf, Oct. 14, 1990.

16. Ibid.

17. Author interview with Emily Alman, Oct. 4, 1990.

18. *New York Times*, Feb. 18, 1953, p. 1.

19. Interview with Emily Alman, Oct. 4, 1990.

20. *New York Times*, Feb. 17, 1953, p. 19.

21. *New York Post*, Feb. 19, 1953, p. 40. This rumor was reported in Lyons's column "The Lyons Den." Lyons also reported that Ethel Greenglass Rosenberg's mother, Tessie Greenglass, had visited her at Sing-Sing. Lyons claimed the elder Greenglass tried to convince her daughter to confess.

22. *Death House Letters*, p. 138.

23. Ibid. For an FBI summary of the broadcast see: FBI memo, (JR), File no: 62-31615, ser. 765, Feb. 24, 1953, p. 3.

24. *Death House Letters*, p. 139.

25. See Walter Schneir and Miriam Schneir, *Invitation to an Inquest*, pp. 278-9.

26. Ibid.

27. Author interview with Leon Summit, Nov. 23, 1990.

28. Ibid.

29. *Death House Letters*, p. 140.

30. Ibid.

31. "Did Ike Offer Rosenbergs Barbarous Deal?" *National Guardian*, March 16, 1953, p. 1.

32. *National Guardian*, March 16, 1953, p. 1.

33. *Death House Letters*, p. 140.

34. Author interview with George S. Trow, April 13, 1991.

35. Author interview with Russell Baker, April 24, 1991.

36. Ibid.

37. Ibid.

38. Summit, interview.

39. Ibid.

40. Ibid.

41. Ibid.

42. "The Missing Table: The Proof that Rosenberg Case Witnesses Lied," *National Guardian*, April 13, 1953, p. 4.

43. Ibid.

44. Ibid.

45. Ibid

46. "High Court Defers Rosenberg Decision," *National Guardian*, April 20, 1953, p. 4.

47. Meeropol and Meeropol, *We are Your Sons*, p. 194.

48. Walter Lippmann, *Public Opinion* (New York: Free Press, 1922), p. 53.

CHAPTER 12

1. "L' Affaire Rosenberg," *Le Monde*, April 19-20, 1953, p. 2; Schneir and Schneir, *Invitation to an Inquest*, p. 196.

2. "Keep Pressing Legal moves in U.S. Court Here," *New York Daily News*, June 6, 1953.

3. Glynn, "L' Affaire Rosenberg in France," p. 513.

4. See "New Evidence in the Rosenberg Case," Records of the National Committee to Secure Justice in the Sobell Case, SHSW, p. 9.

5. *Le Monde*, April 19-20, 1953, p. 2. (This refers to Greenglass's alleged inability to recall who sent spy courier Harry Gold to his home in New Mexico in 1945).

6. For example, surviving Rosenberg Committee members Emily Arnow Alman and William Wolf both say they do not know how the Rogge documents got to France. Emily Alman, interview; Wolf, interview.

7. "New Rosenberg Proof Is Heard by 10,000," *National Guardian*, May 11, 1953, p. 6. Nevertheless, authors Radosh and Milton discovered in their research of O. John Rogge's files that page 2 of the memorandum was omitted from published reports in *Le Combat* and the *National Guardian*. They contend that the missing page contained a statement by David Greenglass that he had received "nearly $5,000 from Julius Rosenberg." *The Rosenberg File*, p. 368.

8. *National Guardian*, May 11, 1953, p. 6.

9. Ibid.

10. *New York Times*, May 4, 1953, p. 7; the May 4 edition of the *New York Herald Tribune* did report on the Randall Island rally but did not discuss the stolen memoranda or the console table. A Rosenberg Committee press release dated May 13, 1953, says the *New York World-Telegram and Sun* reported that O. John Rogge had "confirmed the existence" of the memoranda, Sobell Committee records, Reel 13, p. 0184. Nevertheless, Judge Kaufman was apprised of the status of the memoranda and what was reported about them in the press. See FBI file, JR, memorandum to HQ, C. E. Hennrich to A. H. Belmont, file. 1641, ser. indecipherable, May 13. 1953.

11. *National Guardian*, May 11, 1953, p. 2.

12. "Robbins, Creator of Broadway Dance Hits, Tells He Was a Red Party Member," *Washington Post*, May 6, 1953, p. 7.

13. "Robins, Showman, Admits He Was a Red, " *New York Times*, May 6, 1953, p. 31.

14. "Robbins . . . Tells;" "Threat to Deport Belfrage Made by Velde Inquisitor," *National Guardian*, May 11, 1953, p. 1; also see Walter Goodman, *The Committee: The Extraordinary Career of the House Committee on Un-American Activities* (New York: Farrar, Straus, and Giroux, 1968), pp. 244ff.

15. Murray Mardner, "McCarthy in Press Probe Demands Names of all Reds who 'Infiltrated' News Media," *Washington Post*, May 7, 1953, p. 7; also, see Paul L. Murphy, *The Constitution in Crisis Times: 1918-1969* (New York: Harper and Row, 1972), pp. 216-17; Michael R. Belknap, *Cold War Political Justice: The Smith Act, the Communist Party, and American Civil Liberties* (Westport, Ct.: Greenwood Press, 1977), p. 37.

16. Ibid.

17. See Bayley, *Joseph McCarthy*, pp. 61-65; Thomas C. Reeves, *The Life and Times of Joe McCarthy: A Biography* (New York: Free Press, 1982); David Oshinsky, *A Conspiracy So Immense: The World of Joe McCarthy* (New York: Free Press, 1983), p. 109; for an interpretive history of the early cold war and the U.S. press see Louis Liebovich, *The Press and the Origins of the Cold War, 1944-47* (New York: Praeger, 1988).

18. "Clash of McCarthy, Wechsler Is Bared," *New York Times*, May 8, 1953, p.; "Wechsler, Editor, Quizzed by McCarthy," *New York World-Telegram and Sun*, April 25, 1953, p. 2; also, see Richard Fried, *Nighmare in Red: The McCarthy Era in Perspective* (New York: Oxford University Press, 1990).

19. "Campaign Against Press: Wechsler Case Leaves No Doubts," *Washington Post*, May 9, 1953, p. 11.

20. David Caute, *The Great Fear: The Anti-Communist Purge Under Truman and Eisenhower (*New York: Simon and Schuster, 1977*)*, pp. 140-51.

21. "Two Editors Balk Inquiry on Reds," *New York Times*, May 15, 1953, p. 4.

22. Ibid.

23. Ibid.

24. "McCarthy Taps *National Guardian* Editors; Renews Deportation Threats, " *National Guardian*, May 18, 1953, p. 1.

25. See Belfrage and Aronson, *Something to Guard*, p. 164.

26. "Fight to Free Belfrage Ellis Island-Arrest Riles Britain, U.S. Press Silent," *National Guardian*, May 25, 1953, p 1.

27. Ibid.

28. Radosh and Milton, *The Rosenberg File*, p. 367.

29. Ibid., p. 5.

30. Ibid.

31. "Rosenbergs Lose 3rd Plea to High Court," *Washington Post*, May 26, 1953, p. 1; "Rosenbergs Lose Appeal for 3rd Time by Supreme Court," *New York Times*, May 26, 1953, p. 1.

32. "Rosenbergs Lose Appeal."

33. Ibid.

34. Ibid.

35. Irwin Edelman, "Freedom's Electrocution," November 1952, SHSW, Sobell collection; for the same author in the same collection see "There Is a Third Side to the Rosenberg Case," and "The Suppressed Facts in the Rosenberg Case,"

36. See Radosh and Milton, *The Rosenberg File*, pp. 383, 563n.

37. Ibid., pp. 383ff.

38. "Rosenberg Fight Goes on Despite 3rd Court Blow," *National Guardian*, June 1, 1953, p. 1.

39. Bradlee, interview. Also, see U.S. Ambassador C. Doluglas Dillon to U.S. Secretary of State John Foster Dulles, May 15, 1953. Ann Whitman File, Dwight D. Eisenhower Presidential Library, Abilene, Kan.

40. "Rosenbergs Spurn Brownell Offer of Life for Lies," *National Guardian*, June 8, 1953, p. 1; "Execution Set, A-Spies Shun Mercy Offer," *Chicago Tribune*, June 3, 1953, p. 1 (AP report).

41. "Rosenbergs Spurn Brownell Offer;" "William Z. Foster Defends the Rosenbergs," *Daily Worker*, June 8, 1953, p. 1.

42. "Rosenbergs Spurn Brownell Offer."

43. "Dulles Moving in Oatis Case," *Albuquerque Tribune*, March 13, 1953, p. 4 (Scripps-Howard Service); "Oatis 'Recited' His Confession in Court," *San Francisco Chronicle*, May 18, 1953, p. 1 (AP report).

44. "Rosenbergs Spurn Brownell Offer," p. 4. The first paragraph of Michael Rosenberg's letter reads: "I saw on t.v. Monday Mr. Oatis is not in prison anymore because the President of the country let him go. It said his wife wrote a letter to the President over there and she told him why Mr: Oatis

should be let go. I think it is a good thing to let him go because I think prison is a bad place for anybody to be."

45. Ibid., p. 1.

46. Ibid.

47. Ibid.

48. Emily Alman, interview. A more likely explanation is that Bloch thought the chances of getting a new trial remote. Also, as Radosh and Milton explain, Bloch was embarrassed by the Rogge memoranda theft because Bloch and Rogge shared office space in the same building. Bloch, of course, was suspected by Rogge and his law partners of having had a connection to the theft.

49. "Dr. Urey Meets the Press," *National Guardian*, July 7, 1953, p. 6.

50. "Rosenbergs Renew Prejudice Review Plea," *Atlanta Constitution*, June 10, 1953, p. 5. "Rosenberg Ruling Due Tommorow," *New York Times*, June 14, 1953, p. 1. See "A-Spies Claim New Evidence, Ask New Trial," *New York Post*, June 7, 1953, p. 5. However, in a "local" sample of four New York City newspapers, the *New York Post* did report and explain the significance of the console table.

51. "Belfrage Free on Bail," *New York Herald Tribune*, June 12, 1953, p. 5.

52. "Fourth Plea to Supreme Court," *St. Louis Post-Dispatch*, June 9, 1953, p. 7 (UP report); "Rosenbergs Lose Appeal," *New York Herald Tribune*, June 12, 1952, p. 6.

53. Meeropol and Meeropoll *We Are Your Sons*, p. 220.

54. "Pickets for Rosenbergs Encircle White House," *New York Herald Tribune*, June 15, 1953, p. 1.

55. "Seven Thousand in Capitol March for Spies," *New York Times*, June 15, 1953, p. 44.

56. *New York Herald Tribune*, June 15, 1953, p. 1.

57. "11th Hour Fight For Rosenbergs," *National Guardian*, June 15, 1953, p. 1.

58. "Two Excellent Report Cards at Sing Sing . . . and Tears," *Daily Worker*, June 17, 1953, p. 1.

59. "Rosenbergs See 2 Sons for Possibly Last Time," *New York World-Telegram and Sun*, June 16, 1953, p. 2.

60. Ibid.

61. "High Court Denies a Rosenberg Stay; New Plea Today, " *New York Times*, June 16, 1953, p. 1.

62. Ibid.

63. Ibid.

64. Ibid.

65. "Ruling by Douglas in Rosenberg Case Delayed Today," *New York Times*, June 17, 1953, p. 1.

66. Ibid.
67. Ibid.
68. "Douglas Set Spy Ruling for Today," *Washington Post*, June 17, 1953, p. 1. For a fuller development of Justice Douglas's role in the Rosenberg decision see Michael Parrish, "Cold War Justice: The Supreme Court and the Rosenbergs," *American Historical Review* 82 (October 1977); 822-24; James Simon, *Independent Journey: The Life of William O. Douglas* (New York: Harper and Row, 1980), pp. 312-13; G. Edward White, *The American Judicial Tradition Profiles of Leading American Judges* (New York: Oxford University Press, 1988), pp. 390-403.
69. "Supreme Court Meets on Plans by U.S. to Vacate Rosenberg Stay," *St. Louis Post-Dispatch*, June 18, 1953, p. 6.
70. FBI file, JR HQ memorandum, A. H. Belmont to D. M. Ladd, File no. indecipherable, ser. 1880, June 16, 1953.
71. Ibid.
72. Ibid.
73. Ibid.
74. Ibid.

CHAPTER 13

1. *New York Post*, June 19, 1953, p. 3.
2. *New York Times*, June 18, 1953, p. 16.
3. Joseph Sharlitt, *Fatal Error: The Miscarriage of Justice that Sealed the Rosenbergs' Fate* (New York Charles Scribners' Sons, 1989), pp. 66-67; seven months after the executions, the *Columbia Law Review* said the Rosenbergs did not receive a full measure of justice. The article pointed to the tumultuous political climate at the time of their trial. "The tremendous significance of the Rosenberg case lay in the fact that defendants were communists and were tried at a time when Soviet Communism poses probably the most serious challenge the American Republic has ever known." The *Review* concluded that the political backgrounds of the three were relevant "as motive for the crime charged." Also in 1954, the *Northwestern University Law Review* questioned whether the Supreme Court erred in permitting the Rosenberg executions under the 1917 Espionage Act. The same year Norman J. Beier and Leonard B. Sand, former law clerks of Irving Kaufman, published an *American Bar Association Journal* article on the publicity tactics of Rosenberg defenders. See "The Rosenberg Case: Some Reflections on Federal Criminal Law," *Columbia Law Review* 54 (February 1954): 220-60; "The Rosenberg Case: A Problem of Statutory Construction," *Northwestern University Law Review* 48 (1954): 751-59; Norman S. Beier and Leonard B. Sand, "The Rosenberg Case: History and Hysteria," *American Bar Association Journal* 40 (December 1954): 1046-50.

4. *San Francisco Chronicle*, June 19, 1953, p. 1.

5. "Win Stay; Court Meets as D. of J. Demands Death," *Daily Worker*, June 18, 1953, p. 1.

6. *New York Daily News*, June 19, 1953, p. 16.

7. *St. Louis Post-Dispatch*, June 18, 1953, p. 1. Stern said that to apply the 1946 Atomic Energy Act to the Rosenberg-Sobell case would have been unconstitutional. He also complained that the latest appeal was a stalling tactic.

8. *New York Times*, June 19, 1953, p. 1.

9. Ibid.

10. *St. Louis Post-Dispatch*, June 18, 1953, p. 6.

11. *New York Times*, June 19, p. 1.

12. "Hushed Courtroom Hears Fate of Rosenbergs Argued," *Oregonian*, June 19, 1953, p. 13 (AP report). However, in a contradictory and evidently hypocritical gesture, Justice Jackson later told Marshall he was "all for you."

13. *St. Louis Post-Dispatch*, June 18, 1953, p. 6.

14. *New York Times*, June 19, 1953, p. 1.

15. Radosh and Milton, *The Rosenberg File*, pp. 406-07.

16. "Rosenbergs Are Executed; Rosenberg Dies First, Both Silent," *New York Herald Tribune*, June 20, 1953, p. 1.

17. Ibid., p. 4.

18. *New York Daily News*, June 19, 1953, p. 6. The lawyer from Kansas was R. Roland Ritchie, who practiced law in Wichita. His request was summarily denied by Judge Sylvester Ryan. A second motion was filed for Manny Bloch by New York attorney Arthur Kinoy. This motion essentially brought the Farmer-Marhsall argument back down to the district court level.

19. "Kaufman Rejects 11th Hour Appeal," *New York Times*, June 20, 1953, p. 6.

20. Ibid.

21. "Text of Mrs. Rosenberg's Letter," *Washington Post*, June 20, 1953, p. 3.

22. "Kafuman Turns Down Appeal at Final Hour," *New York Herald Tribune*, June 20, 1953, p. 5.

23. *Daily Worker*, June 22, 1953, p. 2.

24. "Kaufman Rejects 11th Hour Appeal."

25. "Rosenbergs Are Executed," p. 1.

26. Ibid.

27. William R. Conklin, "Rosenbergs Executed as Atom Spies After Supreme Court Vacates Stay," *New York Times*, June 20, 1953, p. 1.

28. "Rosenbergs Are Excited as Spies for Russia, Each Seems Calm, Neither Talks," *St. Louis Post-Dispatch*, June 20, 1953, p. 1.

29. "Kaufman Turns Down Appeal," p. 5.

30. "One Shot, 400 Jailed in Paris," *New York Times*, June 20, 1953, p. 8.

31. "Parisian Is Shot at Protest Rally," *Baltimore Sun*, June 20, 1953, p. 1; "Reds Hail Rosenbergs Abroad," *New York Herald Tribune*, June 21, 1953, p. 15.

32. Baker, interview.

33. *Baltimore Sun*, June 20, 1953, p. 5.

34. "And in a Jersey Town Little Boys Played; Older, 10, Shields Brother from Bad News," *New York Daily News*, June 20, 1953, p. 3.

35. "The Boys . . . the Families," *New York Post*, June 21, 1953, p. 11-M.

36. Max Lerner, "The Last Long Day," *New York Post*, June 21, 1953, p. 8-M.

37. Ralph McGill, "Many a Poor Devil Waiting," *Atlanta Constitution*, June 20, 1953, p. 1.

38. "The Rosenbergs and Their Crimes," *Detroit News*, June 20, 1953, p. 4.

39. "From the Highest Court," *Minneapolis Tribune*, June 20, 1953, p. 4.

40. "Contrast," *Baltimore Sun*, June 20, 1953, p. 10.

41. "The Last Appeal," *Time*, June 29, 1953, p. 10. The name of the East German man shot for insurrection was Willi Göettling.

42. "It Could Never Happen in Russia-How Law Protected Rights of Rosenbergs," *U.S. News and World Report*, June 26, 1953, p. 32.

43. Glynn, "L' Affaire Rosenberg in France, " p. 518.

44. Ibid.

45. "The Animals Sick with Rabies-a European Looks at America," *National Guardian*, July 6, 1953, p. 1. Sartre's article first appeared in the June 20, 1953, issue of *Libération*.

46. "A-Spies Killed by 'FBI Thugs' Says Red Press," *Chicago Tribune*, June 21, 1953, p. 5.

47. "June 19, 1953," *National Guardian*, June 22, 1953, p. 3.

48. *Daily Worker*, June 20, 1953, p. 1.

49. *Chicago Tribune*, June 21, 1953, p. 5.

50. "U.S. Assailed at Rites for Rosenbergs," *San Francisco Chronicle*, June 22, 1953, p. 1.

51. Ibid.

52. "Rosenbergs Eulogized as Martyrs at Funeral," *New York Herald Tribune*, June 22, 1953, p. 3.

53. Emanuel Bloch, "The Guardian and the Rosenbergs," *National Guardian*, June 29, 1953, p. 10. For the subject of press "black outs" in the United States in the 1960s and 1970s see Bagdikian, *The Effete Conspiracy*, pp. 40ff.

54. James Aronson, "The Rotten Role of the U.S. Press," *National Guardian*, June 29, 1953, p. 4.

55. Ibid.

56. Ibid.

57. Ibid.

58. Ibid.

EPILOGUE

1. "The Last Letters of Ethel and Julius Rosenberg," *National Guardian*, July 13, 1953, p. 1.

2. Roland Sawyer, "Spy Case Puts Focus on Aims," *Christian Science Monitor*, June 20, 1953, p. 1.

3. "Court Asked to Discipline Attorney for Rosenbergs," *New York Herald Tribune*, Jan. 20, 1954, p. 7; "Act to Disbar Bloch," National Guardian, Jan. 25, 1954, p. 1.

4. "A-Spies' Attorney Found in Home," *New York Post*, Jan, 31, 1954, p. 1.

5. "Rosenberg Sons Aided," *New York Times*, Sept. 23, 1953, p. 23; "Plea for Rosenberg Boys," *New York Times*, Dec. 22, 1953, p. 24.

6. "Rosenberg Boys Moved," *New York Times*, Jan. 7, 1954, p. 32; "Rosenberg Children Seized," *National Guardian*, Feb. 22, 1953, p. 8; "Rosenberg Mother Gets Children," *New York Herald Tribune*, April 16, 1954, p. 3.

7. For information on the government investigation of the U.S. Rosenberg Committee see U.S. House Committee on Un-American Activities, *Investigation of Communist Activities* (the Committee to Secure Justice in the Rosenberg Case and affiliates), 84th Cong., 1st sess., 1955; also; see "A Request to the Judiciary Committee to Investigate the conduct of the U.S. Attorney General's Office in the Rosenberg-Sobell Case." Submitted by the National Rosenberg-Sobell Committee, Bruxelles: International Association of Democratic Lawyers, 1954. For news stories regarding David Greenglass's life in prison see *Washington Evening Star*, Nov. 24, 1953, p. 1; *New York Mirror*, June 8, 1954, p. 4.

8. Ruth Printz Greenglass to U.S. Parole Board, Bureau of Prisons, Notorious File, David Greenglass. This letter is available at the National Archives, Washington, D.C.

9. "Lane Reveals Spies Gave 'Moon' Data to Reds," *New York Herald Tribune*, Oct. 13, 1957, p. 26; "U.S. May Reopen Spy Claim Hunt," *Chicago Tribune*, Oct. 18, 1957, p. 1; "Rosenberg Cited as Missile Spy," *New York Times*, Nov. 22, 1957, p. 9 (UP report).

10. "Return of the Traitor," *Time*, July 6, 1959, p. 20.

11. "Greenglass Asks Only to Be Forgottten," *New York Post*, Nov. 16, 1960, p. 4.

12. "Two Spies Freed after 17 Years in Prison as Spy for Russians," *Baltimore Sun*, Jan. 15, 1969, p. 1.

13. Wolf, interview.

14. Cohen, *The Press and Foreign Policy*, p. 13.

15. *Hearings*.

16. Tuchman, *Making News*, p. 49; Gitlin, *The Whole World Is Watching*, p. 7.; Doris Graber, *Mass Media and American Politics*, 3rd ed., (Washington D.C.: Congressional Quarterly, 1989), p. 323; Warren Breed, "Mass Communication and Socio-Cultural Integration," *Social Forces* (1958) 37; also, see Daniel Yergin, *Shattered Peace: The Origins of the Cold War and the National Security State* (Boston: Houghton Mifflin Co., 1977).

17. Brigitte Lebens Nacos, *The Press, Presidents, and Crises* (New York: Columbia University Press, 1990), p. 2; Marion Tuttle Marzolf, *Civilized Voices: American Press Criticism, 1880-1950* (New York: Longman, 1991). Marzolf devotes a chapter to the Hutchins Commission's Report: "Press Responsibility Confronted, 1942-50," pp. 163-64.

18. "Frankfurter Belatedly Adds Footnote to A-Spy Dissent," *New York Times*, June 23, 1953, p. 9.

Select Bibliography

BOOKS

Aaron, Daniel, ed. *Writers on the Left.* New York: Harcourt, Brace and World.

Ambrose, Stephen E. *Eisenhower: The President*, vol. 2. New York: Harper and Row, 1972.

Armstrong, David. *A Trumpet to Arms: Alternative Media in America.* Boston: South End Press, 1981.

Aronson, James. *The Press and the Cold War.* Indianapolis: Bobbs-Merrill, 1970.

Babbie, Earl. *Research Methods in the Social Sciences.* Belmont, Calif: Wadsworth, 1980.

Bagdikian, Ben. *The Effete Conspiracy and Other Crimes of the Press.* New York: Harper and Row, 1972.

Bagdikian, Ben. *The Media Monopoly*, Boston: Beacon Press, 1983.

Baughman, James. *Henry R. Luce and the Rise of the American Century.* Boston: Twayne, 1987.

Bayley, Edwin R. *Joe McCarthy and the Press.* Madison: University of Wisconsin Press, 1981.

Belfrage, Cedric. *The American Inquisition, 1945-60.* New York: Columbia University Press, 1973.

Belfrage, Cedric and James Aronson. *Something to Guard: The Stormy Life of the National Guardian.* New York: Columbia University Press, 1973.

Bentley, Elizabeth. *Out of Bondage.* New York: Devin-Adair Co., 1951.

Blum, John Morton. *V was for Victory: Politics and American Culture During World War II.* New York: Harcourt Brace Jovanovich, 1976.

Bredin, Jean-Denis. *The Affair: The Case of Alfred Dreyfus.* New York: George Braziller, 1986.

Brooks, John. *The Great Leap: The Past Twenty-Five Years in America.* New York: Harper and Row, 1966.

Byrnes, Robert R. *Anti-Semitism in Modern France: The Prologue to the Dreyfus Affair*, vol. I. New Brunswick, N.J.: Rutgers University Press, 1950.

Carol, Peter N. and David W. Noble. *Twentieth Century Limited.* Boston: Houghton Mifflin Co., 1980.

Carter, Dan T. *Scottsboro: A Tragedy of the American South.* Baton Rouge: L.A.: Louisiana State University Press, 1969.

Chambers, Whittaker. *Witness.* New York: Random House, 1952.

Cohen, Bernard C. *The Press and Foreign Policy.* Princeton: Princeton University Press, 1963.

Conlin, Joseph. ed. *The American Radical Press*, vol. 2. Westport, Ct.: Greenwood Press, 1974.

Conrad, Earl and Haywood Patterson, *Scottsboro Boys.* Garden City, N.Y.: Doubleday and Co., 1950.

Cook, Fred J. *The FBI Nobody Knows.* New York: Macmillan Co., 1964.

Curti, Merle. *The Roots of American Loyalty.* New York: Columbia University Press, 1946.

Dallin, David J. *Soviet Espionage.* New Haven: Yale University Press, 1955.

Death House Letters of Ethel and Julius Rosenberg. New York: Jero Publishing Co., 1953.

Degler, Carl M. *Affluence and Anxiety: 1945-Present.* Glencoe, Il.: Scott Foresman and Co., 1968.

Demaris, Ovid. *An Oral History of J. Edgar Hoover.* New York: Harper Magazine Press, 1975.

DeToledano, Ralph. *The Greatest Plot in History.* New York: Duell, Sloan and Pearce, 1963.

Donner, Frank J. *The Age of Surveillance: The Aims and Methods of America's Political Intelligence System.* New York: Alfred A. Knopf, 1980.

Donovan, Robert J. *The Tumultuous Years: The Presidency of Harry S Truman, 1949-1953.* New York: W.W. Norton and Co., 1982.

Dos Passos, John. *The Best of Times: An Informal Memoir.* New York: New American Library, 1966.

Draper, Theodore. *The Roots of American Communism.* New York: Viking Press, 1957.

Emery, Edwin and Michael Emery. *The Press and America: An Interpretive History of the Mass Media.* Englewood Cliffs, N.J.: Prentice Hall, 1988.

Fast, Howard. *On Being Red.* Boston: Houghton Mifflin, 1990.

Fineberg, S. Andhill. *The Rosenberg Case: Fact and Fiction.* New York: Oceana Publication, 1953.

Frankfurter, Felix. *The Case of Sacco and Vanzetti: A Critical Analysis for Lawyers and Laymen*. Boston: Little, Brown and Co., 1929.

Fried, Richard. *Nightmare in Red: The.McCarthy Era in Perspective*. New York: Oxford University Press, 1990.

Friendly, Alfred, and Ronald Goldfarb. *Crime and Publicity: The Impact of News and the Administration of Justice*. New York: Twentieth Century Fund, 1967.

Gans, Herbert J. *Deciding What's News: A Study of CBS Evening News, NBC Nightly News, "Newsweek" and "Time."* New York: Pantheon, 1979.

Gardner, Virginia. *The Rosenberg Story*. New York: Masses and Mainstream, 1954.

Garrow, David. *The FBI and Martin Luther King, Jr.* New York: W. W. Norton and Co., 1981.

Gentry, Curt J. *J. Edgar Hoover: The Man and His Secrets*. New York: W. W. Norton, 1991.

Gillmor, Donald. *Free Press and Fair Trial*. Washington D.C.: Public Affairs Press, 1966.

Gitlin, Todd. *The Whole World Is Watching: Mass Media in the Making and Unmaking of the New Left*. Berkeley: University of California Press, 1980.

Goldman, Eric F. *The Crucial Decade and After: America, 1945-60*. New York: Vintage Books, 1960.

Goldwater, Walter. ed. *Radical Periodicals in America, 1890-1950: A Bibliography with Brief Notes*. New Haven: Yale University Press, 1966.

Goodman, Walter. *The Committee: The Extraordinary Career of the House Committee on Un-American Activities*. New York: Farrar Straus and Giroux, 1968.

Graber, Doris. *Mass Media and American Politics*, 3rd ed., Washington, D.C.: Congressional Quarterly, 1989.

Hallin, Daniel, *The Uncensored War: The Media and Vietnam*. New York: Oxford University Press, 1986.

Hastings, Max. *The Korean War*. New York: Simon and Schuster, 1987.

Haynes, John Earl. *Communism and Anti-Semitism in the U.S.: an Annotated Guide to Historical Writings*. New York: Garlalnd Publishing, 1987.

Heale, M .J. *American Anti-Communism: Combatting the Enemy Within, 1830-1970*. Baltimore: Johns Hopkins University Press, 1990.

Healy, Dorothy and Maurice Isserman. *Dorothy Healy Remembers: A Life in the American Communist Party*. New York: Oxford University Press, 1990.

Herken, Greg. *The Winning Weapon: The Atomic Bomb in the Cold War, 1945-1950*. New York: Knopf, 1980.

Hoffmann, Robert L. *More Than a Trial: The Struggle Over Captain Dreyfus.* New York: Free Press, 1980.

Howe, Irving, and Lewis Coser. *The American Communist Party: A Critical History.* New York: Praeger, 1962.

Hoyt, Edwin P. *The Day the Chinese Attacked Korea, 1950.* New York: McGraw-Hill, 1990.

Hunter, Earl. *A Sociological Analysis of Certain Types of Patriotism.* New York:1932.

Hyde, H. Montgomery. *The Atom Spies.* New York: Athenaeum, 1980.

Johnson, Walter. *Sixteen Hundred Pennsylvania Avenue: Presidents and People, 1919-59.* Boston: Little, Brown and Co., 1960.

Joughin, Louis G. and Edmund R. Morgan.. *The Legacy of Sacco and Vanzetti.* New York: Harcourt, Brace and Co., 1948.

Kaufman, Burton I. *The Korean War: Challenges in Crisis, Credibility and Command.* Philadelphia: Temple University Press, 1986.

Kayser, Jacques. *The Dreyfus Affair.* New York: Covici, Friede Publishers, 1931.

Kessler, Lauren. *The Dissident Press: Alternative Journalism in American History.* Beverly Hills, Calif.: Sage Publications, 1984.

Knightley, Phillip. *The First Casualty: From the Crimea to Vietnam-the War Correspondent as Hero, Propagandist and Mythmaker.* New York: Harcourt, Brace Jovanovich, 1975.

Kobler, John. *Luce: His Time, Life and Fortune.* New York: Doubleday and Co., 1968.

Lamphere, Robert J. and Tom Shachtman. *The FBI-KGB War: A Special Agent's Story.* New York: Random House, 1986.

Lang, Kurt and Gladys Engel. "The Mass Media and Voting" in *Reader in Public Opinion and Communication*, 2nd ed., edited by Bernard Berelson and Morris Janowitz, New York: Free Press, 1966.

Latham, Earl. *The Communist Conspiracy in Washington: From the New Deal to McCarthy.* Harvard University Press, 1966.

Leuchtenberg, William E. *A Troubled Feast: American Society Since 1945.* Boston: Little, Brown and Co., 1979.

Liebling, A. J. *The Press.* 2nd ed. New York: Franklin Watts, 1988.

Liebovich, Louis. *The Press and the Origins of the Cold War, 1944-47.* New York: Praeger, 1988.

Lofton, John. *Justice and the Press.* Boston: Beacon Press, 1991.

Lowenthal, Max. *The Federal Bureau of Investigation.* New York: William Sloane Associates, Inc., 1950.

Lowery, Shearon. and DeFleur, Melvin. *Milestones in Mass Communication Research: Media Effects.* New York: Longman, 1983.

Luce, Henry R. *The American Century.* New York: Farrar and Rinehart Inc., 1941.

MacDougal, Curtis. *Interpretive Reporting*. New York: MacMillan, 1938.

May, Elaine Tyler. *Homeward Bound: American Families in the Cold War*. New York: Books, Inc., 1988.

McCombs, Maxwell and Donald L. Shaw with the assistance of Lee E. Becker. *The Emergence of American Political Issues: The Agenda-Setting Function of the Press*. St.Paul, MN: West Publishing Co., 1977.

Meeropol, Michael, and Robert Meeropol. *We Are Your Sons: The Legacy of Ethel and Julius Rosenberg*. 2nd ed. Champagne, IL: University of Illinois Press, 1986.

Messick, Hank. *An Inquiry into the Life and Times of John Edgar Hoover and His Relationship to the Continuing Partnership of Crime, Business and Politics*. New York: McKay Co., 1972.

Miller, Arthur. *Timebends: A Life*. New York: Grove Press, 1987.

Miller, Merle. *Plain Speaking: An Oral Biography of Harry S Truman*. New York: G. P.Putnam's Sons, 1973.

Miller, Perry. *The New England Mind: From Colony to Promise*. Cambridge: Harvard University Press, 1953.

Moorehead, Alan. *The Traitors*. New York: Charles Scribner's Sons, 1952.

Moss, Norman. *The Man Who Stole the Atom Bomb*. New York: St. Martin's Press, 1987.

Mott, Frank Luther. *American Journalism*. Rev. ed. New York: MacMillan, 1950.

Murphy, Paul L. *The Constitution in Crisis Times: 1918-1969*. New York: Harper and Row. 1972.

Nacos, Brigitte Lebens. *The Press, Presidents and Crises*. New York: Columbia University Press. 1990.

Navasky, Victor. *Naming Names*. New York: Viking. 1980.

Nizer, Louis. *The Implosion Conspiracy*. Garden City, NY.: Doubleday, 1973.

O'Neill, William L. *A Better World: The Great Schism, Stalinism and the American Intellectuals*. New York: Simon and Schuster, 1982.

O'Reilly, Kenneth. *Hoover and the Un-Americans: The FBI, HUAC and the Red Menace*. Philadelphia: Temple University Press, 1983.

Oshinsky, David. *A Conspiracy So Immense: The World of Joe McCarthy*. New York: Free Press, 1983.

Philbrick, Herbert. *I Led Three Lives: Citizen, Communist, Counterspy*. New York: McGraw-Hill, 1952.

Philipson, Ilene. *Ethel Rosenberg: Beyond the Myths*. New York: Franklin Watts,1988.

Pilat, Oliver. *The Atom Spies*. New York: Van Rees Press, 1952.

Powers, Richard Gid. *Secrecy and Power: The Life of J. Edgar Hoover*. New York: Free Press, 1987.

Radosh, Ronald and Joyce Milton. *The Rosenberg File: A Search for the Truth*. New York: Holt, Rinehart, and Winston, 1983.

Reeves, Thomas C. *The Life and Times of Joe McCarthy: A Biography*. New York: Free Press, 1982.

Reuben, William A. *The Atom Spy Hoax*. New York: Action Books, 1955.

Roberts, Nancy L. *Dorothy Day and the Catholic Worker*. Albany: State University of New York Press, 1984.

Root, Jonathan. *The Betrayers: the Rosenberg Case-A Reappraisal of an American Crisis*. New York: New York: Coward-McCann, 1963.

Roscho, Bernard. *Newsmaking*. Chicago: University of Chicago Press, 1975.

Ross, Andrew. "Reading the Rosenberg Letters" in *No Respect: Intellectuals and Popular Culture*. New York: Routledge, 1989.

Russell, Francis. *Tragedy in Dedham: The Story of the Sacco-Vanzetti Case*. New York: McGraw-Hill Co., 1962.

Schiller, Dan. *Objectivity and the News: The Public Rise of Commercial Journalism*. Philadelphia: University of Pennsylvania,1981.

Schneir, Walter and Miriam Schneir. *Invitation to an Inquest*. 4th ed. New York: Pantheon Books, 1983.

Schudson, Michael. *Discovering the News: A Social History of American Newspapers*. New York: Basic Books, 1978.

Shannon, David A. *The Decline of American Communism: A History of the Communist Party Since 1945*. New York: Charles Scribner's Sons, 1989.

Sharlitt, Joseph. *Fatal Error: The Miscarriage of Justice That Sealed the Rosenbergs' Fate*. New York: Charles Scribner's Sons, 1989.

Sharp, Malcolm. *Was Justice Done: The Rosenberg Case*. New York: Monthly Review Press, 1956.

Sigal, Leon V. *Reporters and Officials: The Organization and Politics of Newsmaking*. Lexington, Mass.: D.C. Heath and Co., 1973.

Simon, James. *Independent Journey: The Life of William O. Douglas*. New York:Harper and Row, 1980.

Smith, John Chabot. *Alger Hiss: The True Story*. New York: Holt, Rilnehart and Winston, 1976.

Sobell, Morton. *On Doing Time*. New York: Charles Scribner's Sons, 1974.

Stevens, John. *Sensationalism and the New York Press*. New York: Columbia University Press, Columbia University Press, 1991.

The Testament of Ethel and Julius Rosenberg. New York: Cameron and Kahn, 1954.

Theoharis, Athan G. and John Stuart Cox. *The Boss: J. Edgar Hoover and the Great American Inquisition*. Philadelphia: Temple University Press, 1988.

Tuchman, Gaye. *Making News: A Study in the Construction of Reality*. New York: Free Press, 1978.

Weinstein, Allen. Perjury: *The Hiss-Chambers Case*. New York: Alfred A. Knopf, 1978.

Wexley, John. *The Judgment of Julius and Ethel Rosenberg*. New York: Cameron and Kahn, 1955.

White, G. Edward. *The American Judicial Tradition: Profiles of Leading American Judges*. New York: Oxford University Press, 1988.

White, G. Edward. *Earl Warren: A Public Life*. New York: Oxford University Press, 1982.

Whitehead, Donald R. *The FBI Story: A Report to the People*. New York: Random House, 1956.

Yergen, Daniel. *Shattered Peace: The Origins of the Cold War and the National Security State*. Boston: Houghton Mifflin, 1977.

Zeligs, Meyer A. *Friendship and Fratricide: An Analysis of Whittaker Chambers and Alger Hiss*. New York: Viking Press, 1967.

JOURNAL ARTICLES

Anders, Roger. "The Rosenberg Case Revisited: the Greenglasses' Testimony and the Protection of Atomic Secrets." *American Historical Review* 83 (April 1978)

Breed, Warren. "Mass Communication and Socio-Cultural Integration." *Social Forces* 37 (1958).

Clark, James C. "Robert Henry Best: The Path to Treason, 1921-1945." *Journalism Quarterly* 67 (Winter 1990).

Folkerts, Jean. "Functions of the Reform Press." *Journalism History* 2 (Spring 1985).

Gaddis, John Lewis. "Intelligence, Espionage, and Cold War Origins." *Diplomatic History* 13 (Spring 1988).

Gamson, W. A. "News as Framing." *American Behavioral Scientist.* 33 (1989-90).

Glynn, Robert B. "L'Affaire Rosenberg in France." *Political Science Quarterly* 70 (December 1955).

Kiplinger, W.M. "Interpret the News." Journalism Quarterly 13 (September 1936).

Markowitz, Gerald E. and Michael Meeropol. "The Crime of the Century Revisited: David Greenglass's Scientific Evidence in the Rosenberg Case." *Science and Society* 44 (Spring 1988).

McCombs, Maxwell E. and Donald L. Shaw. "Structuring the Unseen Community." *Journal of Communication* 26 (Spring 1976).

McCombs, Maxwell and Donald L. Shaw."The Agenda-Setting Function of Mass Media." *Public Opinion Quarterly* 36 (Summer 1972).

Parrish, Michael "Cold War Justice: The Supreme Court and the Rosenbergs."*American Historical Review* 82 (October 1977).

Rogers, Everett M., James W. Dearing, and Soonbum Chang. "Aids in the 1980s: The Agenda Setting Process for a Public Issue." *Journalism Monographs* (June 1991).

Wolfsfeld, Gadi. "Media Protest and Political Violence: A Transactional Analysis." *Journalism Monographs* (June 1991).

PAMPHLETS AND CIRCULARS

New Evidence in the Rosenberg Case." Sobell Committee Records, National Committee to Secure Justice in the Rosenberg Case. State Historical Society of Wisconsin, (hereafter referred to as Sobell Committee Records).

"The Vatican and the Rosenberg Case." Sobell Committee records.   This document features a reprint of "The Significance of an Intervention," about Pius XII's intervention, from the April 16, 1953, issue of *L 'Osservatore Romano.*

Edelman, Irwin. "Religion, the Left and the Rosenberg Case." Sobell Committee Records.

Edelman, Irwin. "Freedom's Electrocution." Sobell Committee Records.

Edelman, Irwin. "There is a Third Side to the Rosenberg Case." Sobell Records.

PERIODICALS AND TRADE PUBLICATION ARTICLES

Dawidowicz, Lucy S. "The Rosenberg Case: 'Hate-America' Weapon." *New Leader*, Dec. 22, 1952.

Glazer, Nathan. "A New Look at the Rosenberg-Sobell Case."*New Leader*, July 2, 1956.

Hofstadter, Richard. "The Paranoid Style in American Politics." *Harper's*, November 1964.

"Lester Markel Thinks Press Neglects Interpretive Role." *Editor and Publisher*, April 3, 1948.

LAW REVIEW ARTICLES

Beier, Norman S., and Leonard B. Sand. The Rosenberg Case: History and Hysteria." *American Bar Association Journal* 40 (December 1954).

Weihoffen, Henry. "Legislative Pardon." *California Law Review,* 27.

"The Rosenberg Case: Some Reflections on Federal Criminal Law." Columbia
Law Review 54 (February 1954).
"The Rosenberg Case: A Problem of Statutory Construction." *Northwestern
University Law Review* 48 (1954).

DISSERTATIONS AND THESES

Ausenhus, Peter. "Journalism in National Crises: A Cultural History of the
Garfield and McKinley Assassinations." Master's thesis. University
of Minnesota, 1992.
Blanchard, Margaret. "Americans First, Newspapermen Second: The Conflict
between Patriotism and Freedom of the Press During the Cold War,
1946-1952. Ph. D. diss., University of North Carolina, Chapel Hill,
1981.
Lutzky, Seymour. "The Reform Editors and Their Press." Ph.D. diss., State
University of Iowa, 1951.
Shilen, Ronald. "The Concept of Objectivity in Journalism in the U.S." Ph.D.
diss., New York University, 1955.

GOVERNMENT DOCUMENTS AND REPORTS

U.S. v. Rosenberg (microform), prepared by the Fund for the Republic,
NewYork City (James P. Kilsheimer III, an assistant U.S. attorney
who helped prosecute the Rosenbergs, assisted in the preparation,
Wilmington, Del.) M. Glazier (1978). "The record of the trial in
which Julius and Ethel Rosenberg were convicted for conspiracy to
commit espionage and proceedings in the U.S. District Court and the
Court of Appeals." Box title: "Conspiracy Trials in America, 1919-
1953, *U.S. v. Rosenberg.*" The transcript is also on file at the
Federal Records Center (FRC) in Bayonne, N.J. (*U.S. v. Rosenberg,
Sobell, Yakovlev and Greenglass* [Cr. No. 134-245]. Trial exhibits
and appeal motions are also available at the FRC. See: Proceedings
under Section 2255, Title 28, U.S. C. Nov. 24 and 25, 1952, CR.
134-245, accession nos: 021.88.124 and 021-59A149; agency box
nos. 4 and 34102 FRC location, So. 520616-701238A, SDNY. The
transcript is also available from government document departments
of many libraries and college and university libraries. For related
archival and legal documents on the case see: accession no.021-
88.124, agency box no. 1, 2, 3. FRC loc, So. 520476-701738A.

FBI files pertaining to the Rosenberg-Sobell case, FBI reading room, Freedom of Information Act, Washington D.C. (These also include various Justice Department and other files on the case).

Atomic Energy Commission, Transcript, 403/1, Feb. 8, 1951. Archives of the AEC.

Library of Congress, Bureau of Prisons,"Notorious File," Washington D.C. (This file refers to David Greenglass's behavior while incarcerated in federal prisons).

"A Request to the Judiciary Committee to Investigate the Conduct of the U.S. Attorney's Office in the Rosenberg-Sobell Case," Submitted by the National Rosenberg-Sobell Committee, Bruxelles: International Association of Democratic Lawyers, 1954.

U.S. House Committee on Un-American Activities, (the Committee to Secure Justice in the Rosenberg case and affiliates). *Investigation of Communist Activities*. 84th Cong., 1st sess., Washington D.C.: Government Printing Office, 1955.

U.S. House Subcommittee of the Committee on Government Operations. *Availability of Information from Federal Departments and Agencies*. Hearings before a Subcommittee of the Committee on Government Operations. 84th Cong., 1st sess., Nov. 7, 1955.

U.S. House Subcommittee on Criminal Justice. *Hearings before the Subcommittee on Criminal Justice of the Committee of the Judiciary*. 97th Cong., 1st and 2nd sess. serial no. 132, app. 2. "The Death Penalty," (Rosenberg case), Dec. 16, 1982.

Index

About the Author

JOHN F. NEVILLE holds a Ph.D. from the University of Minnesota. He has also worked as a regional freelance newspaper and magazine reporter and as a public relations writer.

CPSIA information can be obtained at www.ICGtesting.com
Printed in the USA
LVOW11*2050130215

427022LV00007B/27/P